Pursuing Citizenship in the Enforcement Era

Pursuing Citizenship in the Enforcement Era

Ming Hsu Chen

Stanford University Press
Stanford, California

Stanford University Press

Stanford, California

© 2020 by Ming Hsu Chen.
All rights reserved.

Printed in the United States of America on acid-free, archival-quality paper

Library of Congress Cataloging-in-Publication Data

Names: Chen, Ming Hsu, author.
Title: Pursuing citizenship in the enforcement era / Ming Hsu Chen.
Description: Stanford, California : Stanford University Press, 2020. |
    Includes bibliographical references and index.
Identifiers: LCCN 2019053660 (print) | LCCN 2019053661 (ebook) |
    ISBN 9781503608160 (cloth) | ISBN 9781503612754 (paperback) |
    ISBN 9781503612761 (ebook)
Subjects: LCSH: Citizenship—United States. | Immigrants—United States. |
    Naturalization—United States. | Emigration and immigration law—
    United States. | United States—Emigration and immigration—Government
    policy.
Classification: LCC JK1759 .C46 2020 (print) | LCC JK1759 (ebook) |
    DDC 323.6/20973—dc23
LC record available at https://lccn.loc.gov/2019053660
LC ebook record available at https://lccn.loc.gov/2019053661

Cover design: Christian Fuenfhausen

Typeset by Westchester Publishing Services in 10/14 Minion Pro

For Maya

Contents

Acknowledgments

This book is based on interviews with more than one hundred immigrants about their experiences pursuing citizenship. So I first want to thank the immigrants, immigration lawyers, and community organizations who talked with me about their challenges and introduced me to others willing to do the same. Thanks especially to Harry Budisidharta from the Asian Pacific Development Center, Claudia Castillo from the Colorado Immigrant Rights Coalition, Kit Taintor from the Colorado Department of Refugee Services, Tracy Harper from the Colorado African Organization, Anita Stuehler from the Boulder Library citizenship class, Leigh Alpert from American Immigration Lawyers Association Naturalization Drives, Carla Castedo from the Mi Familia Vota citizenship workshops, and David Aragon and Diana Salazar from the University of Colorado. Second, I want to acknowledge the law students who worked tirelessly to help recruit participants for interviews, conduct them, and transcribe them: Edyael Casaperalta, Ashlyn Kahler-Rios, Fernanda Loza, Zak New, Julie Schneider, Daimeon Shanks, Ryan Thompson, Tierney Tobin, and Travis Weiner. Edelina Burciaga partnered with me on DACA interviews.

Interpreting immigrant experiences and weaving them into the narratives needed for a book has involved countless conversations. Many of these sense-making conversations occurred in workshops and conferences on immigrant integration: a University of Colorado Law School book workshop and faculty colloquium, University of California Berkeley Interdisciplinary Immigration Workshop, the Center for the Study of Law and Society, the Colorado Immigration Scholars Network, the University of Colorado Immigration and Citizenship Law Program, the University of Colorado Institute for Behavioral Science, the Law and Society Association's Annual Meeting panels on citizenship and migration, American Association of Law Schools Immigration

Law Scholars Workshops at BYU Law and Texas A&M Law, e-CRT conferences at Northwestern Law and Yale Law, faculty colloquia at Fordham Law, Chapman Law, UC Davis Law, UC Irvine Law, and Seattle University. Friends and colleagues who have improved the manuscript with their insightful feedback include Kathy Abrams, KT Albiston, Jim Anaya, Sofya Aptekar, Angela Banks, Steve Bender, Irene Bloemraad, Linda Bosniak, Edelina Burciaga, Deb Cantrell, Kristen Carpenter, Jennifer Chacon, Robert Chang, Violeta Chapin, Elizabeth Cohen, David Cook-Martin, Susan Coutin, Stella Burch Elias, Cybelle Fox, Kristelia Garcia, Charlotte Garden, Eric Gerding, Shannon Gleeson, Laura Gomez, Rosann Greenspan, John Griffin, Pratheepan Gulasekaram, Megan Hall, Cesar Garcia Hernandez, Ernesto Hernandez, Sharon and Tilman Jacobs, Kevin Johnson, Kit Johnson, Anil Kalhan, Dan Kanstroom, Jae Yeon Kim, Sarah Krakoff, Stephen Lee, Taeku Lee, Ben Levin, Aaron Malone, Lisa Martinez, Cecilia Menjivar, Joy Milligan, Hiroshi Motomura, Helen Norton, D. Carolina Nunez, Osagie Obasogie, Anne Joseph O'Connell, Michael Olivas, Huyen Pham, Doris Marie Provine, Fernando Riosmena, Reuel Schiller, Jonathan Simon, Scott Skinner-Thompson, Sarah Song, Rachel Stern, Karen Tani, Monica Varsanyi, Rose Cuison-Villazor, Leti Volpp, Shoba Wadhia, and Josh Wilson. Additional research, editorial, and technical assistance was provided by Jane Thompson and Matt Zafiratos in the University of Colorado Law library, Maggie Reuter and Kathryn Yazgulian in the University of Colorado Law School faculty coordinator office, and Jon Sibray and his team in the University of Colorado IT Department.

Special thanks to Michelle Lipinski, who nurtured the project from seed to fruit. I chose to publish with Stanford University Press because of her enthusiasm and steadfast commitment. She and four thoughtful peer reviewers provided comments on multiple drafts, and colleagues at Stanford ably moved the book through the production process.

Resources and funding came from University of Colorado Law School summer research grants, the University of Colorado Immigration and Citizenship Law Program, University of Colorado diversity grants, a University of Colorado community engagement grant, and the Colorado Immigrant Integration Study. While I was on a research sabbatical, I benefited from the institutional resources of Berkeley's Center for the Study of Law and Society, Interdisciplinary Immigration Workshop, and D-Lab.

Many thanks to my family members, each of whom has been shaped by the immigrant experience: Ken and Gina Hsu, Woei and Mei Chen, Shayna

Source: Maya Hsu Chen (age 6).

Hsu, and Stephen Chen. Stephen knew of my desire to write this book and supported my efforts at every step, whether by serving as a sounding board for ideas, accompanying me on my research sabbatical, or checking bibliographic entries in the final manuscript. The book is dedicated to our daughter, Maya, a US-born citizen and third-generation immigrant who treasures her immigrant heritage. She learned to read, think, and care about immigrants as she overheard dinner-table conversations and witnessed images of border walls, family separation, and immigrant exclusion on the nightly news. Through it all, she cheered on her mother's efforts to imagine a better world by writing a book: "Go, Professor Mommy!" Her child's-eye drawings of a community welcoming an immigrant family across the border and into schools, churches, and town centers capture the essence of this project. Every parent wants to make her child's dreams come true, and I hope the ideas in these pages play a part in making her vision of a welcoming society a reality.

Pursuing Citizenship in the Enforcement Era

CHAPTER 1

Pursuing Citizenship in the Enforcement Era

THE SCHOOL CAFETERIA was filled with rows of tables, at least four wide and four deep with approximately 250 seats in total. It was a Saturday morning in 2016, and a place that buzzed with the chatter of teenagers all week now hummed with hundreds of immigrants looking for help on their path to citizenship. This was one of many Colorado citizenship workshops I visited while researching this book. As I waited for the lines to inch forward and the seats to fill, I spoke with some of these would-be citizens about their reasons for coming. Many were longtime residents of the United States: Latinos who had come from Mexico and Central America ten, fifteen, or twenty years ago and who have held green cards for five or more years. Why had they come out today, clutching the N-400 forms that are required to file for naturalized citizenship, to take the next step toward officially becoming American? Why did two million others similarly file for citizenship that year? There were a record number of citizenship applications filed in the 2016 election year, and they have remained high years into the Donald J. Trump presidency, though spikes normally tail off months after an election.

One reason these immigrants seek citizenship comes from Mercedes, a Latino green card holder, who is seeking citizenship. She explained that while she was not usually one to get involved in politics, the election awakened her to the need to become part of the country. More pointedly, she remarked, "Now we may have a president who does not get along [with the immigrant community]. I said that if I could vote, I wouldn't vote for him. We would have another vote against him: mine."[1] Mercedes immigrated from Mexico in 1977 and received her green card in 1990, meaning she had been eligible for citizenship for sixteen years before feeling that the right to vote was necessary to her sense of belonging. This desire for legal status and the right to vote, emblems of formal citizenship, is commonly discussed. It was evident in the fall of 2016, one month before the presidential election that would usher in Donald Trump, who put immigration enforcement front and center in his campaign promises: to build a wall at the border; to capture and return immigrants who are murderers, rapists, and gangsters; to restrict entry from Muslim-majority countries; to end humanitarian programs for asylum seekers; and to curtail legal migration through trimming of family-based migration, diversity visas, and high-skilled worker visas.[2] Immigrants felt they needed the formal rights of citizenship to serve as an insurance policy against federal policies to close the borders—not only to immigrants singled out by the government as threats to the United States but also to immigrants seeking economic stability and safety, to high-skilled workers and international students seeking to learn and contribute to their professions, to refugees and veterans seeking to give back to their country, and to all manner of immigrants seeking to reunite with their families after many years spent waiting for a visa to become available.

While central to questions at the heart of this book, focusing only on the formal rights of citizenship misses a key component. After all, it was too late for many of the applicants at the workshops I attended to register for the November 2016 election in many parts of the country. Most were green card holders, but in a normal year, the naturalization process takes an average of six months.[3] In the 2016 election year, the higher volume of applications and changes to processing increased processing times to one year or more,[4] before tacking on additional time for residency requirements. Perhaps these immigrants did not realize that despite signing up to become citizens, they would not be able to vote in the 2016 election cycle. If that were the case, however, the lines should have shortened after the election results were announced in November 2016. They did not, nor did they shorten once the presidential inauguration had taken place in January 2017, or following the issuance of three executive actions and several policy reversals that negatively affected immigrant rights in the following years. Moreover, immigrants are making claims for social, economic, and political inclusion that go beyond formal legal status in their appeals for access to education, fair wages, and good jobs. These claims are all substantive dimensions of citizenship that speak to immigrants' broader desire for integration into American society. While formal rights of citizenship, such as voting, are crucial motivators, the push for citizenship is also a push for cultural belonging. Take Ruth, who immigrated to the United States from China as a young adult and attended American universities for two degrees before qualifying for a green card through marriage. She is an example of successful integration; she already felt that the United States was her country, so pursuing citizenship was "natural."[5]

The young undocumented immigrants colloquially known as DREAMers (from the Development, Relief, and Education for Alien Minors Act that would grant them a path to citizenship, had it passed), many of whom migrated as children and came of age in the United States, feel similarly to Ruth. Some DREAMers said their sense of belonging does not depend on papers and that they are already American, having attended American schools, befriended American classmates, and built American lives. Others feel "trapped" by their uncertain futures, caught in a holding pattern and unable to move forward or go back to countries they scarcely know.[6] Nonetheless, they take on an activist role. They encourage those who are eligible to naturalize and register to vote, even though they themselves cannot do so.

By and large, the immigrants who came to the Colorado citizenship workshop filed their N-400 applications for citizenship and got involved in American politics because they felt they needed citizenship's protections, even more than its benefits, and they had to stake out a place for themselves in their communities. Although many had been eligible to naturalize for years, they were filing their paperwork now because it had become too costly *not* to do so. All around their communities, they saw noncitizens being arrested, detained, and threatened with deportation for trivial offenses. Family members and neighbors who had lived peacefully for many years were being questioned by law enforcement, threatened with government raids, and heckled by neighbors and strangers at their schools and workplaces about their immigration status. They felt insecure about their legal status and were seeking *defensive* citizenship.

This book is about why immigrants pursue citizenship in the enforcement era and how the experience varies for immigrants with different legal statuses. The desire for legal protection felt by green card holders I met at naturalization workshops affects all citizens. In this enforcement-minded climate, immigrants of every legal status feel insecure about being noncitizens in America. They feel insecure whether legally admitted or undocumented and whether they possess criminal backgrounds or college degrees. This citizenship insecurity shapes the trajectories of immigrants as they make choices about their present lives and future investments in America. Green card holders, technically known as legal permanent residents or lawful permanent residents (LPRs), must debate whether to make a life in the United States or keep open the option to return to their home countries. Meanwhile, family unity is eluded by reduced caps on refugee admission, travel bans for those from Muslim-majority countries, and the turning away of asylum seekers at the US border. Noncitizens stationed abroad or waiting to enlist, whom recruiters had promised citizenship for their military service, find themselves in limbo with heightened security clearances and burdensome application requirements delaying and derailing their naturalization. High-skilled temporary workers and relatives confront new uncertainty about their ability to legally migrate, as Congress debates the caps on temporary visas and the president proposes a point system altering the criteria for immigrant admission. In sum, across the citizenship spectrum, it is now more difficult to be an immigrant and more difficult to feel included as an American.

Various types of noncitizens are also feeling the effects of their precarious status through social exclusion, economic challenges, and political disengagement. Refugee agencies are seeing dwindling numbers of clients and diminished resources for their settlement.[7] Muslims and Middle Eastern immigrants throughout the nation face increased scrutiny.[8] Mexican and Central American youth are being pulled over and arrested as suspected gang members.[9] The federal government's immigrant serving agency, the US Citizenship and Immigration Services, has deleted "nation of immigrants" from its mission statement.[10] The White House and Census Bureau have sought information about citizenship status to assist immigration enforcement and to restrict public benefits, purposes that may impede integration.[11] Federal immigration policy makes deportation possible for immigrants who were previously considered low priorities for enforcement, putting everyone who is not a US citizen at risk of exclusion and deportation.[12] Even naturalized citizens are vulnerable to denaturalization.[13] More than ever, immigrants are being told they are not welcome in the United States.

The Meaning of Membership for Semi-Citizens

Studying a range of immigrants with different legal statuses shows how status affects the substantive belonging of immigrants and why some struggle more than others to integrate. The law says that everyone who is not US-born or naturalized is a noncitizen alien,[14] but the social reality is more complicated. The

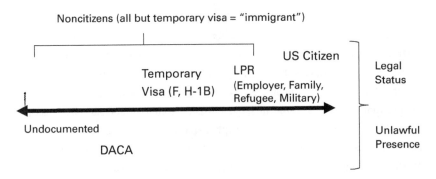

FIGURE 1.1. Citizenship spectrum. LPR = lawful permanent resident.

citizen/alien binary should be reframed as a *spectrum* of citizenship. As figure 1.1 shows, categories of immigrants can be arrayed on a spectrum ranging from US citizenship to undocumented immigrants. The interview groups fall within this spectrum: green card holders (e.g., lawful permanent residents, refugees, service members), temporary visa holders (e.g., temporary workers and international students), and DACA recipients. Placing the groups on a spectrum emphasizes continuities between the experiences of citizenship.

The experiences of these immigrant groups can be further differentiated along *formal* and *substantive* dimensions of citizenship.[15] *Formal citizenship* is a legal status that permits an individual to attain naturalized citizenship and state-conferred rights and benefits, such as the ability to sponsor family migration, travel without restraint, participate in the political process, and not be deported for committing a crime. It encompasses a spectrum of citizenship statuses, from naturalized citizens to green card holders to temporary visa holders to those with limited or no status.[16] *Substantive citizenship* consists of more informal claims to social belonging and might be accompanied by appeals for economic, social, political, and in some cases legal incorporation.[17] While some dispute the desirability of making formal citizenship a prerequisite to substantive belonging,[18] this book argues that formal citizenship is a necessary but not sufficient condition for full citizenship in a nation governed by immigration laws that favor enforcement at the expense of membership and integration.

The context of enforcement sharpens the meaning and increases the necessity of formal citizenship. This is troublesome for citizens and noncitizens alike, as the federal government's obsession with citizenship status renders noncitizens insecure about their rights and benefits. National communities certainly have the right to define their membership, but once the community draws those boundaries, those living within the society—members or not— are entitled to occupy a protected space.[19] The federal government's decades-long emphasis on enforcing the legal status of noncitizens treats them as outsiders living inside a bounded geographic space. Legal status becomes a social construct, as the experiences of different groups of noncitizens consolidate around feelings of insecurity across the citizenship spectrum.

The enforcement bias also erodes substantive citizenship. The sense of insecurity around citizenship status inhibits many dimensions of immigrant integration.[20] My interviews with immigrants reveal that the enforcement bias has negative effects on their sense of social belonging, economic opportunities, civic participation, and interactions with legal institutions. As law and society scholars have argued time and again, legal categories operate within and are constituted by social, economic, and political forces in society. Because noncitizen status takes on negative social meaning during periods of enforcement, noncitizens are constructed as outsiders and excluded from many spheres of life.

In an enforcement regime, noncitizen status produces substantive and formal barriers to belonging. Formal citizenship can positively affect socioeconomic well-being, political participation, social identification, and feelings of legal security. And yet, while data shows *increases* in naturalization applications due to fear of enforcement in the short term, the longer-term repercussions of such enforcement are concerning.[21] Legal noncitizens could come to view citizenship as a transactional decision rather than an opportunity to cultivate meaningful ties to a nation. Refugees and military service members could fall off the path to naturalization and fail to integrate into mainstream life. Burdened pathways to citizenship could lead many temporary visa holders to return to their home countries with their skills and experiences. The collective result is a socially *dis*integrated polity rather than a socially cohesive one fueled by shared purpose and values.

This is not to downplay the benefits of a substantive citizenship uncoupled from formal citizenship. Some advocates say that striving for formal citizenship is a distraction from the more urgent task of integrating *all* people.[22] This emerging view, common among non-legal scholars, holds up the example of the DREAMers' social movement. DREAMers' assertion that they are Americans, just not legally,[23] illustrates a claim to substantive citizenship without legal status. Substantive citizenship fosters a sense of belonging and of deservingness: DREAMers are owed the same basic rights and protections as formal citizens, including access to public education and freedom from threat of family separation. Over time these social membership claims become more than an expression of identity. Civic engagement and social protest—forms of political expression for those without voting rights—have led directly to federal executive policies forestalling deportation for unlawful presence and permitting lawful employment, state and municipal policies providing driver's licenses and public benefits, and community shelter and support from churches and nonprofits.[24] Despite their lack of formal citizenship status, formerly undocumented immigrants laying claim to membership in American society have become semi-citizens, possessing "status non-citizenship," "liminal legality," and "DACA-mentation" (from the Deferred Action for Childhood Arrivals or DACA program).[25] Still, DREAMers' sense of substantive belonging is precarious and can be undermined by repeated failures to obtain legal security, demonstrating the fragility of their formal status.

Contrary to recent scholarship announcing the declining significance of citizenship, this book recognizes the continuing importance of the institution of citizenship. I argue that formal citizenship carries real weight because anything less than formal belonging is insufficient when borders are fortified by expanding immigration enforcement and rising nationalism. Formal citizenship ensures that threshold rights to membership within a society are respected. As semi-citizens living along a spectrum of membership, immigrants are necessarily unequal to one another and to citizens in vital respects, legal status most of all.

Granted, semi-citizens possess constitutional rights to equal protection and due process. They have the opportunity to become more substantively equal. These equality rights are not contingent on formal citizenship and should be strengthened. However, this book argues that to challenge immigration law's traditional acceptance of substantive inequality as the natural by-product of geopolitical boundaries, we must broaden and strengthen pathways to formal citizenship for semi-citizens. Formal and substantive citizenship are both prerequisites to *full* citizenship, which is why pathways to citizenship are vital. Citizenship confers legitimacy, socialization, investment, mobilization, and a sense of social belonging.[26] Full membership is impossible without legal status, and as such, the federal government serves as the grantor or withholder of formal citizenship as it sees fit. This book argues that it should be obligated to address citizenship inequality, and that it should do so in proactive ways—providing affirmative institutional support and demonstrating a commitment to citizenship equality rather than adopting the laissez-faire approach that defers to the expansion of enforcement in immigration policy.

Institutional Pathways to Citizenship

Despite its importance to integration, formal citizenship is understudied and underspecified. Social scientists who empirically study immigrant integration focus on individual attributes as predictors of successful integration.[27] An immigrant possessing more education, greater income, better health, or stronger family dynamics is more likely to integrate successfully.[28] A newer strand of scholarship recognizes legal status as another important determinant of integration.[29] Enhanced enforcement amplifies the effect of legal status on integration. Enforcement-focused regimes stoke social exclusion and impose economic constraints on those targeted, worsening inequality and hindering integration.

Recognizing status as one factor of integration is an improvement. But I consider legal status as a structural determinant of integration.[30] If status is merely one factor, it contributes to successful integration independently of institutional context. My view recognizes that status is paramount and that its effects depend on the surrounding context. Different legal statuses provide differing levels of institutional support to immigrants, and these institutional differences shape the experience of immigrants as well as their integration outcomes. Grasping the structural importance of status to integration reveals the role played by institutions—schools, workplaces, and the government—in bolstering, or hindering, immigrant incorporation.

Immigrants of varying legal status receive different levels of institutional support, producing different integrative outcomes.[31] Lawful permanent residents receive comparatively less support from the federal government than refugees, and perhaps as a result, their naturalization rates are lower.[32] Immigrants who serve in the armed forces have traditionally received substantial assistance from the federal government and have been naturalized at high rates, but they are losing their ability to naturalize as a result of changing policies that heighten front-end criteria for eligibility and back-end consequences for substance abuse and other criminal convictions, resulting in lower naturalization rates.[33] Temporary visitors on short-term visas and undocumented immigrants enjoy no institutional support for citizenship. Their pathway is blocked in ways that dwarf the generalized burdens of integration. The difficulty, or even impossibility, of traversing pathways to formal citizenship poses an insurmountable challenge without changes to immigration law. The specific examples vary, but the larger point remains: a lack of institutional support inhibits immigrant integration. Improving the daily lives and future prospects for those immigrants who have been excluded from society requires affirmative institutional support that fosters both formal membership and substantive belonging.

By interviewing immigrants in multiple legal categories about their pursuit of citizenship, I can examine the hypothesis that differences in the institutional support for each status influence immigrant integration. In the ten years since the foundational literature on citizenship argued that institutions affect citizen belonging, government policies have intensified immigration enforcement in every category of citizenship status.[34] I argue that enforcement environments condition substantive and formal membership, and that this intensifying environment necessitates a sustained focus on the effects of immigration enforcement policies on the citizenship experiences of immigrants. This focus reveals specific policies that negatively affect the integration of each type of immigrant with a degree of detail not possible in more generalized studies of immigrant integration.

Restoring Integration in Immigration Policy

Readers can agree that US immigration policy's fixation on immigration enforcement is misguided, yet scholars seem unable to shift the policy focus from enforcement to integration. Traditionally, the federal government has done little to help immigrants integrate into American society. The laissez-faire approach sometimes works well enough, permitting immigrant integration to proceed "steadily, but unevenly."[35] However, the laissez-faire strategy is an ineffective catalyst for national policy, and it does not shield against the exclusionary effects of virulent anti-immigrant political sentiment.

The documented and undocumented immigrants seeking to integrate need pathways to citizenship. Constructing these pathways requires the federal government to assume center stage. Granting formal citizenship is the province of the federal government, and it is responsible for assisting the integration of green card holders, refugees, veterans, and even undocumented immigrants.[36] I argue that while the federal government must be proactive in these duties, efforts to integrate should be conducted in partnership with local governments and nonprofit organizations, building on efforts in communities nationwide to facilitate social, economic, political, and legal incorporation.

Communities foster substantive citizenship through a decentralized patchwork of policies and practices that vary from place to place.[37] Investments in immigrants in the social and economic sphere are routinely delegated to voluntary efforts of nonprofit organizations, churches, or local communities. Outside of K–12 public schools, society expects immigrants to integrate through their own initiative: to learn English, to become familiar with American customs, to acquire job skills, and to cultivate ties to their newly adopted communities. These decentralized efforts are salutary, but they can not replace coordinated national initiatives. Immigrants often subordinate their higher, civic-minded aspirations to the daily struggle to survive, laying their hopes on future generations rather than making their own claims on the present. Insufficient government support particularly affects poorer, older, less educated, and less fluent immigrants.[38] Those who share the racial identity of native-born citizens who have historically been subjugated in the United States also encounter greater difficulties.[39]

Toward Full Citizenship

Owing to this uneven patchwork of institutional support, integration needs to be restored to a place of prominence in US citizenship and immigration policy. Over the thirty years since the last significant immigration reform, the federal government has kept its focus on enforcement of formal status rather than promoting substantive forms of membership and belonging for immigrants. This imbalance is harmful to immigrants, society, and the enforcement apparatus itself.

There has been a tension between integration and enforcement since the federal government began regulating immigration in the late nineteenth century. The federal immigration laws were not generous to immigrants during the era of Chinese exclusion, racial prerequisites to naturalization, or national origin quotas. Though laws became more accommodating of immigrants in the mid-twentieth century, with a rewriting of the major immigration statute in 1954 and a refinement in 1965 to eliminate national origin quotas, they have since grown more punitive with each subsequent wave of legislation.[40] The 1986 Immigration Reform and Control Act restricted employment opportunities. The 1996 Illegal Immigration Reform and Immigrant Responsibility Act and the 1996 Antiterrorism and Effective Death Penalty Act fortified borders and instituted long waiting periods for immigration violations. The 1996 Personal Responsibility and Work Opportunity Reconciliation Act restricted welfare benefits. Finally, the 2002 Homeland Security Act and the 2005 REAL ID Act entangled immigration law with national security issues, further weakening immigrant rights.

As Congress entered into a political stalemate on forging national immigration legislation following September 11, 2001, still unbroken nearly two decades later, states entered the fray.[41] Between 2001 and 2012, Arizona, Georgia, and Texas enacted severely restrictive laws to compensate for the federal government's failure to secure the border. Arizona's Save Our State legislation (SB 1070), which deputized local law enforcement to take over federal enforcement functions, exemplifies these efforts.[42] Federal enforcement ramped up to unprecedented levels during these years, reaching four hundred thousand detentions, apprehensions, and removals per year. There was a brief reprieve in the second term of the Obama administration (2012–16), when President Barack Obama used executive action to shield some categories of immigrants from federal enforcement and liberal states created inclusionary policies for immigrants. However, conservative states filed lawsuits to challenge these inclusionary policies. At the national level, the Trump administration rolled back President Obama's categorical exceptions and pushed for ever more restrictive immigration policies.

Since 2016, increased immigration enforcement has been the rule, and enforcement discretion has been eliminated.[43] The enforcement regime leaves immigrants vulnerable in many ways. Immigrants' opportunities are curtailed and their aspirations crushed. Societal innovation, cultural diversity, and social cohesion are limited. Under such conditions, the very meaning of citizenship shrinks, becoming more transactional and less vigorous. Moreover, the institutional enforcement infrastructure crumbles under its own weight, with overstretched immigration agencies on the verge of collapse.

Localized voluntary community efforts to integrate noncitizens into their communities counter some of these federal enforcement excesses.[44] A decentralized safety net of pro-immigrant policies improves the substantive aspects of immigrants' daily lives. Cities extend identification cards or encourage state driver's licenses to plug status-related gaps in their community safety net. States offer in-state tuition for public colleges and universities to help undocumented immigrants stabilize their presence, even if they do not address their status. Counties establish sanctuary policies to shield their undocumented residents from federal enforcement. Nonprofit organizations and churches engage in refugee resettlement. These local voluntary integrative efforts function primarily to plug holes in federal immigration policy, though some actively defy federal policies. Despite their promise, these efforts can be stymied by litigation or countervailing federal policies.

Responding to this state of affairs, this book argues that the federal government's approach toward immigrants should encompass integration. I argue that recalibrating immigration policy involves problematizing the stark divide between integration and enforcement in immigration and citizenship law, and that regulating citizenship status should be seen as part of a larger effort to govern the formal and substantive membership of immigrants. Immigration enforcement is overwhelmingly concerned with legal status. Membership, by contrast, is a broader concept that entails incorporating immigrant newcomers into mainstream society economically, socially, politically, and legally. Reducing the meaning of citizenship to legal status creates a skewed immigration policy that unduly harms noncitizens. Beneath the diversity of immigrant backgrounds and experiences, noncitizens by definition possess limited legal statuses that leave them vulnerable to the enforcement of membership rules and border laws. This is precisely why the burden of immigrant integration cannot be placed solely on the shoulders of newcomers. Attaining citizenship equality means society will need to extend institutional support to its newest members.

Some argue that immigrants do not possess an equal claim to live in America and that the terms of their stay depend on the rules for membership determined by the political community they seek to join.[45] Others believe immigrants are members of the community, even if they lack formal citizenship, and they are entitled to basic rights and conditions of equality while living in the community.[46] Considering formal legal status in the frame of the broader concept of membership harmonizes the rules for living in America. Scholars and policy makers from across the political spectrum routinely agree that immigration law is "broken" and that citizenship is becoming eroded in an era of excessive enforcement, yet they lack the conceptual foundation and the policy tools to fix what is broken or restore what is missing.[47] This book sets forth an affirmative vision for citizenship and immigration law based on a foundation of national immigrant integration.

Realistically, comprehensive federal legislation promoting immigrant integration is not forthcoming in a climate marred by political polarization and anti-immigrant rhetoric. For the last thirty years, national legislators have not blocked good immigration policies so much as they have weaponized broken policies and used them toward destructive ends. These broken policies weaken the foundations of a shared society and harm those most vulnerable. This book surveys this modern landscape of expanding federal immigration enforcement but it also imagines new possibilities for less destructive, and more integrative, policies.

Research Methods

This book uses a comparative approach to study immigrant integration in the United States. This approach uncovers the distinct experiences of citizenship for immigrants of various legal statuses: green card holders, temporary workers, international students, and undocumented immigrants with DACA status. To convey these experiences of citizenship, I present and analyze three years of my participant observations, interviews, and surveys with everyday immigrants. The interview data was primarily collected from 2016 to 2018 and follow-up surveys were conducted in 2019, a period of intensifying immigration enforcement nationwide.

Engaging in participant observation and conducting interviews with immigrants about living, working, and participating in a society where they do not formally belong provides a bottom-up perspective on how citizenship shapes immigrant integration. I conducted field work at numerous citizenship and naturalization workshops, citizenship classes, and organizational meetings. My in-depth interviews with more than one hundred immigrants, as well as the follow-up surveys, queried immigrants on their sense of social belonging, their economic integration, their political participation, and their interactions with legal institutions. I spoke with immigrants in multiple categories of legal status to home in on the institutional effects of status. These included family-sponsored immigrants, employer-sponsored immigrants, refugees, and military green card holders with a "straight path" to citizenship, albeit with differing levels of institutional support; high-skilled workers whose temporary status permits them a qualified level of support; and DACA recipients whose limited legal status provides permission to work and temporary relief from deportation but no path to citizenship.

Most of these interviews were conducted in my home state of Colorado, which displays diverse social attitudes toward immigrant integration and has ushered in some of the most regressive *and* most progressive state and local policies. Nearly one in ten Colorado residents is an immigrant, and it has one of the fastest-growing immigrant populations in the country. It is home to many immigrant communities, including well-established multigenerational Latino families and more recently migrated immigrants. There are high-skilled workers, military service members, and refugees. Its urban areas rival the integration polities in famously liberal states, while its rural areas are more conservative. Statewide it has evolved toward immigrant integration. Colorado sheltered Jeanette Vizguerra, an undocumented immigrant, in a Denver church for several months to prevent her deportation, and nearly all of its counties adopted sanctuary policies to defy ICE (Immigration and Customs Enforcement) enforcement at jails. This is not to say that Colorado is representative of the national landscape of immigrant integration—no single state can be—but it is more representative of the nation's ambivalence around immigrant inclusion than, say, California or New York. The field work and interviews paint a picture of citizenship inequality that starkly illustrates common institutional dynamics between integration and enforcement.[48]

Why It Matters . . . and to Whom

Historically speaking, when states have engaged in immigration policy their involvement has swung like a pendulum between pro- and anti-immigrant policies. California, for example, is today considered a pioneer for inclusionary immigration policies that could inspire the federal government to follow suit. However, I attended a California public high school in the 1990s, when voters approved ballot initiatives to restrict public benefits for undocumented immigrants, curtail affirmative action for racial minorities, and effectively end bilingual education in public schools. These initiatives spread to federal policy in 1996, then gained momentum after September 11, 2001. Between 2001 and 2011, state legislators enacted mostly exclusionary laws, intending to close gaps in federal enforcement. The tide turned around 2012 with a wave of inclusionary measures led by California. Based on this firsthand experience, I know the local political conditions that produce pro- or anti-immigrant legislation can shift.

These pendulum shifts at the state level show the problem with the federal government taking a laissez-faire approach toward integration. Though state measures helped immigrants in some parts of the country, they hindered immigrants in others. And they have not resulted in a national plan for integration. State action did prompt some inclusionary executive actions, like President Obama's DACA program, but those have since been rolled back under the Trump administration. Without a national commitment to integration, the inclusion of immigrants is left to the whims of politics. The political branches of the government and local communities will be left to decide for themselves whether they will include immigrants. Courts are usually deferential to political determinations about the boundaries of citizenship.

The federal government's laissez-faire approach toward immigrant rights contrasts with the affirmative role it played in the historic civil rights movement. Early in my career, I was inspired by the civil rights movement to study the potential of law and government to effect social change and embolden citizenship. Studying the failure to extend those civil rights to immigrants has revealed a darker side of the law: law can be a sword rather than a shield; an obstacle rather than a pathway to social justice. The federal government, for all its imperfections, was an engine of change and a force for good for racial minorities and women during the civil rights movement. In immigration, however, the government seems content to play the role of antagonist. Even the 1965 Hart-Celler Immigration Act, which passed with the same egalitarian spirit that marked passage of the 1964 Civil Rights Act, has been transformed into a federal immigration statute that hinders rather than helps immigrants integrate into society. Subsequent federal laws have further divided immigrants from citizens and signaled the federal government's abdication of responsibility for integrating its newcomers.

This book argues that the federal government's lax attitude toward immigrant integration is a mistake, and that immigration lawyers, scholars, and policy makers concede too much when they focus all of their energies on immigration enforcement. The federal bias against immigrants, so vividly on display in the Trump administration, is not new, even if it is more pronounced. Immigrant scholarship and advocacy has been reactive, focused on damage control and defense. It has turned away from engaging the federal government. Given past disappointments, this is understandable. Yet it forfeits an opportunity to define the vision for immigration policy in an affirmative—and affirming—way. In the midst of modern history's era of enforcement, this book explains the cost of abandoning the federal government's commitment to immigrants—for immigrants, for citizens, and for the institution of citizenship—and charts an alternative vision for immigration policy that is premised on making easier each stage of the journey from new-comer to resident to citizen.

Chapter Outline

Part I of this book focuses on the concept of citizenship inequality and the institutional shortcomings that produce it. Chapter 2, "Unequal Citizenship: Gaps in Formal and Substantive Citizenship," frames the problem of inequality for immigrants as the by-product of US citizenship and immigration law. This chapter paints a portrait of immigrants' unequal membership in social, economic, civic, and legal life. It asks whether those lacking formal citizenship should be viewed as noncitizens—unprotected by laws that provide for substantive equality—or semi-citizens deserving of substantive equality, in recognition of their partial legal status. I develop a two-by-two matrix that describes the relationship of formal and substantive citizenship for immigrants that will serve as the conceptual and organizational scheme of the book.

Chapter 3, "Winding Pathways to Citizenship," delves deeper into the claim that citizenship inequality flows from institutional deficits by focusing on the existing citizenship and immigration laws. More specifically, it explains how citizenship law operates for immigrants in multiple legal statuses. Analyzing each category of noncitizen in turn, the chapter examines the effect of institutional support by explaining *how* legal categories influence immigrant integration. As part of this exploration, I study how obstacles stymie integration for each category and the possibility of constructing new pathways.

After providing the theoretical framework for understanding the relationship between citizenship status and integration, in part II of the book I present empirical studies of immigrants who seek to integrate into society and encounter formal and substantive barriers that hinder their efforts. A lack of institutional support constrains integration for each immigrant category, both when pathways to formal citizenship are available to them and when they are not. Chapter 4, "Barriers to Formal Citizenship," examines lawful permanent residents with green cards and a path to formal citizenship. The immigrants in this chapter discuss their reasons for seeking, or declining to seek, citizenship through naturalization, and their challenges navigating the pursuit in a political climate that prioritizes enforcement.

Chapter 5, "Blocked Pathways to Full Citizenship," shifts the focus to immigrants who lack formal citizenship and who cannot seek it. Looking at integration and equality in the places where it is most severely needed, the chapter reports on interviews with temporary visa holders and undocumented immigrants who study, work, and live in America while immigration law blocks or limits their legal status. Interviews with international students, highly skilled workers on temporary visas, and DACA recipients show that the benefits of substantive citizenship are constrained by a lack of formal legal status. The uncertainty about the future conveyed by these immigrant have-nots starkly illustrates what is true for all immigrants during the age of enforcement: lacking legal status produces a tenuous hold on life that inhibits economic, social, and political belonging.

Chapter 6, "Constructing Pathways to Full Citizenship," revisits the opening dilemma of how to integrate immigrants during an era of enforcement. The chapter challenges an emerging perception in citizenship studies that formal citizenship is becoming less important by recounting how immigrants in every legal category suffer citizenship insecurity. This sense of insecurity hampers their present and future investments in social, economic, and civic life. The book closes with recommendations for strengthening immigrant integration into American life. Assuming that institutional problems require institutional fixes, I propose a hub-and-spokes model that places the federal government in the center of a national immigrant integration policy agenda. Building on the most promising examples of immigrant integration in the United States and abroad, this book prescribes government initiatives that extend access to formal citizenship by coordinating and incentivizing civics and language training, equalizing application fees for naturalization, and drawing on the resources of other immigrant-serving agencies to encourage naturalization. These initiatives would complement voluntary and localized efforts to support citizenship and integration. Ultimately, the book calls for a recalibration of immigration policy that takes integration as its north star and injects a measure of equity into enforcement, altering the goal from enforcement to the protection and promotion of citizenship.

PART I

INSTITUTIONAL SHORTCOMINGS

CHAPTER 2

Unequal Citizenship

Gaps in Formal and Substantive Citizenship

THE IMMIGRANTS FEATURED in this book are tremendously diverse: they are wealthy and poor, educated and unschooled, highly skilled and inexperienced workers, married with children and living alone, and culturally mainstream and racially distinct. Yet their noncitizen experiences are fundamentally similar in other ways: they cannot travel freely outside the country, they are separated from family members, and they cannot vote. Their futures remain stuck in limbo unless and until they become citizens.

This chapter paints a portrait of citizenship inequality. While individual immigrant experiences vary, noncitizens as a group lag behind citizens in terms of integration, suggesting that citizenship status influences their successful incorporation into US society. The chapter begins with a portrait of citizenship inequality across multiple indicators of immigrant integration and substantive equality: social, economic, political, and legal. It draws on citizenship theory to explain these variations in belonging as the by-product of structural inequalities, in particular gaps between substantive citizenship and formal citizenship. Framed as a structural issue, the question becomes: Should noncitizens be left unprotected by laws or treated as semi-citizens deserving of the substantive rights and protections of societal membership, notwithstanding their partial legal status? Highlighting the shifting and variegated nature of legal status fills a gap in our understanding of citizenship inequality and lays a foundation for understanding how to construct full citizenship for noncitizens.

An Empirical Portrait of Unequal Citizenship

According to the National Academy of Sciences, immigrants lag behind US citizens on social, economic, political, and legal measures of integration.[1] While their performance on most of those measures improves with time spent in the United States, and their children catch up to native-born Americans in the second or third generation,[2] these gaps in well-being are cause for concern. The gaps are particularly severe for immigrants who bear characteristics of traditionally disadvantaged Americans upon arrival, such as poor, black, and Latino newcomers. Each have a harder time acquiring language skills and obtaining employment in well-paid or professional occupations.[3] This book stresses, however, that the social integration gap is significant *across* citizenship categories as well. Irrespective of the citizenship category to which they belong, immigrant groups are rendered "categorically unequal" in terms of their eligibility for those rights and benefits positively associated with integration.[4] These categories solidify further distinctions until they become social markers and not merely legal ones.[5] In effect, the law constructs immigrants as semi-citizens who are partial members of society and who only partially belong.[6]

This is not to say that we should put blind faith in the power of formal status to generate equality. Critical theorists who are skeptical of the centrality of state power have long argued that formal status does not by itself bring about equality. Immigration scholars studying undocumented immigrants, especially DREAMers, similarly claim that formal status is not the be-all and end-all.[7] These scholars downplay the role of federal law, believing that nongovernmental or local support can compensate for inequalities among formal legal categories. That substantive equality is not guaranteed, even after formal citizenship has been attained, is the point well taken.[8] Racial minorities and women who have obtained formal citizenship equality still lag behind native-born citizens. Still, there is no denying the crucial role of formal citizenship status in achieving equality. Therefore, examining the social construction of that status is critical to understanding immigrant inequality.

Critical race scholars also point out that formal status has often been used to promote racial inequality within citizenship law. For example, in the US Supreme Court case *Dredd Scott v. Sandford* (1857), in which a black former slave unsuccessfully sued for his freedom and that of his wife and two daughters, the court infamously pronounced that "a negro, whose ancestors were imported into [the United States], and sold as slaves, could not be an American citizen."[9] The Fourteenth Amendment's citizenship clause would reverse the *Dredd Scott* ruling a decade later, granting African Americans formal citizenship and stating, "All persons born or naturalized in the United States, and subject to the jurisdiction thereof, are citizens of the United States and of the State wherein they reside."[10] However, several landmark court decisions and immigration statutes supporting race-based immigration exclusions were passed even after the Citizenship Clause.

In 1898, a Chinese-American man born in San Francisco to Chinese immigrant parents was barred from reentering the United States following his travel abroad, despite the Citizenship Clause's promise of citizenship to anyone born on US soil. In *United States v. Wong Kim Ark* (1898),[11] the lower courts upheld the government's position until the Supreme Court ruled that Wong Kim Ark had been illegally denied entry because birthright citizenship applied to the US-born child of Chinese immigrants. The Fourteenth Amendment, the Court argued, meant to "put it beyond doubt that all blacks, as well as whites, born or naturalized within the jurisdiction of the United States are citizens of the United States . . . restricted only by place and jurisdiction, and not by color or race,"[12] thus affirming Wong Kim Ark's birthright citizenship. In this case, formal citizenship law protected Wong Kim Ark, but the government had attempted to use this citizenship law to exclude a disfavored racial minority group, reinforcing and extending social realities.

Race-specific naturalization requirements were codified in immigration law for decades before they were eliminated by the 1965 Hart-Celler Immigration Act. Ian Haney Lopez's seminal work about the legal construction of race, *White by Law*, studies pre-1952 naturalization law to discern the dynamics of racial exclusion.[13] He uses the history of immigration law to show that Asian and Arab immigrants were excluded from citizenship by virtue of being nonwhite. His work demonstrates how law constructs race in society as opposed to codifying natural inferiority: it shapes social meanings and renders concrete the inequality experienced by immigrants seeking to fit into the United States. Citizenship law in particular constructs inequalities between citizens and noncitizens and among categories of noncitizens.

The government also wielded immigration and citizenship law as an exclusionary force during the internment of Japanese-Americans during World War II, the reduction of Latin American migration in 1965, the denials of the rights of Muslims post–September 11, 2001, the ban on the entry of immigrants from Muslim-majority countries in 2016, and more recent proposals to limit Central American, Caribbean, and African migration.[14] History shows that despite achievements such as the Fourteenth Amendment, an exclusionary thread runs through the federal government's regulation of the membership of black, Asian, Latino, and Muslim immigrants in the United States.[15] Many of these historical episodes of racialized immigrant exclusion promoted distinctions in formal citizenship law that reinforced inequality.

Race is one of several sites of inequality in substantive citizenship, yet it is insufficiently analyzed in the immigration context.[16] Latinos, who are the largest noncitizen group, especially lack the means to close the gap in economic achievement. There is evidence that similar trends exist within the Asian population, the fastest-growing foreign-born group, as well. Though there are significant variations across immigrant groups, the overall portrait is of a group of noncitizens who experience more inequality than native-born citizens—at least within their own lifetimes.[17] These substantive gaps in equality give rise to empirical puzzles about the degree to which citizenship matters.[18] They also raise normative questions about what is owed to immigrants—especially immigrants of minority races—and whether their differential treatment can be justified because they are "semi-citizens" of the community or perpetual foreigners outside the political community.[19]

Blurring the Citizen/Noncitizen Dichotomy

To some extent, competing interpretations about *how* citizenship affects conditions of equality stem from the contested nature and multiple uses of the term *citizenship*. Citizenship is frequently thought of in formal terms—as legal status, rights, and material benefits. However, theorists have broadened this definition. J. G. A. Pocock emphasizes political participation,[20] T. H. Marshall emphasizes social citizenship,[21] Judith Shklar emphasizes economic citizenship or the right to earn,[22] and Michael Walzer defines citizenship in terms of membership, belonging, and identity.[23] My definition of citizenship encompasses each of these concepts as components of full citizenship, as shown in figure 2.1. Along the *formal* dimension of the citizenship spectrum, I take note of various statuses: naturalized US citizens; green card holders; refugees; noncitizens in the military; temporary visa holders; and undocumented immigrants, including Deferred Action for Childhood Arrivals (DACA) recipients with limited legal rights such as temporary protection against deportation. Those eligible to naturalize stand at the threshold of for-

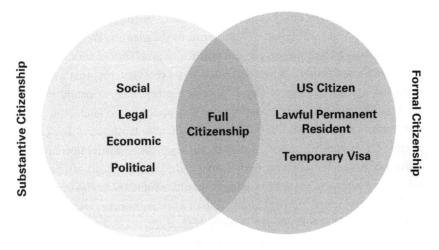

Substantive Citizenship

Social

Legal

Economic

Political

Full
Citizenship

US Citizen

Lawful Permanent
Resident

Temporary Visa

Formal Citizenship

FIGURE 2.1.   Substantive and formal components of full citizenship.

mal citizenship, which is defined as the highest level of legal status. There are also those who lack the ability to ever attain formal citizenship. In between, green card and temporary visa holders follow a progression of increasing formality in legal status. I contrast these legal categories of citizenship with the four major dimensions of *substantive* citizenship that are commonly used in studies of social stratification, integration, and refugee settlement to gauge immigrant parity compared with native-born or naturalized citizens: economic, social, political, and legal rights.[24] Economic incorporation includes employment, education, income, and welfare benefits. Social incorporation includes aspects of individual identity and group belonging. Political incorporation includes civic engagement and political activities such as participating in protests, speaking at community meetings, contacting elected representatives, and voting. Legal incorporation refers to immigrants' formal rights, such as the constitutional rights of due process and equal protection, or immigration benefits such as the freedom to travel or not be deported. Unlike historical accounts of immigrant assimilation, my analysis emphasizes that immigrant integration is a two-track path along which immigrants progress toward citizenship as they access mainstream institutions and begin to resemble native-born citizens.[25]

This book's definition of formal citizenship as a spectrum contrasts with several other definitions in common use. Everyday conversations about immigration during the era of enforcement tend to distinguish "illegal immigrants" from "legal immigrants."[26] The terms *illegal alien* and *illegal immigrant* are both descriptively imprecise and politically problematic: *undocumented status* and *unauthorized status* are much more precise terms that avoid the stigmatizing connotations of *illegal*.[27] While legality is an important marker, the legal/illegal dichotomy oversimplifies that immigration landscape. Legal immigrants, for example, can be either permanent or temporary; they can be eligible for citizenship or not. Moreover, the legal/illegal distinction can be a difference in kind or a difference in degree.[28] Illegal immigrants can be out of status for a variety of reasons, ranging from unlawful entry to visa expiration, working without a permit, or commission of a crime. Another reality masked by the dichotomy is that illegality largely depends on the shifting tides of official recognition. In *Immigration Outside the Law*, Hiroshi Motomura explains that "unlawful presence is inconclusive in several key respects, and that immigration status is just the start of deciding how unauthorized migrants should be treated."[29] Lawful presence is murky because changing policies can excuse, permit, award discretionary relief to, or adjust the status of seemingly illegal immigrants. Only 19 percent of lawful permanent residents originally crossed the border without permission, and another 12 percent came with permission and then overstayed their visas.[30] These statistics suggest that it is necessary to reframe "illegality" as a contingent rather than categorical status.[31]

As an alternative to the language of illegality in formal status, Linda Bosniak, in *The Citizen and Alien*, distinguishes between citizens and noncitizens.[32] She describes the issue in terms of citizenship rather than illegality, which makes it an affirmative rather than a negative designation. This focus on citizenship acknowledges how various statuses create critical differences among society's various members in terms of their rights and obligations. Traditionally, citizens can participate in formal politics: they can vote, contribute to campaigns, serve on juries, and hold public office.[33] These rights are particularly significant for citizenship theorists, who believe that political activity is the root of a self-governing citizenry or well-functioning representative democracy. Formal citizens additionally enjoy greater freedom of travel, capacity to sponsor family members for permanent migration, eligibility for social welfare benefits, and protection from the threat of deportation, even after committing crimes or other offenses that would trigger removal for a noncitizen.[34] These aspects of formal citizenship become most salient in eras of enforcement, where being on one side or the other side of the dividing line produces even starker differences in rights.

Noncitizens, in contrast, lack many of these formal rights and they are also deprived of other forms of economic, social, and political belonging. The term *semi-citizenship*, used by scholars such as Elizabeth Cohen, nicely captures the gradient quality of their in-between status. Cohen, in *Semi-Citizenship in Democratic Politics*, explains the differences in kind and degree that attend semi-citizenship categories, and she disaggregates of semi-citizen rights into relative and autonomous rights.[35] Extending her framework to legal classifications on the citizenship spectrum, the law affords different rights and benefits to permanent, temporary, limited, or undocumented statuses. US-born citizens and naturalized citizens have largely the same economic, social, political, and legal rights, with minor differences in their ability to resist denaturalization. Green card holders enjoy many of the same economic and social rights but cannot vote and are susceptible to losing their green cards if they commit a deportable offense. Undocumented immigrants cannot work unless they obtain a work permit by virtue of a special designation such as DACA or asylum. The noncitizen category, therefore, comprises a variety of partial statuses arrayed along a spectrum. Whereas a citizen/noncitizen or legal/illegal immigrant binary implies fixed differences between two groups, semi-citizen categories can shift with changes in the law or in practice as enforcement around certain rights or benefits weakens or intensifies.

The formal differences between groups along the citizenship spectrum ultimately stem from the sovereignty of nations to determine their membership and to control their borders. In a world that is carved into nation-states, borders are "both the product and precondition" of citizenship rights.[36] To say that borders are a precondition of citizenship means that they differentiate a priori an American from a Canadian, Mexican, Chinese, or Filipino national. This disparity is most obvious in the rules governing acquisition of citizenship at birth. It is present in the rules governing naturalization and the lives of immigrants living inside the United States as well. Borders, in short, reinforce boundaries of membership,[37] and heavy border enforcement further entrenches the citizen/noncitizen distinction, allowing legal status to overshadow other social, economic, and political differences.

The enforcement epidemic that distinguishes documented from undocumented immigrants amplifies the citizen/noncitizen binary intrinsic to the nation-state. Qualitative evidence suggests that the most important motivation for becoming a citizen is no longer the right to vote, which has long been seen as the sine qua non of citizenship. Rather, avoiding immigration enforcement, or maintaining territorial security, is now the most common reason cited for obtaining formal citizenship. For this reason, immigration scholars have started referring to undocumented status as a "master status"—that is, as the defining quality of immigrants' identities.[38] My argument takes an additional step: I contend that during an enforcement era, formal status becomes the master status for virtually *all* noncitizens, even green card holders and temporary visa holders. The reason is that the defining characteristic of noncitizenship is no longer the right to vote, which separates green card holders from US citizens, or the right to work, which separated citizens from slaves. Rather, in an age of travel bans and mass raids the defining characteristic is ever-present insecurity, most vividly crystallized in the fear of deportation. Recall that many criminal aliens who become a priority for deportation are first green card holders. Recognizing their lineage gives one a sense of the particular vulnerability—distinct from race, gender, and class vulnerability—experienced by semi-citizens.

Despite the general insecurity felt by noncitizens, there are legal distinctions within the noncitizen category that make some feel more included and better protected than others. Compare, for example, the eligibility of permanent residents and ineligibility of temporary migrants for social welfare benefits. Analyzing the laws restricting welfare benefits for immigrants in the 1990s reveals that green card holders and citizens are often covered, whereas noncitizens with lesser forms of status are not.[39] The permanent/temporary migrant divide in welfare laws is subtler than the citizen/noncitizen divide, yet it is consequential for understanding citizenship inequality. Further dividing lines are found in the official justifications given to support or deprive immigrant workers of rights. Undocumented immigrants are generally not entitled to work, whereas immigrants on temporary visas may work in some circumstances. Yet in the enforcement context, some claim that longtime undocumented immigrants are entitled to a right to remain in the United States, whereas guest workers, be they low-wage fruit pickers or high-skilled technology workers, have not sufficiently demonstrated their intention to settle and thus should not be allowed to remain.[40]

Another status-based legal distinction focuses on criminality rather than illegality. This distinction implies that the major problem with immigrants is that they are lawbreakers.[41] Enforcement choices reflect this presumption.

During the 1990s, raids targeting fraud, abuse, and unlawful work led the federal government to focus on worksite violations and interior enforcement.[42] After September 11, 2001, however, immigration law shifted its focus to anti-terrorism and the US-Mexico border, and the rhetoric shifted to distinguishing good and bad immigrants.[43] Denying access to so-called criminal aliens and foreign-born terrorists (i.e., the bad immigrants) became the enforcement priority under presidents George W. Bush and Barack Obama.

The Donald J. Trump administration expanded immigration enforcement to include virtually all present or former immigrants—that is, everyone who is not a US-born citizen. By restricting legal immigrants with green cards, H-1B visas, F visas, and asylum claims alongside undocumented immigrants, the government sent a strong message that no immigrant is safe from enforcement. These actual or perceived threats to the security of all noncitizens reinforce the citizen/noncitizen divide that I adopt in lieu of legality or criminality. The shifting parameters of contemporary immigration enforcement have led to a reconstruction of the citizen/noncitizen divide that pits US-born citizens against everybody else—legal or illegal, good or bad.

The Structural Gap between Formal and Substantive Citizenship

To occupy a position between undocumented status and full citizenship means living in the gap between formal and substantive citizenship. Immigrants are, by definition, formal noncitizens, falling short of the full legal status of US citizens. Immigrants additionally lack substantive citizenship, enjoying diminished access to social, economic, and political belonging and rights that are reserved for native-born and naturalized citizens. Some legal migrants are eligible for formal citizenship, yet they are denied social or economic membership by virtue of their racial minority status, lack of social or professional networks, low education, modest job skills, income, or experiences. For example, a Latino green card holder might be routinely stopped while driving, suggesting that he is not substantively equal to a European technology worker on a temporary visa in social terms. A Chinese engineer who is kept out of upper management as a result of suspicion regarding her ties to China is substantively unequal in economic terms. In this sense, the experience of an immigrant with formal citizenship but low substantive citizenship mirrors that of African Americans, who were once classified as a formal noncitizens under *Dredd Scott* in 1857, were disenfranchised under Jim Crow laws in the 1950s, and are still disproportionately targeted by police years after obtaining formal citizenship.

Consistent with critical race theorists' claim that formal citizenship is not enough for full membership and belonging, my argument is that *formal citizenship status* is consequential for substantive belonging. Substantive citizenship is the end goal of the integration process, but substantive citizenship cannot be obtained without formal citizenship. It is necessary but not sufficient. Obtaining formal citizenship facilitates fuller inclusion at the final stages of membership and belonging. It would have been quixotic for slaves to attain economic equality without first securing the right to vote or being considered formal citizens. Legal rights are an important prerequisite for "belonging" for racial minorities in American society.[44]

Noncitizens can be considered semi-citizens when their partial legal status lends itself to substantive inequality. These gaps in formal and substantive citizenship produce inferior positions for immigrants as compared with someone with full formal and substantive citizenship. Table 2.1 presents a conceptual diagram of how formal and substantive citizenship relate to each other for noncitizens in the empirical studies that follow. Each dimension of citizenship is displayed as low or high in a 2 × 2 matrix. Formal citizenship is displayed horizontally, demonstrating high or low legal status. The matrix is an ideal type that simplifies the categories within it. While the high and low designations appear to be dichotomous, the categories actually run along a spectrum: formal citizenship in decreasing measure on the horizontal x-axis and substantive inequality on the vertical y-axis. Extending the concept of formal citizenship to the end points of the horizontal spectrum, a US-born citizen would have the highest formal citizenship and a foreigner living abroad with no ties to the United States the lowest. In my empirical study, a lawful permanent resident is considered high formal, a temporary visa holder is considered medium formal, and an undocumented immigrant with a limited legal protection like DACA is considered low formal.

Substantive citizenship is displayed vertically in table 2.1. Once again, the high and low degrees of citizenship are visually represented within the grid as ideal types, though they could be envisioned along a vertical spectrum (on the y-axis) that ranges from complete belonging to none at all. Here, the high-low distinction illustrates the more complex notion of substantive citizenship. As the chapter has described, substantive citizenship is composed of multiple facets and ranges from complete social, economic, political, or legal

TABLE 2.1. Intersection of formal and substantive belonging.

		Formal	
		−	+
Substantive +		(4) Low formal, high substantive	(1) High formal, high substantive
−		(3) Low formal, low substantive	(2) High formal, low substantive

belonging to none at all. Someone who is rich, white, and well connected socially would be considered high on this measure. Someone who is poor, black, socially isolated, and civically disengaged would be low. While the 2 × 2 grid cannot precisely compare each facet of substantive citizenship, the specific measure of one's combined economic, social, or political level of integration is less important than seeing how substantive belonging is distinct from formal citizenship.

Thus, in this stylized 2 × 2 grid, the intersection of the formal and substantive dimensions of citizenship creates four possible grid placements among noncitizen groups: box 1 (+, +), box 2 (+, −), box 3 (−, −), and box 4 (−, +). Each of the immigrants interviewed for this book falls into one of the boxes:

- Box 1 (+, +): The lawful permanent residents in box 1 register high on both formal and substantive dimensions of citizenship. For example, green card holders with family or economic sponsors on the brink of naturalized citizenship would rank highest. A European or Canadian technology worker or veteran might also occupy a high position because of his or her high formal and substantive belonging. A Latino green card holder who faces racial discrimination might fall lower within the same box. (Chapter 4)
- Box 2 (+, −): The lawful permanent resident immigrants in box 2 share the high formal status of those in box 1, but they lack a sense of substantive belonging. For example, a refugee who feels socially isolated might fall lower in box 2. (Chapter 4)

- Box 3 (−, −): An immigrant with medium to low formal and substantive citizenship falls into box 3. For example, temporary visitors with nonimmigrant visas would fall in the middle range on formal citizenship since they have lawful status but lack an automatic pathway to citizenship; H-1B temporary workers would rank relatively higher than international students given their greater prospect for adjusting to permanent residence. Both the H-1B worker and F-1 international student would rank low on substantive citizenship given their social isolation and ambivalence about future US affiliation, despite relatively strong economic prospects. (Chapter 5)
- Box 4 (−, +): In box 4 are noncitizens with low formal citizenship but high substantive belonging. The high substantive belonging deviates from expectations given the presumed importance of formal citizenship to integration. An undocumented immigrant with DACA is low on the formal dimension but higher on the substantive axis given his or her longtime residence in the United States. (Chapter 5)

Structural Barriers to Citizenship Equality

Formal citizenship, manifested in legal status, is a structural feature that contributes to substantive differences. By structural, I mean that it is an overarching force that produces inequality through the unequal distribution of opportunities and the generation of hierarchies. It is not merely one factor within the larger set of forces affecting immigrant integration. Yet the relationship between formal and substantive citizenship is not necessarily causal in the sense that quantitative studies might imply. Rather, it is constitutive. Substantive citizenship speaks to economic, social, political, or legal membership in ways that materially affect membership within a society, extending or undercutting the law's provisions. A green card holder may be eligible for welfare benefits for which an undocumented immigrant is not, and is therefore in an economically privileged position—notwithstanding the fact that both lack full legal status. The temporary worker, though possessing legal status, may feel socially alienated in a way that discourages taking further steps along the path to citizenship.

The deficiencies of semi-citizenship produce material gaps in integration for immigrants. The most obvious example is the economic premium that attaches to increased wages for citizen workers, though the differences are not confined to the economic.[45] As compared with disadvantaged groups whose members are formal citizens, immigrants still have not obtained full civil, political, economic, and social rights, and this renders them vulnerable. As we have seen, territorial security and freedom from deportation is another key deficit in the enforcement climate. Moreover, immigrants are formally ineligible for a host of social welfare benefits, and they can be socially excluded by virtue of discrimination that uses their lack of formal citizenship as a proxy for their race, national origin, or foreign-born status.

Immigrants often differ from citizens in substantive ways: physical appearance, language, religion, cultural values, income, and social networks. Those differences are socially significant, even if morally irrelevant to their claim of equality. Yet the key is that immigrants are *legally* vulnerable—in addition to being socially, economically, or politically different—and these differences are legally significant. Dark skinned or light, rich or poor, educated or not, they constitute a peculiar kind of vulnerable minority within a majoritarian, democratic society because of this structural deficiency. These legally relevant inequalities give rise to institutional concerns and require institutional interventions.

The basic worry is that, without such government intervention, immigrants will become an underclass of foreign residents who can never become equal to citizens.[46] This concern is complicated by the close association between legal inequality and economic, social, and political insecurities.[47] Policies about voting and political participation, language gaps, eligibility for social welfare, and employability differentiate citizens and noncitizens and exacerbate substantive inequality.

This inequality reaches across the citizenship spectrum. Cecilia Menjívar, Roberto Gonzales, and other scholars speak of legal liminality to describe undocumented immigrants, including those who hold Temporary Protected Status or DACA status.[48] I extend their concept by arguing that liminal legality[49] befits all immigrants. My interviews show that immigrants with incomplete citizenship status experience both subjective and material barriers to integration during their time in the United States. They live in "gray areas," and their "legal status shapes who they are, how they relate to others, their participation in local communities, and their continued relationship with their homelands."[50] For those who hold a partial legal status that blocks their path to citizenship, they can remain in a state of limbo for an extended amount of time or even indefinitely. This underlying sense of citizenship insecurity affects all immigrants and binds them together by virtue of their shared status as noncitizens.

My empirical data shows that the enforcement era binds noncitizens socially as well. My interviews with legal immigrants show permanent residents and temporary visitors to be acutely aware that their rights might be curtailed by changes in policy or shifts in enforcement emphasis. Green card holders were cognizant that their eligibility for naturalization can be stripped, their rights limited, and their territorial security vulnerable despite having settled in the United States years ago. This is especially true for Latino green card holders, who have been in the crosshairs of interior enforcement policies and are scrutinized during the naturalization process. International students and technology workers with provisional paths to citizenship had to rethink their plans in light of the Trump administration's travel ban on temporary visitors from Muslim-majority countries and its curbing of the number of H-1B visas. As DACA is rescinded, leaving recipients with precarious protections that could be withdrawn, DREAMers report worrying about being unable to lawfully work once their work permits expire. They express frustration at being unable to vote for legislative proposals that would stabilize their lives in the United States, even after protracted advocacy to block the rescission and create a legislative path to citizenship. The liminal experience of all these immigrants is defined by a series of cumbersome transitions and heightened uncertainty.

As a normative matter, citizens need not be the same in every respect, but the "democratic ideal of equal citizenship entails more than formal legal equality."[51] Indeed, formal laws requiring too much sameness can be undesirable and encroach on individual freedom and encourage cultural assimilation rather tolerating differences. The notion of equal citizenship is an idealized rendering of an equality ideal. US immigration law sanctions citizenship and national origin discrimination pre-admission. Alienage law applies constitutional ideals in less protective ways post-admission, sometimes in violation of the general rule that the Due Process and Equal Protection Clauses apply to noncitizens. Moreover, a society can legitimately afford different rights to citizens and noncitizens. We do not owe a formal education to tourists who are passing through or to short-term workers who retain strong ties to other countries.

However, those living within the United States possess claims to inclusion in many spheres of life, even if they lack legal claims under citizenship and immigration law. For the category of temporary visitors who hold weak claims on the United States, short stays may become long ones. Withholding important rights throughout this period is ethically problematic. Also, the premise that a migrant can only be rooted to a single place ignores that transnational migrants can and do have meaningful ties in multiple places. Intent distinguishes the guest from the transnational and is an important concept in immigration law. If a guest intends to make a life in the United States, his claim to belonging should begin at day one, even if it takes time for his stakes and ties to be fully realized. If a visitor intends to pass through, her claim is weaker from the outset. Further complicating matters, individuals migrate for many reasons and their intentions change over time. Yet the blunt functioning of laws that divide citizen from noncitizen and permanent from temporary migrant does not capture these nuances.

Strictly enforcing citizenship law and maintaining the clear divisions between categories loses sight of the purpose of citizenship: to build a national community. The experience of citizenship insecurity, or liminality, interferes with the task of individual integration and societal cohesion. For example, green card holders may not want to naturalize. DACA recipients and temporary visa holders may experience a "sense of foreshortened future" that inhibits their social investments while living in the United States.[52] Insecurity inhibits social cohesion as well. Studies have shown that racial diversity presents challenges to social cohesion.[53] The same may be true for legal status diversity, especially given the racialized nature of citizenship status.[54]

My encouragement of more naturalization and integration will have critics asking, Why should every immigrant become a citizen?[55] Why should the government ensure that semi-citizens become equal to US citizens? To narrow my claim, I am arguing that *some* groups should be allowed this opportunity to integrate who are denied the chance under current law. Among them are temporary visitors and DACA recipients, two categories of legal status not granted a path to citizenship under citizenship law. It is possible that other groups deserve this opportunity, too: migrants who cannot qualify for temporary or permanent statuses, undocumented immigrants ineligible for deferred action, or immigrants who have lost their eligibility for citizenship based on their conduct inside the United States. My argument does not extend to these groups because I have not studied them. While I am sympathetic to the inclinations of those who feel immigrants would fare better without border constraints, I am also a realist and believe that enforcement is an enduring feature of a bounded society rather than a feature peculiar to our times. In this book, therefore, I make the narrower argument that a pathway to citizenship would improve the individual standing for the immigrants living in the United States whom I interviewed.

The Social Construction of Citizenship

The integration of immigrants can be improved because citizenship is a socially produced category of legal status, and not a fixed concept. As critical race scholars have long explained, race is a social construct.[56] It is created and solidified by legal categories.[57] Citizenship is similarly a social construct. Citizenship law articulates legal categories such as the green card; the H-1B, F, or J visa; or DACA. A green card holder becomes a de facto citizen. An H-1B, F, or J visa holder develops an expatriate identity as someone living temporarily abroad. These legal categories, which are initially devoid of social meaning become meaningful as they take root in everyday experience. Over time, the legal construct takes on social meaning: a highly skilled worker with an H-1B or DACA is considered a "good immigrant," whereas an undocumented immigrant ineligible for DACA is considered an "illegal" or a "bad hombre."[58]

Moreover, everyday social practices can sustain, undermine, or otherwise transform formal legal categories.[59] For example, the historical process of racial formation transforms a social category into a legal one. As with race, stereotypes of noncitizens can be deployed to justify exclusionary citizenship laws. The explicit justifications for such statutes were historically racist and xenophobic, then became subtler as overt racism was increasingly condemned. In this subtler form, lawmakers would proclaim that though they were committed to equality, the United States is not responsible for those outside its political boundaries or who have been deemed unfit for membership. In more extreme times of racism and anti-immigrant enforcement, the racialized undertones of immigration law are glaringly evident. The immigrant group is "racialized" by a social process that chips away at the guarantees of formal equality and fixes racial identities to legal categories.[60] An H-1B worker becomes a white university professor or an Asian engineer; a DREAMer becomes an undocumented Mexican immigrant. A refugee becomes a migrant from an economically developing, politically unstable, "Third World" country: perhaps Africa, if the migrant is black, or a Middle Eastern national security threat, if the migrant is Muslim. The foreign identities transform into citizenship categories, even as the language of citizenship law permits noncitizens to naturalize into US citizens.[61] As such, arbitrary classifications make their way into immigration statutes.

Citizenship inequality is the product of racial associations *and* legal status, not merely epiphenomenal of a biological trait. This understanding of citizenship law and inequality is different from the conventional understanding of citizenship law as a translation of black letter law. The category of citizenship is authored by lawmakers and then imposed, construed, and constructed in society so as to justify and promote inequality. The implementation of inequitable immigration policies translates formal distinctions into material differences. The enforcement-first or enforcement-only culture exacerbates these tendencies. Enforcement does not operate neutrally among groups but rather disfavors already mistrusted groups. Even when it does operate neutrally, enforcement exaggerates the importance of formal belonging at the expense of substantive belonging. As a result, a citizenship policy that is fixated on legal status and uncritically accepting of citizenship inequality lets status displace social, economic, and political belonging.

This problematic distortion is common to all immigrants, including those who are on the pathway to citizenship. My interviews show that because restrictions in their formal rights and benefits generate a lack of substantive and social belonging, legal immigrants experience partial citizenship as a result of their noncitizen status. The current immigration policy climate magnifies the feeling of exclusion and limits their full integration into society. Temporary and especially undocumented immigrants, who are the main target of enforcement policies, exhibit the same feelings. Enforcement-driven distortions against undocumented immigrants who reside without the permission of society or temporary migrants who overstay their visas might be tolerated to some extent. However, the distorted focus on status obscures other claims to belonging. Despite their status, immigrants are bearers of economic, social, and political rights. This is equally true for permanent and temporary migrants, both documented and undocumented.

Integrating Semi-Citizens

Legal categories can become imbued with social significance that perpetuates citizenship inequality. On the flip side, changes in legal citizenship status can lead to improved integration outcomes. I argue that the law provides crucial institutional pathways to these improved integration outcomes. Legal immigrants can transition between temporary and permanent categories of legal status under citizenship law. For example, an international student can marry a US citizen or obtain an employer-sponsored visa. Undocumented immigrants can obtain deferred action or become eligible for legalization, meaning their legal status can be and sometimes is "indeterminate."[62] Gaining access to formal citizenship can help close equality gaps, even though it does not solve everything: formal citizenship is *necessary*, even if it is not *sufficient* for immigrants to feel as if they fully belong.

Conversely, citizenship statuses can be undone, and the social experience of a legal category can shift as a result of the enforcement climate without a formal change in status. Many criminal aliens were formerly green card holders. Longtime undocumented immigrants can become enforcement priorities when they are denied stays of removal. A refugee or veteran who receives economic support and a presumptive green card can face hurdles that ultimately block their adjustment to formal citizenship, or result in the loss of their green card. High-skilled workers on temporary visas, such as the H-1B, can become ineligible for citizenship based on shifting policies that make visas less available or more highly scrutinized. Family-sponsored permanent residents, such as the elderly parents of a US citizen, have similarly become more vulnerable as policy proposals to limit chain migration have surfaced. Even naturalized citizens are within the crosshairs of the Trump administration.

My empirical claim, therefore, is that the enforcement climate produces a social category of noncitizen defined by legal insecurity and that this category is expanding. I argue that legal immigrants are now part of the contested group, and so they are legally vulnerable outsiders to society. Legal immigrants need not be placed in competition with undocumented immigrants or criminal aliens to see who has it worse. There are continuities of insecurity in the immigrant experience. That such a diverse set of individuals—of various ages, races, genders, religions, class backgrounds, and national origins—can even be lumped together in a single category of noncitizen is telling. Being a noncitizen should be a residual legal category that has no independent meaning, but it now carries social meaning and legal significance. In the current enforcement-dominated climate, legal status is a primary identity marker, not merely a penultimate stage in a progression of belonging. The legal-status divide poses substantive barriers in its own right. Immigrants, even lawful permanent residents, cannot vote, run for office, or seek representation in Congress. The citizen/noncitizen status divide also erodes social, economic, and political belonging.

My interviews highlight the role of immigration enforcement and reveal that formal and substantive citizenship both figure into the analysis of integration during an era of enforcement. The sequencing by which one obtains full citizenship may not be the same for all groups of noncitizens. Formal citizenship is merely the threshold for full citizenship, a prerequisite that must be fulfilled before true substantive equality can be attained. It is the beginning and not the end of the conversation if one's goal is to enable *full* citizenship that goes beyond the traditional citizen/noncitizen dichotomy and embraces social, economic, political, and legal integration.

The citizenship spectrum described in this book combines the critical and socio-legal framework for understanding noncitizens as semi-citizens. It recognizes noncitizens as being on a pathway to citizenship that acknowledges the nonbinary, contingent nature of semi-citizenship and its relationship to formal belonging. It attends to both social process and legal mechanisms undergirding the integration of noncitizens as full members of society. The next chapter describes this spectrum in greater detail. It focuses on the connective tissue between the legal categories, detailing the mechanisms for transitioning between statuses and identifying the potholes that block transition to higher levels of formal affiliation for each immigrant subgroup.

CHAPTER 3

Winding Pathways to Citizenship

RALLIES FOR UNDOCUMENTED IMMIGRANTS routinely feature signs and chants calling for a pathway to citizenship. However, during the enforcement era, many immigrants have lowered their expectations. As one Deferred Action for Childhood Arrivals (DACA) recipient said during an interview, "If I had a green card, I would have citizenship eventually."[1] Those immigrants who *do* have a green card and are seeking citizenship express continuing discontent with their legal status. Rattled by the images of deportation they see on television and the stories they hear in the community about being detained for minor offenses, many permanent residents fear that their green cards will be threatened. One permanent resident, Guy, said, "The president is so strict, they can take away your residency for any little thing."[2] Luis agreed, explaining that "as a [legal permanent resident], one day you could be here and the next you could be deported. There is no security. You're still just a guest."[3] Each believed formal citizenship was necessary to make him secure. Another resident, Carmen, worried that were she to keep renewing her residency instead of pursuing the path to citizenship, the government would question why she had not naturalized already.[4]

These immigrants all express concern over the lack of an institutional pathway to citizenship. This chapter builds on the observation that current laws impose a citizen/noncitizen binary in the formal classification of immigrants. And it shows how these classifications impose structural barriers to full integration. Drawing on citizenship and immigration law, it explains the potholes in existing citizenship law that impede the smooth transition between different categories: undocumented to documented, temporary to permanent, green card to naturalized citizen. These impediments in-hibit social, economic, political, and legal integration for every category of noncitizen. The combination of the United States' laissez-faire approach to citizenship and its heightened enforcement hinders integration by creating a negative feedback loop that amplifies the importance of legal status.

The Normative Case for Pathways to Citizenship

Before turning to *how* we can reduce citizenship inequalities, we should ad-dress *why* they arise and why we should try to mitigate them. A nation can regulate its boundaries based on criteria of its choosing, within the parameters of certain norms and laws.[5] Those criteria are hotly contested in both the schol-arly and public discourse. Those who would restrict citizenship point out theo-retical and practical problems with a "come one, come all" approach. People concerned about national sovereignty prioritize the right to control borders over admitting more immigrants, while those who are concerned about maintaining a particular national culture in the United States prioritize their right to maintain the current population mix over demographic transforma-tion.[6] Others worry about the financial obligations of supporting newcomers, fearing that admitting too many will put an unmanageable strain on a limited pool of resources.[7]

The normative ideal of establishing pathways to full membership and be-longing for semi-citizens rests on an ethical premise: the United States owes semi-citizens the opportunity to integrate while living in the United States and the chance to become equal with citizens over time. This does not mean that all immigrants will choose to take that option. But the aspiration of the liberal legal norm of inclusion includes opportunities for expanding mem-bership and inclusion. The government might condition the opportunity on certain qualifications or caveats, such as an agreement from an immigrant to abide by American values or announce an intention to reside permanently in the United States provided the ability to do so under immigration law. The immigrant might need to remediate prior transgressions of immigration law, whether through fines or other demonstrations of commitment to the nation.

Earlier chapters pointed out that immigrants are arrayed on a spectrum of semi-citizenship. If not all who come are allowed to stay, how should the government choose whom to settle? Citizens and noncitizens have always been treated differently, the distinctive rights of the former stemming from political boundaries.[8] Citizens within a political community enjoy a set of rights and owe one another reciprocal obligations. Noncitizens reside outside that political community, even if they might be included for some social matters. It is a principle of national sovereignty that the community chooses where to draw the line between the political community and its outsiders. National boundaries, therefore, create societies in which conditions of equality can flourish.

The level of equality for noncitizens depends on society's stance toward newcomers. Theorists make several kinds of distinctions among the rights of noncitizens. In the social contract view, the United States consents to the presence of lawful immigrants and, conversely, withholds consent to those who enter unlawfully or who violate the terms of their temporary stay.[9] This view is illustrated by US immigration policies to restrict welfare benefits for undocumented immigrants and movements to end birthright citizenship for children of undocumented immigrants. The more welcoming affiliation view treats immigrants as political insiders from the start.[10] It respects their personhood as members of the community and grants them a presumption of equality, as seen in *Yick Wo* (1886), the Supreme Court ruling that equal protection applies to noncitizens and citizens, or in laws affording immigrants access to local services and K–12 public schools such as *Plyler v. Doe* (1982).

The transitional view of citizenship treats immigrants as political insiders once they declare an intention to become American. Hiroshi Motomura's historical work, *Americans in Waiting*, describes a forgotten provision in citizenship law from 1795 to 1952 that exemplifies the transitional view.[11] It permitted "near citizens" to declare their intention to eventually naturalize and then be granted numerous rights and benefits over the course of their transition to formal citizenship. Though this declaration-of-intent provision remains on the books, its use was curtailed after the elimination of racial quotas resulted in more diversity among immigrants. It is now lost to immigrants as a functional option, though some public benefits and nondiscrimination protections do exist for the small number of "intending citizens" who file each year.[12] Instead, modern immigration law privileges those who arrive with a visa that permits an intention to permanently reside in the United States, such as an employer-sponsored visa, a family-sponsored visa, or a refugee determination. Modern immigration law requires that immigrants who arrive outside of these avenues, such as temporary visa holders, stay for a limited purpose or duration and demonstrate their intention to return to their home country rather than remain in the United States.[13] In most cases, there is no path to citizenship.

This book adopts a model of integration based on affiliation, with greater prospects for transitions that lead to substantive and formal integration. Because the United States has wavered between these three views (social contract, affiliation, transition), the standing of temporary visitors and undocumented immigrants remains in flux. Much ink has spilled on societal responsibilities to undocumented immigrants who entered without documents or consent of society and have since become longtime residents of the United States, particularly the children who did not share in the decision to enter without inspection and who consider themselves American. So, too, for immigrants who have opted to remain in the United States beyond the terms of their visa. Many theorists and laypersons, as polls would tell us, think guest workers and longtime residents who are undocumented have a strong moral case for regularization of their status, if not also legalization. For guest workers who overstay their visas and intend to remain and work in the United States, critics of enforcement argue that society has tacitly consented to their integration.[14] For undocumented immigrants, the worry is that stigmatizing them will create an underclass without prospects for integration.[15]

And what of those immigrants, here for shorter stays, who cannot express an intention to remain or who do not intend to become US citizens? This was the case with many of the international students, Asian temporary workers, and Canadian green card holders in my interviews. Dazhen, a Chinese scientist on an H-1B temporary worker visa and weeks away from receiving a green card, said he is not sure whether he will pursue citizenship following his receipt of a green card; the decision will depend on the economic benefits of obtaining US citizenship.[16] Deepti, an Indian professor on an H-1B visa, has been in the United States for seventeen years on temporary visas and filed for a green card nine years ago. Despite her impatience after many years of waiting, she explained that for her, "citizenship is not emotional," stating, "My Indian citizenship is a document, not an identity."[17] Both of the Canadian green card holders whom I interviewed, Rob and Bob, said they may eventually take the next step toward naturalized citizenship so as to share a common national identity with their US-citizen families, but they were in no rush and so far they had not felt the need. Collectively, these interviews—which are presented in greater detail in the following chapters—reveal that not everyone who is eligible wants to become a citizen. Their hesitation might stem from a sense of continued affiliation with their home country, the lack of a pressing need, or social and legal barriers to new membership.

Theorists have not historically focused on these temporary visa holders, and when they do, they tend to assume that their nonpermanent residency limits their legal rights and integration.[18] For example, David Miller writes, "Their human rights must of course be protected. But beyond that, their position is better understood in contractual terms: what rights they get should depend on what agreements they have made (or are in place) before they enter. . . . Otherwise, it is their responsibility to ensure that the work contracts they sign are adequate to provide for their needs. Equally, they are under no obligation to contribute to the society they work in, other than by complying with its laws and rules of social behavior."[19]

Along similar lines, Motomura writes in *Americans in Waiting* that the transitional view he favors would permit benefits to immigrants closer to arrival but deny public benefits to intending citizens once it becomes clear they do not intend to naturalize.[20] I argue that the federal government should extend to these immigrants greater opportunities to integrate during their temporary stay and permit visitors who will live in the United States for a significant amount of time the ability to express an intention to reside permanently, unlocking the benefits of formal citizenship with increased time and affiliation. As a formal matter, the government should rethink the non-immigrant intent doctrine that bars a temporary visa holder who lives in the United States from signaling an intention to reside and instead make it easier to demonstrate changing or dual immigration intentions. Also, to promote substantive belonging, the government should provide temporary visa holders eligible for and wishing to reside permanently, social, economic, and civic opportunities to integrate while they wait to adjust their status. This approach emulates the H-1B visa program that permits high-skilled workers to declare a dual intention to pursue work and to settle in the United States, and it models the historical declaration of intent.[21] It contrasts with the F-1 visa program, which requires students to depart after completing their studies.[22] The government could offer less to temporary immigrants on short-term tourist visas that do not permit residency for a significant time—say, five years factoring in extensions—or who do not declare an intention to remain in the United States. Aligning formal requirements with the empirical reality that intentions evolve while immigrants are living, working, and studying will lessen the impulse to violate the nonimmigrant intent requirement or overstay a temporary visa—thereby reducing the need for enforcement.

Employers, universities, and other voluntary institutions can and should supplement government efforts by encouraging substantive integration for temporary visitors. Doing so would improve the day-to-day experience for immigrants and pave the way for long-term integration and substantive equality. While there is much to be gained by becoming a US citizen, those who must give up their original citizenship—and even those who can keep their citizenship—have something to lose as well. In my view, it is not a problem per se if Latino green card holders and Chinese or Canadian technology workers who live in the United States for many years prefer to retain their original citizenship and decline to become US citizens. Maintaining such a choice protects them against pressures to assimilate against their will. The problem is immigrants being unable to transition when they so wish. Immigrants should be able to choose whether to avail themselves of the opportunity based on the pull of their home country or the push of an unwelcoming climate.

Is it problematic for immigrants to opt for citizenship for purely transactional or pragmatic reasons? Some theorists argue that "thin citizenship"—that is, formal citizenship without deep investments in economic, social, and political life—is enough.[23] However, given the exclusionary nature of the nation-state, which becomes even more restrictive in times of heavy enforcement, thin citizenship may not suffice. In such times, there is a diminished possibility for "thicker" substantive engagement with the United States without formal affiliation.[24]

In presenting a normative case for citizenship based on an inclusionary ideal and commitment to formal equality, I argue that US institutions, including the federal government, should assist noncitizens with integration during their stay and with their eventual transitions to citizenship. Integration should be a two-way process, but it is often seen to be one-way. The terms and conditions of naturalization show the immigrants' obligation—a language requirement, a civics requirement, a loyalty oath, and a period of residence to demonstrate genuine ties in the United States—but the government bears no reciprocal responsibility. Inclusion abets integration. Indifference and exclusion inhibit it.

The pursuit of equality is part of the liberal ideal of citizenship. Creating the conditions that lead to broad and inclusive citizenship requires rethinking current approaches. The next section provides background on how citizenship law currently operates and offers new ideas for moving from the government's laissez-faire approach to an affirmative approach.

Background on Immigration and Citizenship Law: Tiered Paths

The institutional paths to formal citizenship are provided for in the US Constitution, Article I Section 8, Clause 4, which requires Congress "to establish a uniform rule of naturalization."[25] According to these rules, citizenship can be obtained by birthright citizenship or naturalization.[26] In general, as figure 3.1 shows, immigrants eligible to become citizens enter on an employment-based or family-sponsored visa. Absent expediting circumstances, they wait three to five years to attain a green card, which renders them lawful permanent residents. At this point, lawful permanent residents face a voluntary choice to become citizens. If they were not born on US soil or to US-citizen parents, qualifying immigrants can *choose* to become citizens through naturalization. Approximately half of immigrants choose to naturalize, and those who naturalize make up approximately 10 percent of the US citizen population. Generally, to be eligible to naturalize, the Immigration and Nationality Act, the immigration statute governing naturalization, requires that the applicant be at least eighteen years old; demonstrate continuous lawful permanent residence for five years, knowledge of civics and the English language, and a good moral character; and pledge loyalty to the United States.[27] Alternatively, immigrants can choose to "stay green" without ever becoming citizens, provided they renew their permanent resident status every ten years by refiling and paying a fee to the US Citizenship and Immigration Services (USCIS). These renewals permit immigrants to keep their resident status without needing to leave the United States.

Despite the similarities in pathways to citizenship for lawful permanent residents, the process differs according to an immigrant's prior legal status. For refugees, the overseas process of determining eligibility is more involved initially and then becomes streamlined as they transition to citizenship in several steps.[28] After obtaining their refugee determination, refugees come to the United States and become eligible for their green card within one year.[29] In their initial settlement period, refugees receive some economic support and cultural orientation through the combined efforts of government-funded social workers, state resettlement agencies, and refugee-serving nonprofits such as Catholic Charities and Lutheran Family Services. Many of these nonprofit organizations

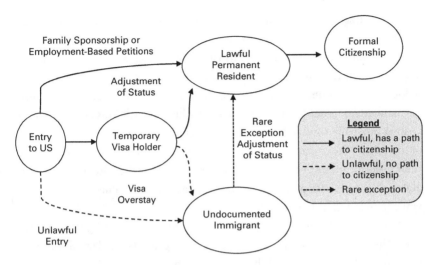

FIGURE 3.1. Pathways to citizenship.

stay in touch when it comes time to naturalize five years later. Asylum seekers, who differ from refugees in that they enter the United States without prior approval, undergo a similar process once their refugee determination has been made.[30] In both cases, while the transition from green card to naturalized citizenship is not required, nearly all refugees take this next step toward formal belonging. Consequently, refugees make impressive strides economically, socially, and legally; they naturalize at higher rates than other immigrants.[31]

Many noncitizen military recruits already have a green card when they enlist. Among those who do not, the immigration laws since September 11, 2001, provide two accelerated paths to citizenship for service members. For those who serve during peacetime, the route provided for in the immigration statute mirrors the refugee process in many respects: service members become green card holders and can naturalize on a fast track.[32] During wartime, service members can file soon after enlistment and are simultaneously eligible for a green card and citizenship once they file a naturalization application.[33] Naturalization programs offered during basic training and waived application fees streamline the process even further.[34] Several veterans in my interviews spoke of helpful military officers and government bureaucrats who shepherded them through the steps. Hiring preferences for government work, college tuition support, and health care facilitate their economic integration. Because of this bundle of support, noncitizen veterans outpaced their civilian counterparts for naturalization by a factor of seven until a reversal of trends in 2017.[35]

Temporary visa holders, by contrast, typically lack a pathway to citizenship as shown in figure 3.1. By statutory requirement, most temporary visa holders must demonstrate that they do not hold the intention of remaining permanently in order to gain entry to the United States.[36] This entails that the visitors prove their intent to return to their country of origin at the expiration of their visa. The insistence ignores the reality that many visa holders extend their visas for many years or overstay their visas to make a life in the United States. Still, the letter of the law treats them as guests who need not integrate while living in their host society.

As for undocumented immigrants in the United States, as figure 3.1 shows, few paths lead to citizenship.[37] Immigration law treats their "unlawful" presence as an anomaly to be corrected through enforcement: a removal hearing, detention, and deportation. There are some equitable paths to a stable legal status or naturalized citizenship for immigrants who enter without inspection or who overstay their visa. However, these options are limited and narrowing under enforcement policies that limit exceptions and restrict exercises of discretion.

Potholes in the Pathway to Citizenship

Reflecting my training as a legal scholar, I view citizenship law as a key facet of the institutional pathway to integrating immigrants. After all, citizenship and immigration status directly determines the pathway from newcomer to green card to formal membership in the United States. Formal citizenship status functions as a structural constraint on integration, determining eligibility for future immigration benefits, welfare, travel permission, and voting rights, among other things. Given the variety of pathways available to green card holders and the absence of options for temporary and undocumented immigrants, we can see how citizenship is a mechanism for integration. It is not merely an outcome of it. My focus on citizenship pathways is also merited for an empirical reason: the majority of naturalized citizens in the United States have transitioned from another legal status—upwards of 60 percent, according to data from the New Immigrant Survey.[38] This transitional character of immigration law explains why debates over entrance criteria, admission caps, or deportation priorities fail to capture the whole picture. It is crucial to examine the process for changing visa categories and adjusting status to improve immigrant integration.[39]

As a matter of law, institutional support along the pathway to citizenship is minimal. Toward the beginning of the immigration journey—when obtaining a green card is often the goal—contacts with immigration authorities occur at least once every two or three years. Once an immigrant has been granted eligibility to naturalize, communication tails off. It is then incumbent on the green card holder to seek citizenship; nobody from the government contacts the green card holder to see if he or she is interested in pursuing the next steps. Facing this communication breakdown and lacking interim milestones, green card holders may only think about the possibility of naturalizing when their green card needs to be renewed nine years after its issuance. During my interviews, several green card holders on the pathway to citizenship said they read online forms themselves, sought help from family members, or consulted with employers and private attorneys about the necessary steps for naturalization. Many more foundered or delayed beyond their eligibility to naturalize because they faced language barriers, were intimidated by the process, or lacked motivation to pursue the benefits of citizenship.[40]

The exception to the United States' prototypical laissez-faire path is the *affirmative* institutional support it offers to refugees and noncitizens in the military. But the support available to these groups is eroding as well. The reduced number of refugees permitted in the United States leads to reduced resources for refugee resettlement agencies to facilitate refugee integration; an executive order permitting states to veto refugee resettlement within their boundaries makes resources even more unstable.[41] Service members remain eligible for streamlined naturalization and fee waivers, but interviewees reported that these institutional supports did not always operate as smoothly in practice as they appear to on paper. Recruiters misrepresented the ease of the process, military officers knew little about immigration, and government bureaucrats were insufficiently attuned to the challenges of completing paperwork between training and deployments. This weakening of institutional support has worsened since I conducted my interviews: 2017 policy changes have cut off the eligibility of immigrants for citizenship through the Military Accessions Vital to the National Interest program (MAVNI), which provided some immigrants with a means of naturalizing through the military that they previously lacked, and increased procedural burdens on the naturalization process have led to fewer applications, longer wait times, and higher denial rates.[42]

Temporary visitors and undocumented immigrants encounter additional barriers to integrating. Temporary visitors may never be eligible for a green card, depending on the terms of their visa.[43] For those who do become eligible for a green card, obtaining one requires strict compliance with the terms of their visas. These requirements can seem obscure to scientists and students who are more focused on their studies than satisfying administrative requirements. Undocumented immigrants are not only passed over for formal citizenship but discouraged from substantively integrating.[44] They are ineligible for most federal benefits and only selectively eligible for state or local benefits. Some undocumented immigrants are eligible to adjust their status—for example, if they marry a US citizen—through an immediate relative exception; others are not able to adjust without departing the country, thereby incurring penalties for having previously entered without inspection.

The divide between temporary visa holders and undocumented immigrants on the one hand, and green card holders eligible for citizenship on the other hand, is not as stark as it initially appears. If two-thirds of lawful permanent residents originally entered the United States with a temporary visa or no documentation, only one-third were newcomers automatically eligible for citizenship.[45] Thus, most lawful permanent residents in the United States take multiple steps along the path to citizenship, beginning with temporary or no status and then gradually moving on to a more permanent status. The notion that immigrants arrive ready to transition to citizenship in a single step is an outdated presumption held over from the era of predominantly European migration.[46] It has little bearing on today's migration patterns, where Asian and Latin American immigrants predominate. Some immigrants succeed in making these numerous transitions; others do not progress or express frustration with the obstacles they encounter.

How Pathways Affect Integration

Under existing law, immigrant integration proceeds steadily but unevenly.[47] Individual immigrants face multiple barriers to social, economic, and political integration upon their arrival.[48] It often takes more than a single generation to overcome these barriers. Different immigrant groups vary significantly in their outcomes, and progress is not always linear.[49] Significant structural barriers and long delays leave certain immigrants in limbo: immigrants without immediate relatives, immigrants without favored skills or professional networks that lead to employer sponsors, and immigrants from oversubscribed countries. Depending on the category of eligibility and country, wait times from these oversubscribed countries can run seven or more years, with Mexico, China, India, the Philippines, and El Salvador showing the longest waits in recent years.

Along the pathway to legal citizenship, there are several moments when the process of transition can break down: obtaining a visa before entry,[50] transitioning from one temporary visa to another temporary visa (i.e., international student to H-1B),[51] transitioning from temporary visa to lawful permanent residence (i.e., H-1B to employer or family sponsor), transitioning from lawful permanent residence to naturalized citizenship, or transitioning to a green card following relief from deportation.[52] As noted earlier, more naturalized immigrants arrive at citizenship via one of these transition processes (530,000) than as newcomers automatically eligible for a green card (460,000), so any disruptions along the way are consequential.[53] These breakdowns in the transition process derive from immigration law, which establishes a dichotomy between citizen and noncitizen rather than a spectrum of citizenship.

The declaration of intent, discussed earlier, was a historical example of how affirmative institutional supports once eased the transition from noncitizen to citizen. The United States' provision of material support for military service members and refugees is another example that, until recently, led to fewer administrative problems, higher naturalization rates, and more positive feelings toward the government. By comparison, green card holders going through the normal process of transition were left to rely on private resources like families, friends, immigration attorneys, and employers. As a group, they experienced more difficulty, held less favorable views of the federal government, and reported lower naturalization rates. The dissatisfaction is more intense for Latino immigrants, who might benefit the most from naturalizing. Yet it was striking how much the federal government is *not* seen to be part of the integration process for all types of green card holders: to most of the noncitizens interviewed, the federal government's involvement in immigration equates to enforcement, not integration. Among temporary visitors and DACA recipients, many voiced complaints about renewal fees, timelines, and delays that impeded their work and created uncertainty. They found themselves relying not on the government but on high school or college administrators who were ill-equipped to help them.[54]

Changes in formal citizenship laws will not by themselves solve the problems of substantive inequality. Formal changes are necessary, but not sufficient, for substantive equality. Recall that, in chapter 2, I argued that everyday social practices can sustain, undermine, or otherwise transform formal citizenship categories. The opposite is true as well: formal laws can shape social possibilities for membership and inclusion. For noncitizens, the terms of their legal categories limit them: their social identities produce and extend inequalities. However, their legal categories are not natural categories and do not fix their identities permanently. Indeed, the formal language of citizenship law permits noncitizens to become US citizens with the same rights and benefits afforded to those who were born in the United States.

What does an affirmative institutional path to immigrant integration enable that a laissez-faire one does not? Addressing this question requires a baseline understanding of how individual attributes of immigrants affect their integration. Immigrants with higher incomes and education, younger immigrants, and those with more social ties are generally more likely to integrate.[55] These observations, however, do not tell the full story of how the institutional approach shapes integration for all immigrants. Immigrants who initially resist naturalizing can change their minds with the help of greater encouragement and resources, such as community organizations making available language and civics classes or the government waiving naturalization fees. In *Becoming a Citizen*, Irene Bloemraad provides an institutionalist explanation for naturalization and summarizes institutional explanations for variations in the pursuit of citizenship across noncitizen categories.[56] Bloemraad compares the United States and Canada to contrast the former's laissez-faire approach (and 40 percent naturalization rate) with Canada's more robust approach (and 60 percent naturalization rate).[57] Her work shows how the United States could improve its institutional commitment to formal citizenship.

How Enforcement Undermines Integration

Institutional barriers are not the only factor inhibiting immigrant integration. A laissez-faire institutional approach leaves immigrants vulnerable to exclusionary policy climates and anti-immigrant sentiments, especially in times of heavy enforcement. This hostile climate generates feelings of exclusion and impedes a sense of belonging. This creates a negative feedback loop, as enforcement policies magnify immigration laws that permit inequality across the citizenship spectrum. Immigrants from Latin American and Muslim-majority countries spoke most frequently about the hostile policy climate,[58] but the sense of unease extended to interviews with migrants from Eastern Europe, Russia, Africa, and Asia as well. This section examines the institutional and social barriers that produce feelings of exclusion and societal *dis*integration.[59]

If institutional support for citizenship positively affects naturalization, the reverse is also true: administrative burdens discourage eligible green card holders from naturalizing. Longtime green card holders from Canada and Europe especially reported feeling that their status was sufficient and that they did not need to go to the hassle of naturalizing.[60] These privileged immigrants contemplating naturalization did not find the process daunting or difficult. Rather, they simply felt it was not worth it, especially if they came from a country that did not permit dual citizenship and required them to forgo their native citizenship to attain a new one.

Latino green card holders, who as a group felt a green card to be sufficient without citizenship, said the enforcement era made them rethink their complacency.[61] Some immigrants compared papers to an "insurance" policy in the face of potential discrimination, and they were more willing to undergo the hassles of naturalizing. Other immigrants expressed skepticism that formal status would safeguard them from racial discrimination because US citizens assume all brown-skinned individuals are noncitizens.[62] The responses of white immigrants from Canada and Europe and Latin American immigrants suggest that race and class cleave the experience of being a semi-citizen, and that enforcement realities have heightened the exclusion for disfavored racial minorities more than for white immigrants.[63]

My interviews also suggest that substantive citizenship is often a precursor to attaining formal citizenship. A sense of social belonging—the feeling that one has a meaningful life in America—precipitated many naturalization decisions, even more frequently than instrumental factors like obtaining the right to vote, travel, or sponsor family members.[64] Other immigrants commented that becoming a naturalized citizen made them feel more American afterward. Consequently, formal citizenship and substantive integration operate in a positive feedback loop, with obtaining formal citizenship comprising an important step to integrating fully and substantive integration facilitating naturalization.

Another important barrier to formal citizenship is language, which also influences prospects for social belonging, naturalization, and civic engagement.[65] This is because of the uncertainty immigrants felt at every point along the citizenship spectrum. Even immigrants who do not suffer from language barriers were rattled by the enforcement-minded policy climate. For example, green card holders from Canada and Germany expressed uncertainty about "what this administration would do" regarding immigration.[66]

In comparison, my interviews with refugees and military service members—those green card holders who, unlike permanent residents in the general population, receive affirmative institutional support—show how institutional support interacts with a hostile environment. Refugees benefited from the certainty of their pathway toward citizenship.[67] This benefit is seen in their impressive naturalization rates and their subjective experiences navigating administrative complexity. Most refugees found the process complicated but counted on institutional mediators for help. They viewed refugee determination as one step toward the longer-term goal of naturalization, without much regard for whether they felt a sense of belonging in their new society.[68] For refugees who had been poorly treated in their home countries, this prioritization of citizenship and its protections makes sense: as Mary, a Burmese refugee, said, "I've never been a citizen of a country."[69] Beneath their high naturalization rates, many refugees lack a sense of belonging and exercise low political participation.

Immigrants who serve in the military exhibit the opposite tendencies: high substantive belonging that is being gradually eroded by decreasing, yet still relatively high formal belonging. Military naturalization rates are historically strong,[70] but my interviews indicated that in this era of enforcement, the pathway is not as smooth as the institutional support hypothesis would predict. Many immigrants did not have citizenship on their mind when they enlisted in the military, and their intermediaries in the Department of Defense were less informed and less committed to helping them naturalize than the nonprofit organizations and state agencies that serve refugees. Some service members said they felt like Americans already, and they thus do not bother to become formal citizens through military service. Frank, a veteran born in Mexico, had been eligible for citizenship for a long time before he was deported. He did not remember why he neglected to apply for his US citizenship before then. Though he was born in Mexico, he had been raised in the United States and never went back to Mexico to visit. He simply did not think he needed to obtain citizenship status because he had never contemplated being deported elsewhere.[71] Indeed, he thought of his military service as a "second passport" for reintegrating into civilian life and was surprised when he subsequently realized that he needed a secure immigration status to be safe in the aggressive enforcement climate. Such jarring realizations are becoming more common as the Trump administration intensifies vetting requirements for service members and reneges on promises to reward service with citizenship. Recent data shows that military naturalization rates have dropped 65 percent with the implementation of more burdensome requirements—suggesting that strong substantive belonging is not enough to buffer a deficiency in formal citizenship.[72]

The importance of legal status to substantive integration increases when immigration enforcement is strong. This can be seen most clearly in the case studies of temporary visa holders and undocumented immigrants. Temporary immigrants on short-term visas, such as international students and high-skilled workers, have limited pathways to citizenship and are considered "guests" rather than residents under US immigration law.[73] When applying for their visas, many of them rely on colleges, employers, and private attorneys for assistance. USCIS is largely absent from the process, and the nonprofits that help other immigrants with lower incomes or specific subethnic groups tend to be less involved as well. Though temporary visa holders manage with their private resources, they frequently complain about administrative complexity and lack of coordination between their university or employer sponsor and USCIS. The resulting delays may disrupt an international student's studies or university researcher's work if one visa expires before the next visa is ready. Those on short-term visas fret over renewal schedules, though high-skilled workers, who hold H-1B visas for three years and can renew fairly simply, do not report this concern as frequently. While many students and high-skilled workers do not seek to stay in the United States, those eligible to stay for longer or those seeking a permanent visa stress the frustration of feeling in limbo or even "stuck" during the process.[74] As one technology worker said, "For me, personally, the [visa outcome] has been positive. But the process has been painful . . . and I'm worried. Is there a box somewhere that was wrongly checked so that the application will get denied and now everything in my life has to change? It's the fear of some rule change tomorrow. I'm at a point now where I feel like I've done everything I was supposed to, I've done everything correctly. I love my job. I've lived my life here. But I'm waiting to see. Someone gets to decide [whether] I stay or not."[75] These institutional barriers can be become unwelcoming signals; bureaucratic forms can feel personal when they determine one's social experience.

Undocumented immigrants experience blocked pathways to formal citizenship. DACA recipients are a subset of undocumented immigrants who possess limited protections from deportation and who are permitted to work, which helps with their legal and economic integration.[76] Their extensive social ties and political engagements in the United States enhance their sense of membership in the community, even if they are not formally US citizens. However, the continuing gap between their substantive and formal citizenship causes hardship for many. Substantive citizenship does not compensate for their lack of legal status, and the hostile climate can erode their sense of belonging. Shan, whose parents overstayed their tourist visas from China, said that she always saw herself as starting a family and retiring in America but "cannot do that without citizenship."[77] Faced with fading hopes for a pathway to citizenship, another DACA recipient said, "If DACA remains, but there [is] no citizenship, we are not moving forward in anything."[78] These remarks reflect a pessimism about the future that inhibits integration in the present.

The DACA recipients I interviewed relied on university services or community clinics that popped up after the DACA rescission to help them gather paperwork, process forms, and pay application fees. Though grateful for these ad hoc resources, they were perplexed by the many rule changes and overwhelmed by the complexity of forms and the seemingly unending renewal applications. Most DACA recipients had applied three times for renewals since 2012 and had another application pending at the time of their interviews for this book. Compare their experience with that of a Canadian green card holder who said his private attorney emailed him when his visa was ready for renewal or another green card holder who received unrequested extensions from USCIS while waiting for renewal appointments. Several DACA recipients lost work permits or felt vulnerable to immigration enforcement while they waited for application renewals, biometrics, or employment authorization documents. Some DREAMers inadvertently let their DACA lapse while waiting for a work permit to come through. Their experience was disjointed across dimensions of substantive citizenship. They could be eligible for a college scholarship while being unable to apply for a credit card or car loan. They worried that their DACA "visa" would be revoked by the government on a whim.[79] Though their situations were more stable than their undocumented family and friends, they were markedly less stable than green card holders or US citizens: DACA started their pathway toward citizenship, but it did not complete it.

Theoretical Framework: How Institutional Pathways Improve Immigrant Integration

This chapter has built on institutional explanations to determine how laws can disrupt citizenship inequality and promote integration. Untangling the tiered pathways for different citizenship statuses reveals the importance of citizenship laws to immigrants' integration experiences and outcomes. Government sponsored integration programs should augment existing informal and decentralized supports with interventions of their own to bolster naturalization and boost social, economic, and civic engagement. As the government data shows, the generally lackluster naturalization rate for US permanent residents is significantly higher for refugees and higher yet for veterans, the two groups who receive coordinated institutional support from the federal government. The immigrants with burdened or blocked pathways to naturalized citizenship struggle with jobs, civic engagement, and social belonging as a result of institutional indifference to their settlement in the United States.

Taking the argument further changes the trajectory of immigrant integration. The hostility of an enforcement-minded climate produces contradictory effects. When immigrants feel unwelcomed and mistrustful of the government, they burrow into their daily lives: cutting themselves off from society, working in an informal economy, and becoming cynical about politics. They may seek informal support from family and friends, but they will expect little and offer little to American society. At the same time, immigrants may seek out formal protections to navigate the challenges of a hostile social environment. The trend toward increased naturalization in the presence of heavy enforcement persists because immigrants who feel threatened by policy changes naturalize to protect themselves. While this defensive mindset positively affects naturalization in the short term and sometimes ignites civic engagement, it can weaken over the long term and negatively affect social belonging and economic opportunity.[80]

This dual finding about the effects of enforcement policies on naturalization rates enhances existing understandings of how citizenship relates to integration. Whereas the seminal work on immigrant incorporation and contexts of reception categorizes the United States' policies as laissez-faire—with the exception of those concerning refugees and military, who receive more support—I would categorize the United States as neglectful or even harmful.[81] The last thirty years have witnessed intensifying immigration enforcement against noncitizens in every legal category. These enforcement policies have altered the context of reception in the United States, and the consequences for the integration of immigrants have been significant. The laissez-faire acceptance of hostile immigration policies worsens citizenship inequality by dampening the desire of immigrants to become full citizens and depressing their economic, social, and political integration.

The framework of tiered pathways explains how citizenship and immigration laws constitute the institutional support structure for immigrant integration. The next part presents empirical studies that delve deeper into the experiences of immigrants pursuing citizenship and describes their varying levels of substantive integration. Chapter 4 presents the experience of lawful permanent residents seeking naturalized citizenship. It illustrates that immigrants find the availability of formal legal status important, but they need more institutional support to do better socially, economically, and politically. Chapter 5 presents stories from immigrants without a pathway to citizenship. Here, the absence of a path to citizenship significantly constrains immigrant integration, especially in a climate of heavy immigration enforcement. Together, the empirical studies in the next part of the book tell a common story of insufficient support for a range of immigrant groups that includes those pursuing their pathway to citizenship, those choosing not to pursue the pathway available to them, and those without a pathway altogether.

PART II

STORIES OF IMMIGRANT
INTEGRATION DURING ENFORCEMENT

CHAPTER 4

Barriers to Formal Citizenship

WHEN WE MET OVER coffee, Canadian green card holder Bob had completed the citizenship application but he was still unsure whether to submit it. He had been content with a green card for more than a decade. In his view, applying for citizenship was not necessary. His aerospace engineering job at the university was secure—there were only a few minor projects he could not work on for security reasons—and he felt a sufficient sense of belonging without formal citizenship, at least most of the time. To the extent that he did feel like an outsider to American culture, he was glad: the anti-immigrant tenor of the Trump administration made him appreciate the multiculturalism of his Canadian identity. For Bob, the reasons to proceed were largely instrumental: procuring the economic benefits and political rights of citizenship that would benefit his career and allow him to be more civically engaged. But now there was something else to consider: the expanding reach of immigration enforcement and hostility toward high-skilled workers served as a wake-up call that his legal status, once considered de facto citizenship, fell short of full citizenship. This had never bothered him before, but it now gnaws at him in unexpected moments. Mercedes, a Latino green card holder, feels a greater sense of urgency to naturalize. In contrast to Bob, she is eager to become a citizen as soon as possible so that she can vote in the next election. She says that she feels scared of Trump's immigration policies. In addition, government suspicion is wearing on her, and she wants to signal to her neighbors that she is not an outsider amid rising racial and anti-immigrant sentiment. These two cases illustrate how two people who are eligible for citizenship respond differently to pressures to naturalize in the enforcement era.

Earlier chapters made the argument that institutions, especially laws governing categories of citizenship, shape immigrant integration. These categories condition the level of institutional support available to help immigrants transition between legal categories and progress toward full citizenship, helping to level structural inequality. Among legal immigrants, citizenship law shapes their substantive trajectories and influences their social, economic, and civic integration. Federal support for refugee resettlement, military pathways to naturalization, and language accommodation illustrate the potential for facilitating substantive citizenship in federal integration programs. Enforcement-minded climates, by contrast, boost the utility of formal affiliation without bringing gains to substantive belonging. Recognizing naturalization as an important site for investigating formal citizenship status, this chapter examines the government's approach toward citizenship and its effect on immigrants' decisions to naturalize. While the strong emphasis on enforcement of legal status could just as easily discourage immigrants from pursuing formal citizenship, quantitative data shows that naturalization rates among immigrants eligible to become US citizens—historically hovering around 50 percent—have risen by 8 percent in the last decade, and even more in the early years of the Trump administration. Between 2016 and 2018 the number of green card holders applying for citizenship increased 25 percent. What does this upward trend reveal about the purpose of naturalization? How does that purpose change under conditions of heightened enforcement and hostility toward immigrants?

This chapter examines the relationship between citizenship as a formal legal status and a substantive realm of belonging for legal immigrants. It focuses, more precisely, on lawful permanent residents—informally known as green card holders—who are eligible for formal citizenship as a result of marriage, family sponsorship, employer sponsorship, refugee status, or service in the military.

The federal government plays a distinctive role integrating green card holders because of its unique ability to regulate their access to naturalized citizenship. Interviews with immigrants considering citizenship suggest that federal policies toward naturalization influence immigrants' decisions to seek formal affiliation with the United States and substantively integrate into American life. When the government supports these efforts, naturalization increases. Yet paradoxically, the number of noncitizens seeking formal citizenship can also rise during time periods with *less* institutional support. Interweaving the immigrant interviews with data on naturalization trends, the book asserts that the enforcement-minded climate puts pressure on immigrants to seek formal citizenship as a strategy for countering exclusion. This theory of defensive naturalization helps reconcile theories of citizenship with quantitative and qualitative data on naturalization. However, immigrants' restricted formal rights deprive them of substantive belonging. Taking the path to formal citizenship, therefore, becomes more necessary and yet less substantively meaningful as immigrants seek citizenship as a defensive strategy for belonging.

Naturalization as Formal Citizenship

This book argues that acquiring formal citizenship status through naturalization is part of becoming a full member of society and is an important measure of integration.[1] Naturalizing, which leads to formal citizenship, assigns legal recognition, making rights and privileges, such as voting, travel, family sponsorship, and protection from deportation, possible. Naturalizing also leads to more job security and opportunities for promotion, more social belonging among family and friends, and more opportunities to be civically engaged.[2] While citizenship does not erase other forms of inequality, it is an important determinant of integration.

Since attaining formal citizenship status is critical to integrating substantively, one would think that immigrants would aggressively pursue naturalization. Surprisingly, though, figure 4.1 shows that the *level* of naturalization

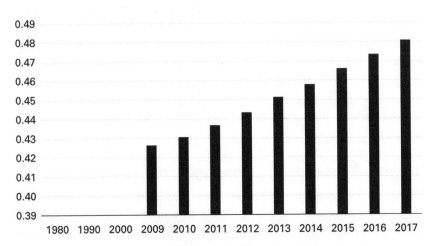

FIGURE 4.1. Rising naturalization levels since 1980. Source: Adapted from Waters and Pineau, *Integration of Immigrants*, fig. 4-2.

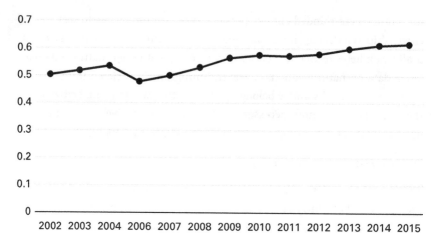

FIGURE 4.2. Rising naturalization rates from 2006 to 2015. Source: Figure by Ming H. Chen, Department of Homeland Security, Office of Immigration Statistics, "Estimates on LPR Population," 2002–15 (2005 missing data). Publication of data ceased in 2016; a 2017 executive order may lead to future publication.

among the *total* foreign-born population has hovered around 40–45 percent over the last twenty years or longer.[3] It is only over the last decade that the *rates* of naturalization, for those eligible to do so, have risen. Since 2011, the rates of permanent residents applying for citizenship have increased to 58 percent, as seen in figure 4.2.[4] Reports based on government data show that applications to US Citizenship and Immigration Services (USCIS) for citizenship increased by 10.5 percent in anticipation of the 2016 presidential election,[5] and that they remained high in the first term of the Trump administration.[6] Because of a backlog in processing naturalization applications and increased denial rates,[7] this does not immediately translate into higher citizenship attainment rates—more on that later—but the increase is a notable and unexpected trend given common beliefs that *more* support boosts naturalization and *less* support diminishes it.

Incomplete Explanations for Changing Trends in Naturalization

To explain the changing trends in the numbers of immigrants seeking citizenship, we must ask a central question about membership: How do institutions influence membership for noncitizens in the United States when enforcement efforts overshadow integration initiatives? The existing hypothesis—that individual, country of origin, and destination country attributes determine membership rates—is not fully adequate.[8] There is robust evidence that institutional support for naturalization matters to naturalization outcomes, and that the lack of institutional support for naturalization that characterizes the United States' laissez-faire approach helps explain the somewhat lackluster historical naturalization rate.[9] But these theories do not explain the rise in naturalization during the enforcement era.[10]

Without understanding how citizenship law and legal status operate in society, scholars cannot understand moments in immigration history when naturalization rates *rise* despite relatively constant institutional support.[11] The interview data suggests that the hostile political climate and negative policies toward immigrants correspond with increased interest in naturalization. On the flip side, these instrumental gains in formal citizenship translate into feelings of exclusion that can degrade the meaning of substantive citizenship. Eventually, depressed substantive citizenship can unravel the short-term gains of formal citizenship and transform the institution of citizenship overall.

Defensive Naturalization as a Strategy for Inclusion

The lives of all immigrants are less secure without formal status: from poor immigrants becoming ineligible for needed social benefits, to refugees relying on fewer resettlement services, to temporary workers worrying about their long-term job security.[12] If the motivations to naturalize can be characterized as thick or thin, defensive naturalization is thin insofar as it is motivated by transactional reasoning. This outlook hollows out the substance of citizenship.

Based on interviews with lawful permanent residents about their reasons for naturalizing, immigrants engage in acts of defensive naturalization in response to a hostile political climate. This drive toward formal citizenship as a protective strategy constitutes a mechanism of integration.[13] The opening vignettes about Bob and Mercedes describe two longtime residents contemplating naturalization for defensive reasons. After so many years of declining to formalize their citizenship, why are they considering it now? Immigrants like Mercedes and Bob may choose to naturalize as a response to an anti-immigrant political climate and a desire to improve their position within it—for example, by voting against specific politicians and policies that hurt immigrants. Next consider a Somali refugee like Hassan, who worries that he will not be able to visit his family members in light of the Trump executive order banning travel because he and his family are Muslim. Hassan has a straightforward path to citizenship as a refugee, yet he feels unsafe and insecure about the future and longs for continuing connection with his loved ones abroad.

Anti-immigrant political climates have catalyzed naturalization before. Most studies documenting this effect focus on Latino naturalization during the 1990s, when California's Proposition 187 sought to bar undocumented immigrants from receiving state public benefits. David Cort found that California's naturalization rate increased after the proposition passed, and that the episode has had lasting effects for the political mobilization of Latinos.[14] Paul Ong found that Chinese immigrants in California naturalized at higher rates than Chinese immigrants in New York during the same time period.[15] Similar studies show that the fear of losing federal public benefits led to increased naturalization in the 1990s for elderly immigrants.[16] Furthermore, qualitative interviews with green card holders conducted immediately after naturalization tests have shown that fear and insecurity were among the motives for naturalization.[17] Most of these studies, however, do not explore the mechanisms behind the increased rates or the integrative effects of policy change. Timing is important to keep in mind because the catalyzing effects of the negative policy environment weaken over time and traditional incentives resume, though the interest in naturalizing remained high throughout the Trump administration.[18]

Defensive naturalization is apparent across immigrant subgroups, race, and national origin. Also, the defensive justifications for seeking citizenship extend beyond threatened immigrant communities to include green card holders. Based on an analysis of the interviews, the meaning of citizenship to naturalized immigrants can be degraded during hostile policy climates. Feelings of societal exclusion trigger a downward spiral that erodes the substantive benefits of naturalization and distorts the meaning and purpose of citizenship.

Why Immigrants Seek Formal Citizenship

Prior studies of immigrants' political integration are limited by their portrayal of naturalization rates as a static number, without acknowledging changes over time and in different policy climates.[19] Policies changed dramatically in the transition between the Obama and Trump administrations. These policies influence the reasons that green card holders choose to naturalize.[20] Also significant is that green card holders confront different obstacles relating to naturalization. Most studies group all permanent residents together and do not differentiate by prior legal status, therefore limiting understanding of immigrant decisions to naturalize in response to those policies. The US government does not maintain longitudinal studies of naturalization, instead using national origin as a proxy for legal status or assuming that naturalization erases differences in the backgrounds and experiences of all permanent residents.[21]

To gain a deeper understanding of formal citizenship, I interviewed green card holders about their decisions to naturalize and gauged how much institutional support they had along the way. The interviews were conducted for three groups of immigrants who are eligible for citizenship and enjoy different levels of support based on their legal categories. Lawful permanent residents eligible for citizenship as a result of employer-based or family-sponsored visas are provided little institutional support. Refugees and asylum seekers have an expedited path to their green card and receive blended support from the federal government, state government, and voluntary organizations.[22] Noncitizens who serve in the military have the fastest track to citizenship and coordinated federal support between the US Department of Defense and USCIS.[23] The findings reveal enforcement strongly influences how these immigrants construe the meaning of formal citizenship and the complex relationship between legal, social, economic, and political belonging for immigrants seeking citizenship.

Darkening Motivations for Seeking Citizenship

Citizenship confers a mix of rights, benefits, and membership to those who seek it. In my interviews, the most commonly cited reasons for naturalizing matched those reported in established studies: the desire to receive benefits, vote, and become American.[24] At the same time, the interviewees framed these motivations in negative terms or as a reaction to the anti-immigrant, enforcement-minded climate. These responses reflected a darkening mood and shift in emphasis. Immigrants are now seeking to *retain* their benefits, vote as a form of civic dissent, and become American to guard against social exclusion or immigration enforcement.

Retaining Immigration and Other Public Benefits Not surprisingly, immigrants valued the tangible economic and legal benefits associated with formal citizenship. Of the immigration benefits made available to citizens through naturalization—the ability to travel, hold a US passport, and sponsor family—the permission to travel freely was among the most frequently mentioned in interviews. Immigrants, by definition, come from another country, and many maintain personal and professional ties that require travel to and from that country.[25] Several immigrants cited the need to care for elderly parents, the desire to maintain connections with friends and relatives, and the wish to introduce their children to their national heritage. In some cases, these trips abroad were numerous. A Chinese immigrant married to a green card holder traveled with her children every summer when school was out of session so that her American-born child would learn her native language and culture and so that she could visit her elderly parents.[26] In the case of Tanya, a Latino immigrant with family responsibilities on both sides of the border, the travel limitation became a hurdle to naturalization.[27] When I met her, she was being turned away from a citizenship workshop. Even though she migrated to the United States nearly ten years ago, she had difficulty satisfying the five-year continuous residence requirement for naturalization because she had returned "home" so much since first migrating to the United States that the immigration attorneys told her she was ineligible to apply that day. A professional athlete who first came to the United States on a student visa traveled back and forth to visit his wife in Africa while he waited five years to qualify for permanent residency; he naturalized because he grew weary of "all of the paperwork" associated with travel.[28]

Business travel enhanced the desirability of naturalization. A Japanese businessman said he intended to pursue citizenship because being able to travel with ease would facilitate his collaborations with partners overseas, a sentiment shared by many professionals involved in international businesses and working on multinational teams.[29]

However common it may be for immigrants to maintain transnational ties that require travel, concerns became especially acute after the Trump administration issued three executive orders limiting travel to the United States for immigrants from Muslim countries, among other places. In our 2017 interviews, immigrants from Muslim countries in all immigration categories were aware of the travel ban that was issued the same year and eventually upheld in the US Supreme Court.[30] In a follow-up survey conducted a year later, refugees overwhelmingly listed travel as one of their top three motivations for seeking citizenship.[31] Latino immigrants, who are mostly not directly subject to the travel ban, seemed aware during their 2016–17 interviews of a general crackdown at the border that made travel and border crossing more burdensome. They described being stopped, being subjected to intense questioning, and having their social media accounts searched. They worried that the travel ban could be amended to include Latin American countries.[32] These findings are consistent with journalistic reports of increased interest in naturalization as an "insurance policy" after the 2016 presidential election and prior studies of increased naturalization following anti-immigrant legislation.[33] Immigration attorneys, who can barely keep up with the needs of immigrants affected by the travel ban, explained that the Trump administration's anti-immigrant rhetoric and travel ban policy functioned as a "scary wake-up call" for many immigrants, including permanent residents—whom administration officials had briefly contemplated including in it.[34] Even though the ban eventually exempted permanent residents, the possibility that lawful permanent residents could be included underscored the tenuousness of anything other than full citizenship, even for those immigrants who typically feel relatively secure in the United States.[35]

Interviewees also expressed the desire for immigration-related and collateral public benefits in similarly defensive ways. Sponsoring family members is a long-standing immigration-related benefit of naturalizing, but an uncertain political environment amplifies its importance. Hassan is a Somali refugee who has his green card but worries about seeing his family after the travel ban: "I have been in the United States for over seventeen years, and despite the fact that I am a citizen of the US, I still fear the worst for me and my family members. So the travel ban, it does affect me. I have family members who live in Somalia and Yemen [two countries on the travel ban list], who now cannot visit us and have, as of late, run into some barriers in applying for refugee status. We don't know how long those barriers may last or when we will see them again."[36] Tanya, the Central American woman who was turned away from a naturalization drive because she lacked the continuous residency requirement, expressed worry that she would not be able to sponsor her adult sister in two years because "policies change so much."[37] Proposals to end "chain migration" and to burden the pipeline from a high-skilled worker visa to a green card raise worries for Chinese immigrants especially.

In addition to immigration-related benefits such as travel and family sponsorship, US citizenship offers a variety of ancillary public benefits. Many are related to economic incorporation, a nonlegal aspect of substantive citizenship. Among higher-income earners and high-skilled workers, one green card holder who recently naturalized reported that she sought to naturalize in order to receive scholarship assistance in pursuing her master's degree.[38]

A scientist felt similarly about how naturalization would increase his odds of obtaining a postdoctoral research position that drew on federal grants; an aerospace engineer mentioned a promotion to a permanent position that required access to data that could only legally be accessed by "US persons."[39] Military service members similarly mentioned the ability to receive higher security clearances, and therefore job promotions, as a benefit of naturalizing, even if this was not their primary reason for doing so.[40] However, some high-skilled workers with green cards from well-developed economies (e.g., China, Germany, and Canada) said they had *less* interest in pursuing US citizenship because their home countries also supplied good jobs.[41] At the lower end of the economic spectrum, refugees and other permanent residents mentioned lower employer regard for noncitizen workers or need for health care and other social welfare programs as reasons to naturalize.[42]

Political Participation as Civic Dissent The right to vote is a distinctive benefit of naturalizing that has sometimes been called the sine qua non of formal citizenship.[43] Immigration scholars and immigrants from stable economic and political backgrounds frequently emphasize the political rights obtained by citizenship as motivations for naturalizing.[44] Studies show that immigrants speak about the ability to vote and participate in politics in varied terms, according to their various characteristics. Generally, immigrants with higher education, income, job skills, and other indicators of elevated integration tend to vote as regularly as the general population once they are eligible. Racial minority voters, especially those who were formerly immigrants, are typically more disengaged from the political process than US-born and white voters. Their lower participation is evident in naturalization rates and voter registration. Latino green card holders, for example, often "stay green" even after decades of naturalization eligibility.[45]

The contemporary climate is catalyzing immigrant interest in political participation and naturalization. Latino immigrants are especially well mobilized to participate in politics, presumably because they developed experience resisting being targets of immigration enforcement for many years.[46] The same desire to vote and participate in democracy is seen in 2018 survey updates for the Latino green card holders, with two-thirds of respondents listing it among their top three reasons for seeking citizenship.[47] In the interviews, Mercedes, the Latino green card holder in the opening vignette, succinctly said that her reason for naturalizing was "to vote!"[48] Other Latino green card holders, such as Luz, spoke pointedly about anti-immigrant policies. Whether or not these policies directly targeted green card holders and their families, Luz shared that she wanted to use her voice to protect the immigrants who could not help themselves.[49]

Beyond voting for specific immigration policies, immigrants spoke of a desire to "be involved" and to "have a say" in politics. Iranian journalist Hamid fled his home country because of pressure he faced following his critical reporting. Shortly after arriving in the United States as a refugee he found work in a grocery store, and he eventually resumed his journalism career with the help of his professional contacts. While he found himself initially fearful of immigration policies targeting immigrants from Muslim-majority countries, he took solace in hearing that the US government was different from the Iranian government. He mentioned the First Amendment specifically as one of the United States' bedrock principles that he appreciated and benefited from in his new country.[50] Bob, the Canadian green card holder and technology worker, came to the United States for college and has stayed while obtaining graduate degrees, working multiple jobs, and starting a family. He explained that he is thinking about naturalizing after twenty years of eligibility because he needs citizenship "in order to do anything: to vote, to be more involved in politics, to persuade elected representatives to vote on your behalf."[51] He urged his wife to give money to various political causes and "wants to do more." He has deep knowledge and strong opinions about politics but has "held back" on expressing his views publicly because he lacked "standing" to speak up as a noncitizen. Bob was aware that noncitizens can participate in politics outside the channels of voting and campaign contributions, and he worked assiduously to influence the opinions of his US-citizen family members. But he felt that direct participation in politics would be improper, even if legally permissible.[52] These views on civic engagement suggest a nuanced relationship between political and legal incorporation.

Many green card holders in my interview sample viewed immigration policy as a partisan issue. This was not the case with many of the refugee and service member interviewees. A Colorado refugee service provider, Kit Taintor, recalled that "the Refugee Act was bipartisan and it passed unanimously."[53] Many immigrants say that the long-standing reputation of America is unchanged by the Trump administration's hostility toward immigrants. More than one Chinese immigrant expressed agreement with government assessments that immigration enforcement is needed to protect the system from fraud and abuse, having personally endured long waits to immigrate legally and then naturalize.[54] When asked whether they were concerned about enforcement going too far, these Chinese immigrants pointed out that they were accustomed to authoritarian governments and social exclusion. All in all, they felt that current circumstances were not entirely unfamiliar and were not nearly as bad as what they had endured in their home country.

Seeking Citizenship as Protection from Enforcement Although concrete rights and material benefits were cited as important reasons for naturalizing, they were not always the most important. Many immigrants in my interviews brought up identity, belonging, or membership in American society as reasons for naturalizing. Several of the Canadian and European green card holders—who came through family sponsorship or employment-based visas and were now eligible to naturalize—said they had long felt that they were American. Becoming a citizen was mostly a formality for them. Other immigrants married to US citizens said they became or planned to become citizens so that they could share a national identity with their family members.[55] This was particularly true when an immigrant had a US-born child. Rob, a high-skilled worker who has long been eligible for US citizenship and is married to a US citizen, shared that the federal childcare facility where his daughter is enrolled has a separate entrance and more vigorous screening process for noncitizens. He felt strange needing to enter through a different gate from the one his US-citizen wife used when dropping off and picking up his daughter.[56] The interviews also revealed that the desire to belong was often accompanied by a desire for knowledge about US politics. Other immigrants reported that after they naturalized, they became more interested in current affairs, even if they had lived in the United States for ten, twenty, or thirty years before becoming citizens. Only after they formalized their citizenship status did they feel that the United States was truly their country.[57]

Immigrants with skin colors or accents that made evident their foreign national origins noted belonging and protection as important motivations for naturalizing. The trend seemed especially prevalent for Latino immigrants, who have felt targeted by immigration enforcement policies for a long time. The extent to which these visible immigrants felt citizenship eclipsed the effects of racism or nativism varied. Luz, a green card holder seeking citizenship in 2017, said citizenship smoothed her interactions with law enforcement: "If you're Latino, it's important that you have your papers and important that you speak English, because you can't defend yourself or anyone else. It's like being mute. People feel nervous, whether legal or illegal, to defend [themselves] and be understood. Having papers helps."[58] Carmen expressed a bleaker view that skin color or accents mattered more than citizenship: "Due to [my] color . . . they'll still call me a wetback and tell me to go back to Mexico."[59] She felt that having official papers would nonetheless counter some race-based discrimination. These noncitizen racial minorities also brought up the issue of being perceived as good or bad immigrants. Luz said she feels "mad that [President Trump] makes us feel like criminals and . . . killers." She continued, "I say that 'we are not all like that!'" Yet she also says that she "understand[s] that there are people who come here to do bad things, but it's not everyone."[60] Luis expressed approval for the thorough vetting that immigrants undergo in the naturalization process, but he objected to how the government will take away "workers . . . who aren't doing any harm in working. They are helping the country."[61] This desire for security and social belonging continued to be very strong for Latino green card holders in a 2018 follow-up survey.[62] It was strong for Muslim immigrants as well, who have to combat stereotypes about their ties to terrorism. Muslim green card holders, though, felt less likely to be perceived as terrorist threats, perhaps because so many of those in the sample were refugees or military interpreters as well as green card holders.

For all the similarities, the effects of enforcement on social belonging vary for immigrant subgroups. Many immigrants still report that naturalization is a meaningful moment and that citizenship is a valuable goal. There are tears at USCIS naturalization ceremonies, and overseas the United States still has a reputation as a land of opportunity.[63] However, some of the more privileged noncitizens are troubled enough by US anti-immigrant sentiment to hold on to their non-US passport. Canadians Rob and Bob are still weighing their decisions to naturalize. Despite their longtime eligibility, each says that the nationalistic backlash makes him more proud to be Canadian and more reluctant to become American.[64] Immigration attorney Leigh Alpert detects a similar attitude among her clients, who increasingly mistrust the United States and are taking pride in their alternate identity as dual citizens.[65] In the extreme, some asylum seekers choose to continue through the United States to Canada, and fewer natives of the Middle East and Mexico are immigrating to the United States because they prefer either to stay home or to settle elsewhere.[66] This increased consciousness about noncitizen status *across* the social markers of race, accent, and legal status is noteworthy.

These immigrants increasingly feel that formal status can not only prevent their exclusion from US society but also allay fears of immigration enforcement. Insulating oneself from the fear of deportation is a critical benefit of naturalizing. But as a legal matter, the lawful permanent residents in this study enjoy a degree of territorial security that would not ordinarily render them vulnerable to enforcement. The salience of semi-citizen status for permanent residents indicates a changed relationship between formal and substantive belonging within and across noncitizen categories.

How Formal Citizenship Status Affects Substantive Belonging

The changing terrain of immigration enforcement influences how, and how much, formal status matters to legal immigrants who hold green cards. Citizenship status is a safeguard against removal and other forms of enforcement. Formal citizenship is the highest level of legal status, and possession of a green card is next highest. For the green card holders who are eligible to naturalize, formal citizenship is attainable, but only if they take the final step. The primary difference between holding formal citizenship and holding a green card is access to political rights, but formal citizenship also matters to one's sense of belonging and other dimensions of integration. The interviews highlight the variation in substantive integration within this group enjoying high formal citizenship.

Citizenship Insecurity for Permanent Residents (Table 4.1, Box 1)

In general, green card holders register high in formal and substantive citizenship. Green card holders with employer sponsors and financial stability may be highly integrated economically, whereas white immigrants from English-speaking nations of origin with long lineages in the United States might be well integrated socially. From my interview sample, a white Canadian technology worker would be marked very high within box 1 of table 4.1. So would a military service member who migrated early in his life and earned a green card, and social respect, through his service. In contrast, a Latino green card holder who faces social discrimination would rank lower within the same box.

For these green card holders, protection from immigration enforcement has become a critical benefit of formal citizenship. Insulation from deportation, or legal security, matters to immigrants for instrumental reasons. However, legal security is also related to the desire to feel "more American" or to belong. Nasim Khansari, citizenship project director at Asian Americans Ad-

TABLE 4.1. Intersection of formal and substantive citizenship: lawful permanent residents, refugees, and veterans.

		Formal	
		−	+
Substantive	+	(4)	(1) Military LPR-EB, LPR-FS
	−	(3)	(2) Refugees

Notes: LPR-EB = Lawful Permanent Resident (Employment-Based); LPR-FS = Lawful Permanent Resident (Family Sponsored).

vancing Justice in Los Angeles, reported, "After the election, the desire to naturalize shifted. It wasn't about opportunity and bringing more family, it was more about, 'there is a new president who is anti-immigrant and we need to do what we can to protect ourselves.'"[67] Even some immigrants who arrived ten to fifteen years ago and have obtained economic and social stability are worried about changes in immigration policy. Those coming from communities that the administration has prioritized for immigration enforcement, such as the Muslim immigrants from countries banned from entry into the United States, expressed this anxiety even if they themselves hold green cards. The concern about formal status among green card holders is striking. A green card is a privileged status that some consider de facto citizenship, which is why it is marked high in formal citizenship in table 4.1. While we would expect undocumented immigrants and Deferred Action for Childhood Arrivals recipients to value formal legal status over and above other forms of belonging, it is surprising that green card holders would value it so much.

Layered over formal citizenship is the experience of substantive integration, which varies along social, economic, and political dimensions—especially by race. For example, a Latino green card holder who feels perennially discriminated against on the basis of race or legal status would register high in formal citizenship but lower in social belonging than a green card holder who is not a disfavored racial minority. Such immigrants lack social belonging. Compounding the problem, they are more likely to become the target of law enforcement, shaking up their supposedly secure status. Luz, a Latina immigrant who gained her green card through a family sponsor, worried about the fate of her children if law enforcement jeopardized her legal status: "If something happened that put me in danger, my kids would be in danger as well."[68] Luz elaborated, "As a citizen, I will feel more secure, for myself and my children," yet she also expressed concern that as her son grows up, he may make mistakes that could subject him to deportation if she does not naturalize and secure citizenship for them both.[69] Compounding the sense of arbitrariness in immigration law, Luz says she has heard that a growing percentage of removals have been based on minor offenses or very old infractions as enforcement expands from specified priorities to zero tolerance.[70] Guy said that "because the president that we have now is so strict . . . they can take away your residency for any little thing."[71] Immigrants fear the threat posed by volatile policies and expanding enforcement targets,[72] which they associate with President Trump's unpredictability. Only naturalizing, they feel, can insulate them against more policy changes.[73] Jose is a Latino green card holder who migrated to the United States in high school. He delayed applying for citizenship for eighteen years, noting that naturalizing had become more difficult since 2001 and speculating that the new immigration policies could make it even harder: "There's a fear amongst [legal permanent residents] that Trump could initiate a law that puts them at risk because they are not citizens."[74] Attaining citizenship would give him "peace of mind."

High-skilled workers showed a similar discomfort with shifting enforcement policies around deportation and exclusion. Historically, many of these high-skilled workers came from privileged economic backgrounds and felt an H-1B visa or green card is sufficient. New worries that federal policies would encumber high-skilled workers arose in interviews. These immigrants now feel that the federal government is serious about excluding *all* noncitizens from full participation in American society, even if they are living in compliance with immigration laws and have been low priorities for enforcement. Stefan, a German green card holder who had been eligible for citizenship for decades, stated, "Who knows what this administration would do?" and called citizenship an "immunization" against future policy changes.[75] While many of these high-skilled workers did not feel directly threatened by enforcement,[76] they all described a growing awareness of the difference between their own privileged legal status and the greater security of naturalized citizenship. On paper, the rights and privileges that distinguish green card holders from citizens may seem small, and these distinctions have not changed. What has changed is the significance of such distinctions for green card holders while living in the enforcement era. This is why I claim that status consciousness is a noteworthy phenomenon.[77]

This gap between formal and substantive citizenship suggests that formal status does not guarantee substantive belonging. Green card holders who have lived in the United States since they were students, like Jose and Rob, had long felt they were "all but" American and enjoyed a substantive sense of belonging. They faced few legal restrictions until enforcement strengthened. Their attitudes toward naturalization changed as a result of the political climate. While some immigrants who are eligible to naturalize opt not to do so because they feel they do not belong and do not consider themselves American, others feel compelled to counteract their feelings of economic, social, and political insecurity. Over time, feelings of exclusion limit other forms of integration. Green card holders who decline to naturalize sometimes return to their home countries to put down roots in places where they feel more welcome. While felt most strongly by Latino, Asian, and Middle Eastern immigrants, the vulnerability of partial citizenship has spread as policies threaten more categories of immigrants.

Noncitizens in the Military: Challenging Formal Citizenship (Table 4.1, Box 1)

Compared with the general lawful permanent resident population, military service members naturalize at high rates and enjoy some of the highest rates of formal citizenship. They benefit from institutional support for naturalization and other material aspects of substantive citizenship such as education, health care, housing, and job placement assistance. When asked why they naturalize, though, many military service members do not mention the material benefits. Instead, they resoundingly speak about feeling American.

Service members' strong sense of social belonging results from serving in the military. Overwhelmingly, noncitizens in the military feel substantively American by the time they apply for citizenship.[78] Their reasons for "feeling American" varied. Some longtime green card holders felt this way before they enlisted, seeing military service as a civic duty to their adopted country. Those who became eligible through military service found that the training and service itself bred a sense of patriotism, solidarity, and identification with America's national culture and identity. Others came to feel this way upon their return to civilian life, as civilians' respect for their sacrifices made them feel welcome despite their former differences. For example, one Sudanese military interpreter said he felt his military service functioned as a "second passport" and helped him escape racial profiling by police officers during traffic stops.[79] Remarkably, the feeling of belonging held regardless of whether the noncitizen service members had been long-term green card holders at enlistment or became eligible through military service.

For these immigrants, formal citizenship status seemed secondary to belonging. Only one immigrant in my sample reported that he enlisted primarily so that he could obtain citizenship. For the rest of the noncitizens who were already eligible or became eligible through their military service, the motivations for enlisting and pursuing citizenship were intertwined. That is, the reason to enlist and the reason to become a citizen were one and the same: to serve or "give back to" one's fellow countrymen. This conjoined motivation could be an artifact of bundled benefits of enlistment during periods of hostility, with simultaneous eligibility for enlisting and applying for citizenship. Many service members, therefore, misunderstand citizenship to be obtained automatically, without realizing they needed to affirmatively file for citizenship.[80] However, the interviews suggested that substantive citizenship usually arises before enlistment and, subsequently, is uniformly enhanced: all of the noncitizen service members reported feeling American and evinced strong indicators of social integration by the time they pursued citizenship. Jose, who came to the United States from Mexico as a child and possessed a green card before enlistment, said that he felt the United States was his country. Therefore, pursuing citizenship was "natural," and he called it "necessary and inevitable."[81] Emir, who became eligible for citizenship through military service, said he was enamored with American ideals and American generosity before migrating, having witnessed the American peacekeeping presence in his home country of Bosnia. He enlisted so that he could "give back" to the United States and became an American during boot camp, both formally and substantively.[82]

That sense of belonging is not altered by lacking, or losing, formal status. Cesar came to the United States from Mexico with a green card and was raised as an American, delighting in reading Captain America comic books. He does not consider citizenship a status to be earned. Because he had a green card and already thought of himself as American, he resisted the military recruiters' appeals to apply for citizenship. He would later regret neglecting to formalize his citizenship status when, struggling with mental health problems, he developed a drug habit that led to a conviction and his deportation.

Yet even following his deportation, Cesar did not blame America. He drew a distinction between the bureaucrats responsible for stripping him of citizenship and the Americans with whom he served and identified. Even after experiencing the consequences of lacking formal citizenship, Cesar shrugged off the discrepancy between his formal identity and his subjective identity.[83] Francisco, who served and was discharged, felt that same way. He knew he was not a citizen, but he believed that he could "never be deported after serving." He reminisced about a fight he had with his sister, a US citizen, upon returning to civilian life. She told him to "get out of this country," and he responded, "I am more American than you because I fought for this country." He still feels that way, even after being deported.[84] The strong sense of patriotism and commitment to a collective endeavor facilitates integration and counteracts other cultural differences among service members and the communities in which they settle.

Still, some feel that the citizenship-for-service model is under threat.[85] Rollbacks of the streamlined enlistment process that used to make naturalizing easier for military service members limits military service as an integrative mechanism. It could be argued that a so-called green card army that relies heavily on racial minorities and immigrants inherently produces inequality and the potential for exploitation, despite the material benefits and emergent sense of solidarity that help soldiers.[86] This inequality could be contributing to the contemporary unraveling of promised immigration benefits for military service. What seems certain is that a political climate that devalues military service disrespects citizenship per se. Latino service members who experienced discrimination, either directly or vicariously through their communities, relied on their military status for respect and were disappointed when it did not trump other social differences. Cesar, the Latino veteran who grew up idolizing Captain America, said it made him angry when people told him, "You don't belong here," and that the United States was "their" country when they did not serve in the military as he did.[87] The feeling is shared among Middle Eastern service members like Emir and Adam, who served and yet felt the suspicions of US-born Americans. It seems doubtful that the high level of social belonging traditionally felt in the military can be sustained in a hostile climate in which popular support for noncitizen service members is eroding.

As a group, noncitizens have been successfully integrated through the military along both formal and substantive dimensions. However, without social support, the institutions of citizenship for service will falter, as witnessed by the gradual removal of the distinctive institutional commitments to noncitizen service members since 2017.[88] Merely restoring institutional support for noncitizen service members, though, will not be sufficient for integration without the immigrant *also* feeling American. If the long-term goal is civic revitalization, the lesson to learn from the military is that the sense of instilling pride in "Team USA" is vital. Eroding the shared identity through a hostile political climate could hinder social cohesion in the longer term, even if it boosts naturalization in the short term through defensive naturalization.[89]

Refugees: Formally Included, Socially Excluded (Table 4.1, Box 2)

Like service members, refugees obtain formal citizenship through naturalization at higher rates than lawful permanent residents.[90] Many receive institutional support for integration in the form of civic education, language learning, job placement, and public benefits. This institutional support produces positive results for formal and substantive citizenship. However, the refugee interviews reveal that a hostile climate presents barriers to substantive integration, especially in terms of social belonging and political engagement. High formal citizenship can yield low substantive citizenship, contrary to the expected trend line for other green card holders.

Refugees reported instrumental reasons to become citizens that mirrored those of other green card holders: immigration benefits such as travel and family sponsorship and collateral benefits such as skills training and job placement. Refugees have much to gain economically given their disadvantaged position entering the United States. Their subjective feelings about belonging, however, are more complicated. In my interviews, I found that all of the refugees came to the United States to escape hardships at home and migrated seeking better opportunities, but they may not have specified the United States as a place for resettlement. Mary, who migrated from Myanmar (Burma), said, "We did not choose the United States. I think they chose us when we went to the camp. . . . We did not choose Texas either . . . some people go to where they are assigned, and then try to move later. . . . We thought about doing that, but I don't think we will now. We are used to Texas now."[91] This sense of ambivalence about the United States was a recurring theme in the interviews. While grateful for the material provisions and enhanced legal protection supplied by the United States, many did not *feel* American.[92]

Refugees not "feeling American" stems from the many barriers they face in the United States. The refugee population is extremely diverse, with groups of refugees resettling in disparate and sometimes remote locales within the United States. Given the differences between their cultures and languages and mainstream America, refugees worried about their *ability* to integrate. Many lacked the education, language abilities, and job skills that typically lead to successful economic and political integration. Also, in contrast to the patriotic feelings of military service members, and despite their gratitude to the United States, refugees were more firmly attached to their native cultures than American culture. Several noted that their migration to the United States was involuntary: leaving their home country for the United States was not their choice. Many missed home to an extent that made it difficult to settle permanently in the United States. Still, few refugees faulted the United States for their feelings of exclusion; many never expected to belong, having felt excluded as disfavored social group members in their home countries as well.[93]

Middle Eastern refugees dramatically illustrate this ambivalence about fitting into American life. Many of these refugees possess significant racial, religious, linguistic, and class differences from mainstream America. Granted, many refugees were persecuted on the basis of these differences and were accustomed to feeling a sense of social distance in their home countries. Yet they expressed unease in a US political climate that sends mixed signals about their acceptance. Despite local campaigns to welcome immigrants, federal policy has limited refugee admissions, especially from Muslim countries.[94] Moreover, some experience survivor's guilt for leaving behind their unstable homes. For example, Hassan, a refugee from Somalia, said, "Although I'm grateful to be here, some days I miss home and yearn to go back one day. In fact, the more I count my blessings the more I feel a sense of sadness and emotionally beat myself up for not doing enough to contribute to the betterment of my home country."[95] None of the Middle Eastern immigrants I interviewed fell under the travel ban because they had already entered the United States by the time of our interview. However, some of them, like Hassan, had left behind family members whose entry would be complicated or barred by the travel ban and changes to refugee admissions, leading to uneasy awareness that they were safe and their family members were not.

This is not to imply that refugees take formal citizenship lightly; rather, they routinely naturalize despite their ambivalence.[96] As one refugee shared, "Every refugee I know, know[s] they will be citizens eventually. None of them have any kind of jealousy about anyone else from their community who has become a citizen. They know they will get there eventually."[97] Even daunting challenges with integration or lacking a sense of belonging do not deter refugees from seeking formal status. Many pursue citizenship dutifully, because they feel it is expected of them and is "the next step" in a long list of government requirements that began with their relocation to refugee camps.[98] Others seek US citizenship in order to ameliorate their feelings of insecurity, especially economic insecurity, and their lack of a sense of belonging.[99] All refugees become lawful permanent residents within one year, and laws guard against their return to unsafe countries, even if they commit a deportable offense. Still, many refugees imagine that documentation will make them feel "safer," though the meaning of "safety" varies. For Hamid, safety meant economic security in the form of public benefits or job placements.[100] For Emir and Mary, safety meant protection from threats of further displacement or the tyranny in their home country.[101] For others, safety involved protection from the US government and its seemingly arbitrary enforcement policies.

Refugees felt legal insecurity in spite of the protections offered by formal law, and these feelings were exacerbated by intensified enforcement policy. While not every immigrant had heard of ramped-up immigration enforcement efforts against refugees and asylum seekers, most refugees from Middle Eastern and Muslim countries were fearful of enforcement efforts.[102] Service providers reported that their reassurances to refugees with green cards that they were safe from enforcement policies targeting undocumented immigrants were not always effective, even for permanent residents without criminal histories[103] and for refugees from countries outside the Trump administration's travel bans.[104] Iraqi refugee Sahar's entire family fled unsafe conditions in her home country. She said that "being a permanent resident is not secure enough anymore with the Trump administration," and her mother agreed that the Trump administration's negative rhetoric and harsh immigration policies made her family more determined to take the citizenship test. Sahar believed that US citizens outside of the government are now emboldened to commit racist acts against noncitizens, and she plans to naturalize as a source of security against discrimination.[105] Many refugees distrust the US government and its protections for legal noncitizens based on their negative experiences in their home countries. As one service provider said, "Refugees know what happens in worse-case scenarios based on their home countries. Syrians, for example, saw a stable country, saw it fracture, and worry that it could be happening again in the United States."[106]

Still, the political climate affected refugees' perception of belonging in similar ways. Refugees generally showed less defensive motivations for citizenship than other categories of immigrants. Many refugees naturalize without regard to their feelings about the United States, and some refugees feel more welcome than they did during the resettlement process or in their home countries.[107] Other refugees show an awareness of US discrimination against race, religion, foreign accents, and immigrants generally, and they see worrisome parallels between the hostile climate in the United States and that of their home country. Still, refugees overwhelmingly go along with the naturalization process as a matter of course, without much feeling or forethought. For most of them, American identity is irrelevant to formal citizenship status. As one refugee said, "I still consider myself a refugee, even though I have citizenship. I have been through terrible times, like genocide. That does not get left behind even though becoming a citizen brings benefits."[108] Refugees in these circumstances simply need somewhere to belong. For them, the United States represents a safe haven, but not necessarily a new identity to embrace. However, others hope that the formal citizenship status will bolster their claim to belonging.[109] Mary, a Burmese refugee who is a member of an indigenous group on the border of Myanmar (Burma) and Thailand, said, "My family and I have been stateless for many years. I am Karen [an indigenous group] and [I] lived in Burma, but I was born in Thailand. Because of the fires that destroyed all of our documents, we couldn't show we were from anywhere. Being a US citizen now, [I am] finally a 'Legal Human.' That is how I feel: I am finally legally somewhere. I have a permanent home."[110] Mary's experience of pursuing formal citizenship without feeling fully American exhibits the social exclusion of refugees.

Formal Citizenship: Inhibiting or Facilitating Integration?

Both institutional and environmental factors influence the pursuit of citizenship. Naturalization rates, a metric of legal incorporation that leads to formal citizenship, rise with institutional support, as can be seen by comparing lawful permanent residents with refugees and military noncitizens. Interviews with immigrants reveal that social support and political climate affect integration as well. *How* these factors influence integration is complicated. On the one hand, a hostile political climate can boost naturalization rates and the acquisition of formal citizenship. From the vantage point of immigrants eligible to naturalize as formal citizens, the cost-benefit calculus changes. The number of reasons to naturalize, and the cost of not naturalizing, increases during a political climate that favors enforcement. Consequently, naturalization rates rise. While some immigrants provide reasons for naturalizing that are not substantially different from the reasons given in normal times, many of their responses during a hostile climate emphasize the costs of not naturalizing over the benefits of naturalizing—for example, emphasizing the right to dissent from the government over the privilege of voting, or emphasizing the importance of avoiding deportation over the ability to build a permanent life in the United States.

Lauding this boost to naturalization rates is shortsighted. Longitudinal research on quantitative metrics of naturalization shows that exclusionary environments depress citizenship rates over time, even if legislative or social threats might generate short-term increases in naturalization.[111] Increased immigration enforcement also delays the timing of naturalization by several months.[112] Moreover, cross-national comparisons with European countries suggest that citizenship acquisition eventually falls when naturalization requirements become more difficult.[113]

Beyond the raw numbers, what do these changing naturalization trends mean to immigrants? If integration requires formal citizenship, a debated presupposition among theorists of citizenship,[114] then boosting naturalization rates is a means to a positive end. A hostile climate that catalyzes formal citizenship acquisition provides a route to integration. The seeds of citizenship can flower into a fuller sense of belonging for the immigrant and strengthen allegiances to mainstream society.

Still, there are reasons to worry about the soil beneath the flower. First, as the interviews reveal, both immigrants who have formal citizenship and those who do not, show ambivalence toward citizenship. For some immigrants, a high formal status does not necessarily translate into a high substantive citizenship. They prioritize the costs of *not* having citizenship over more positive motivations to pursue it, and this can distort and degrade the meaning of citizenship. Longtime permanent residents like Jose, the Latino green card holder, feel pressed to naturalize to guard against enforcement actions or to be able to express political views that would otherwise go unvoiced. More privileged permanent residents like Bob, the Canadian scientist, reject citizenship in order to disavow intolerant American attitudes. Refugees, who become formal citizens soon after their arrival, wrestle with feeling unwelcome and un-American, notwithstanding their official legal status.

The disjuncture between one's formal status and substantive belonging can also be disintegrative for society. The mythical progression from formal to substantive citizenship is disrupted when a newcomer who joins society feels alienated and the pathway to citizenship is obstructed by fear and mistrust. Immigrants like Ruth, a Chinese immigrant from Indonesia who migrated on a student visa and then naturalized through marriage to a US citizen, lack the citizenship status privileges and entitlements to institutional support enjoyed by refugees and service members.[115] She expressed some jealousy toward those who have those privileges, some of whom obtained refugee status based on the same home-country persecution she endured. Native-born citizens express skepticism over the integrity of the naturalization process, and naturalized citizens may develop cynicism for a system that coerces rather than compels citizenship.[116] Recall the cautionary tale of Francisco, who neglected to naturalize and was deported after serving in the navy: his story suggests that the integrative potential of belonging is eroding in an enforcement climate that discounts the value of service to the nation.

Overemphasizing immigration enforcement undermines the institutions of citizenship. If the intense focus on legal status is meant to reinforce membership for insiders, then it is backfiring. In theory, immigration enforcement strengthens the significance of citizenship. On the ground, heavy enforcement can alienate immigrants whose voluntary cooperation is needed to maintain safe neighborhoods and stoke economic and security threats.[117] Immigration policies that celebrate nationalism can undermine the social capital and social cohesiveness that ensure the smooth functioning of social welfare programs and democratic institutions.[118] As a practical matter, heavy immigration enforcement can upset necessary compromises in immigration policy and cause institutional collapse in the immigration courts[119] and other immigration agencies.[120] This process is being seen in the transformation of USCIS from an integration agency into an enforcement agency. When the pursuit of citizenship involves a risk of removal, it prompts immigrants to remain partial citizens—to "stay green," as one immigration attorney put it—or to leave the United States.

Spiraling Insecurity

Three findings emerge from the interviews in this chapter. First, there is growing insecurity among green card holders that cuts across their individual circumstances and legal categories. Second, the service of noncitizens in the military is discounted and formal citizenship is eroded while the government overemphasizes immigration enforcement. Third, refugees are not fully citizens because they feel socially excluded, even if they formally belong.

As of late, legal immigrants feel more like outsiders than semi-citizens. The insecurity that accompanies their partial belonging is expanding to other immigrant subgroups, most notably to those who cannot obtain formal citizenship because of their burdened or broken pathways to citizenship. As the next chapter shows, temporary visitors and undocumented immigrants experience exclusion most keenly of all: not only socially but also economically, politically, and legally. Unlike the lawful permanent resident immigrants profiled in this chapter, undocumented immigrants and temporary visa holders do not have the option to naturalize as a defensive strategy that insulates them from immigration enforcement.

CHAPTER 5

Blocked Pathways to Full Citizenship

THOUGH DIFFERENT FROM EACH OTHER in many ways, Mei and Natalia are both struggling with blocked pathways to citizenship. Their stories show what happens when institutions not only neglect immigrant integration but actively obstruct it. Mei is an international student from China who recently graduated from a public university. She entered the United States legally, has since earned two advanced degrees, and now has an offer to work in a law firm on an H-1B visa. However, she is not sure if the job will lead to a green card and is making plans to return to China in the meantime. Natalia, in contrast, has lived in the United States most of her life and cannot imagine living anywhere else. She has excelled at school, and in life, and was fortunate enough to receive Deferred Action for Childhood Arrivals (DACA) three times after having crossed into the United States without documentation as a child. However, because DACA has been rescinded, she is nervous that she could lose it all. If she is deported, she will need to leave friends and family and she will not be able to use her education and work permit to pay her and her family's bills. She fears needing to upend her life in America.

This chapter examines the meaning of citizenship for those temporary visitors and undocumented immigrants who, like Mei and Natalia, lack a formal pathway to citizenship. For them, the quandary of citizenship insecurity is harder to resolve than for the lawful permanent residents we encountered in the previous chapter because the law constrains both their formal and substantive integration.

After explaining the scenarios that block the pathway to formal citizenship for temporary visa holders and undocumented migrants, this chapter examines the daily experiences of those who cannot attain formal citizenship. It considers the effects of limited legal status on immigrant integration using mixed-method studies that document the integrative effects of DACA and temporary visas, including interviews with DACA recipients, international students, and high-skilled workers about their legal uncertainty and their reasons for desiring, or not desiring, more formal pathways to citizenship. It then observes how the existing enforcement-dominated policy approaches negatively affect the sense of immigrant belonging by blocking their pathways to citizenship. The chapter concludes by prescribing policies and institutional supports that could unblock those pathways.

A note on terminology: While the lawful permanent resident and undocumented immigrant categories on either side of the immigrant spectrum are relatively clear, the "middle" categories—including temporary and nonimmigrant visitors—vary in usage. In this chapter, the terms *temporary visitors, temporary visa holders, temporary workers,* and *temporary migrants* are used interchangeably to describe international students and high-skilled workers on H-1B visas, who are considered "nonimmigrants" in the immigration statute.[1] DACA recipients are considered a subset of undocumented immigrants because they were formerly undocumented and possess some of the same demographic characteristics, though their work permits and legal protections improve their prospects for integration temporarily.[2]

Blocked and Broken Pathways to Citizenship

Similar to the lawful permanent residents discussed in the last chapter, temporary visa holders and undocumented immigrants receive little institutional support and face steep barriers to integration. Indeed, the barriers they face are considerably steeper. These limitations create legal, social, economic, and political barriers.

In terms of impediments to formal citizenship, immigrants with temporary visas and undocumented immigrants hold partial legal rights. Most notably, temporary visitors cannot vote and have limited access to public benefits. The issuance and terms of their visas are subject to the government's discretion, and visas can be revoked. Their ability to reside in the United States over the long term is constrained: international students on F visas must demonstrate that they are planning to return to their country at the end of the visa term, whereas high-skilled workers on H-1B visas can express dual intent if they can overcome presumptions that they are presently seeking permanent residence—keeping open their options to stay temporarily or adjust to a green card should they become eligible. And finally, temporary visitors' ability to work is constrained because most federal government jobs require citizenship, visiting students cannot work off-campus, and technology jobs might require security clearances not available to noncitizens.[3]

As for undocumented immigrants, they also cannot vote and have limited access to public benefits and health care.[4] They cannot work lawfully.[5] They are subject to deportation for unlawful presence. DACA creates a limited protection to forestall deportation and work lawfully, but the program's rescission leaves these rights in limbo.[6] Though it is a matter of ongoing discussion, DACA recipients do not have a pathway to permanent residence or citizenship; few qualify for the limited avenues for adjustment of status because they entered without inspection or overstayed visas and have lived without status for a long period of time.

The contingent nature of these limited statuses can be seen clearly in the process for adjusting status, which theoretically lays out a smooth path from temporary status to permanent status and then naturalized citizenship.[7] The smoothness is misleading. In reality, the process for temporary visa holders to become green card holders is complex, uncertain, and cumbersome. It offers few guarantees. International students face obstacles to adjusting status unless and until they find an employer to sponsor them for a green card. Therefore, if Mei, the international student, enters on an F visa, she must find an employer to sponsor her for an H-1B visa in order to work after completing her degree. Then she must find a sponsor for her green card before she sets out on a path to citizenship. Undocumented immigrants face even greater barriers, with immigration law barring adjustment of status for those who entered without inspection and carving narrow exceptions for those who have overstayed their visas.[8] DACA recipients who entered without inspection and whose limited legal protections have been rescinded will remain in limbo without legislative reforms that would alter their pathway to citizenship.[9] Nancy, who entered without documents and obtained DACA in high school, would not be able to obtain a green card under current law. Had she entered on a temporary visa and overstayed, she might be able to adjust status later upon subsequent eligibility—for example, if she married a US citizen.

*Blocked Pathways for High-Skilled Temporary Workers
and International Students*

Mei's winding path from a temporary student visa to a green card is becoming increasingly common. The presence of international students and scholars in American universities has dramatically increased in the last two decades, doubling from 547,000 in 2000–2001 to 1.8 million in 2016–17, though there have been signs of modest decreases since 2017.[10] This increase is driven by intensive recruiting from American universities seeking revenue, since international students pay high fees and receive little to no financial aid, and it will continue to expand as domestic investments in higher education flatten. The increase is also driven by foreign countries' desire to expand the education of their students and the global reach of their workforce. International students and scholars hold F-1, J-1, and H-1B visas that provide temporary permission to reside in the United States during their studies and for a one-year Optional Practical Training work period following graduation.[11] The temporary nature of the visas means that students are not eligible to remain in the United States without obtaining another type of visa. According to the New Immigrant Survey, 25 percent of international students on F visas eventually acquire H-1B visas, and a rising share (50–60 percent) of high-skilled workers on H-1B visas eventually obtain green cards through a family member or permanent employer.[12] The background characteristics of these high-skilled temporary visa holders vary considerably, but typically their income, education, and skills would otherwise correlate with positive integration and naturalization indicators if they were immigrants.[13] However, temporary visa holders confront uncertain pathways to citizenship.

Temporary visa holders enter the United States lawfully for a specified purpose or time period for tourism (B-1), work (H-1B, H-2A), or education (F or J visa).[14] Others, such as those with Temporary Protected Status, enter on humanitarian grounds with visa terms that are similarly constrained.[15] Temporary visa holders are not presumed to be seeking a pathway to citizenship since the short duration of their time in the United States is not meant to displace deeper ties in their home country. Still, they might be able to extend their stay through qualifying circumstances, such as by marrying a US citizen or by switching to a job that offers a green card. Most of the temporary visa holders in this book have or are on track for high-skilled visas such as the H-1B. An H-1B worker might find an employer who is willing to sponsor them for a green card. Typically, though, the government invests little in the temporary workers' initial adjustment of status or in their long-term integration because their stays are supposed to be of limited duration. Those workers who overstay their visas must navigate numerous administrative obstacles and penalties to adjust their status, much like immigrants who enter without documents.

Little scholarship has been written about these students and high-skilled temporary workers.[16] Existing studies view temporary visa holders such as international students, scholars, and high-skilled workers as privileged guest workers, who, because of their robust economic characteristics, do not require institutional support for integration.[17] This outlook focuses on economic integration at the expense of other dimensions of substantive integration: social, political, and legal. It especially overlooks the legal uncertainty that stems from their temporary status and a volatile political climate that includes multiple proposed or enacted policy shifts: the travel ban, the Buy American and Hire American executive order, H-1B caps, and limits on Chinese scientists and students.[18] Given this uncertainty about the future, many students and technology workers either do not want to remain in the United States or do not intend, once eligible, to pursue citizenship beyond their green card; such reluctance is the ultimate sign of disconnection and nonintegration. Contrary to conventional wisdom, international students and high-skilled workers experience incomplete integration once factors other than economic integration are considered. Socially, politically, and legally, their limited legal status constrains and erodes whatever measure of integration they may have obtained on their own. These are the result of lacking assistance or encouragement from US institutions.

Blocked Pathways for DACA Recipients and Undocumented Immigrants

Natalia's experience is typical of a DREAMer. Natalia crossed into the United States at the age of nine with her family in search of economic opportunity. She is one of 11.3 million undocumented immigrants in the United States and, more specifically, one of 800,000 immigrants who received DACA after 2012.[19] Just as these DACA recipients are transitioning from school to the working world, the DACA program is being shelved. This shift in circumstances is emblematic of the uncertainty that the undocumented face.

The undocumented population is not a fixed category but a composite of groups that do not fit into other categories of legal immigration. As a group, they make up 26 percent of the foreign-born population.[20] Immigrants who enter the country without inspection and official documentation (55 percent of the undocumented population) lack the ability to subsequently become lawful permanent residents and US citizens.[21] Some unauthorized immigrants, meanwhile, initially arrive on a valid temporary visa but then stay beyond the terms permitted (45 percent of the undocumented population).[22] Shan, who migrated with her family to the United States from China on a tourist visa, falls into the latter category. Both undocumented immigrants who enter without inspection and those who overstay a visa lack a pathway to citizenship and face delays and penalties if they try to leave, return, and resume their residency. However, immigrants who overstay their visa may be able to adjust status under certain statutory exceptions,[23] whereas immigration laws may bar those who enter without documents from ever attaining citizenship.

DACA recipients, a subset of the undocumented population, possess limited legal protections despite sharing many of the characteristics of undocumented immigrants. Following years of pressure, President Barack Obama in 2012 granted DREAMers limited legal protection in the form of deferred action on deportation. President Donald Trump rescinded those protections in 2018, leading the way for the program's extinction.[24] By the terms of the program, DACA recipients migrated from their home countries as children and have been raised largely in the United States. All of them have clean criminal records and many are high achieving, with bright prospects for their futures.

Existing studies of DREAMers emphasize the high degree of substantive integration for this group as compared with undocumented immigrants without legal protection. They report that immigrants' participation in the 2006 social movements to lobby for a DREAM Act demonstrates their high degree of social citizenship,[25] or argue that DREAMers are already American.[26] The National UnDACAmented Research Project study indicates that DACA recipients benefited economically, socially, and politically from their legal protections.[27] Indicators of economic progress include the finding that 61 percent of DACA recipients took on new jobs as a result of their work permits, most with higher earnings and a better fit to their training and credentials; 70 percent became financially independent or able to help support their families; and 94 percent pursued educational opportunities they previously could not.[28] On political and legal integration, 55 percent reported they had or felt they could influence national politics, and 94 percent said they would apply for citizenship if they became eligible.[29] Social engagement is more mixed, with National UnDACAmented Research Project surveys finding that DACA recipients feel legitimized by their status and, though they fear less for their own safety, continue to worry about family members and friends.[30] A 2019 report update shows that their worries are intensifying in the face of uncertainty over the rescission of DACA and continuing heavy immigration enforcement.[31]

Despite their inspiring stories of belonging, I contend that the optimism surrounding the DREAMers masks a more troubling reality. By definition, DREAMers come from mixed-status families. Undocumented parents typically migrate with low levels of education, weak English language skills, and little work experience, and they struggle to find steady, remunerative work. Qualitative studies describe the DREAMers as children who cannot go forward and cannot go backward to stabilize their legal status. These lives in "limbo" are constrained by citizenship status.[32] I contend that the importance of obtaining formal citizenship has been undervalued in studies conducted during a more auspicious policy climate.[33] Whether positive indicators of integration can withstand a retraction of DACA, and with it the opportunities for legal status, is the key question. As this book shows, DACA recipients retain improved economic, social, and political integration as compared with other undocumented immigrants. This is because they can obtain a work permit and become eligible for a variety of public benefits at the state or local level, such as driver's licenses, financial support for college, or health care. However, each measure of integration remains limited by the lack of a pathway to formal citizenship and is further eroded by uncertainty about DACA's future after its 2017 rescission.

Studying Legal Liminality and Formal Citizenship

US immigration policy reflects an enforcement bias that prioritizes exclusion over inclusion. Lost in the obsession with enforcement is the mission of integrating noncitizens during their migration and settlement. As a result, pathways to formal citizenship are burdened or blocked, and the ties between formal and substantive citizenship fray as a result of legal uncertainty.

Supplementing objective indicators of integration, interviews with immigrants present the subjective experience of how liminality diminishes their integration. Scholars use theories of liminality to explain the uncertainty experienced by immigrants who face blocked pathways as a result of their citizenship status. Cecilia Menjívar, for example, discusses the "liminal legality" of Guatemalan and Salvadoran immigrants who possess Temporary Protected Status within the United States.[34] The term applies not only because their legal status is temporary and subject to revocation but also because they move in and out of statuses, between lawfulness and marginalization. The same is true of temporary visa holders such as international students and scholars who can be denied entry to the United States or prevented from transitioning to a more permanent status. Socio-legal scholars have since applied Menjívar's notion of liminal legality to DACA recipients, with one reversing the phrase—thus, *legal* liminality—to emphasize the role of the law in creating this uncertainty.[35]

As an empirical matter, I identify three crucial aspects of legal liminality: (1) limited legal status or partial rights, (2) temporariness, and (3) contingency. *Limited legal status* refers to the partial rights supplied by DACA, which provides work permits and social support but no pathway to citizenship or means of formal political participation.[36] *Temporariness* refers to the immigrant's awareness of the time-limited nature of a status that requires ongoing renewal.[37] *Contingency* refers to legal status being dependent on arbitrary events such as bureaucratic discretion and changing immigration policies.[38] The interviews reveal that the lived experience of liminality is profoundly unsettling for immigrants. Temporary visitors and immigrants with limited legal protections experience multiple points of vulnerability as a result of their legal liminality. Immigrants with temporary or limited legal status can go to school but not obtain all types of work (partial liminality). They can enjoy these partial rights for only a few years at a time (temporal liminality). Their ability to extend their status beyond these limited terms is contingent on further approval and the continuing availability of the visa, which are not certainties in a tumultuous policy climate where immigration laws and enforcement priorities constantly change.

I apply these three aspects of liminality to interviews with international students, high-skilled workers on temporary work visas, and undocumented immigrants with DACA in Colorado. I asked these migrants about their daily lives in the United States and their future plans. For international students, the "future" refers to their plans following graduation; for technology workers on an H-1B visa, their possible plans to acquire a green card, permanent residency, and possible citizenship. For DACA recipients, I asked about their plans to stay or depart upon expiration of their two-year DACA and work permits. By including these three groups of migrants, this chapter presents multiple challenges along the citizenship spectrum and avoids the legal/illegal binary.[39] Still more citizenship statuses could have been included, such as agricultural workers with temporary visas or permanent residents who lost their status after committing a deportable offense, but the larger point would remain unchanged: legal constraints condition economic, social, and civic integration in the United States.

Legal Constraints Condition Integration

All three migrant groups feel limited by their partial citizenship status or legal liminality. Each group possesses some legal protections—to work, to study, and to reside in the United States—even if their protections fall short of those enjoyed by green card holders or US citizens. DACA recipients feel the effects of their partial, contingent, and conditional legal status through the bureaucratic hassle of renewing their visa or DACA application, their circumscribed ability to work, and the uncertainty of applying for immigration benefits without being sure of the result or even the continuing availability of the benefit. International students and high-skilled workers experience the administrative hassle of short-term renewals and uncertain prospects for adjusting status, and they are dependent on finding a university or an employer sponsor who will petition on their behalf and complete burdensome paperwork in a timely fashion. They recognize limitations on the types of jobs they can seek and their ineligibility for necessary grants and security clearances. They refrain from participating in social life and politics because they, and the government, consider themselves guests in the country. These feelings of legal liminality inhibit full integration for all three groups of immigrants. They pertain even though none of the groups faces the harshest outcomes of immigration enforcement, such as deportation.

Within Low Formal Citizenship, Differences in Substantive Belonging

Highlighting the experiences of immigrants blocked from attaining citizenship drives home the significance of citizenship status during times of enforcement. Those who lack or are low in formal citizenship most keenly sense how this deficiency impedes their successful integration. Still, key differences arise among the three blocked groups around *which* aspects of integration are most inhibited by partial legal status. These impediments affect the types of institutional interventions that could fix the blocked pathways they encounter.

Inhibiting Social Belonging and Civic Engagement All three blocked groups experience limited social belonging, albeit to differing extents. International students and high-skilled workers self-identify as foreigners or transnational migrants, whereas DACA recipients identify as Americans. This reveals an important difference in the way that a partial legal status affects social integration. For international students and high-skilled workers, holding a partial legal status works against a sense of belonging. Most of these temporary visa holders evince weak social and political ties to the United States. They are guests rather than residents, and they feel like outsiders.[40] These weak ties produce a transitory outlook on their stay in the United States and a transactional way of thinking about the future. This lack of durable national identification impedes meaningful engagement with institutions that control their status. Many temporary visa holders are not civically engaged: they remain more connected to home country politics, they desire a green card without necessarily coveting formal citizenship or the associated right to vote, and they intend to retain ties in both countries and perhaps return to their home country. Most would choose dual citizenship if available. Despite temporary visitors' lawful status, which derives from a legislatively created category that can lead to citizenship as a matter of law, this lack of substantive belonging erodes their desire to pursue full citizenship. In essence, they divert from the path rather than forging ahead.

For undocumented immigrants, in contrast, a partial legal status such as DACA facilitates substantive belonging. In comparison to international students, DACA recipients are better socially integrated, having spent most of their adult lives in the United States. Most DACA recipients cannot fathom living in another country, even though they have relatives abroad. As an extension of social belonging, many DACA recipients contact their congressional representatives to advocate for policies that would improve their standing. Overwhelmingly, they desire permanent residency and formal citizenship, even though some were unclear about the technical differences. Still, their social status is challenged by their legal liminality, which inhibits their continuing social, economic, and political belonging by reorienting their thoughts from future success to present anxiety. It produces skepticism about the possibility of fully belonging and erodes their trust in the institutions of citizenship.

Granted, temporary workers can become more like permanent residents as they develop family ties in the United States, and DACA recipients can become more open to living in their countries of birth as they reckon with the limitations of life in the United States and the transferability of their talents that creates possibilities in their home countries. An immigrant's sense of present belonging and the future are highly salient to integration.

Economic Citizenship: Hitting Ceilings, Clearing Floors The economic positions of temporary visa holders and undocumented immigrants differ dramatically. International students and high-skilled workers occupy positions of economic privilege given the skills, degrees, and income they must possess in order to meet admissions criteria. Undocumented immigrants, however, typically come from poorer countries with fewer resources. They often come to the United States without documentation precisely because they could not readily qualify for a visa based on educational credentials or employment prospects. A minority of immigrants come on visas and overstay.

This is not to suggest that temporary visa holders do not struggle. A blocked security clearance or the need to find an employee sponsor can hold back a high-skilled worker's career. For international scholars, restrictions on funding sources hamper their research. In contrast, DACA recipients worry about obtaining basic income to support themselves or their families. DACA does provide a work permit that facilitates economic integration, and it can lead to tuition discounts that make educational attainment easier in some states. Still, the rescission of DACA renders those economic benefits insecure.

Divergent Feelings about Legal Status One of the starkest differences between the three groups is their feelings about pursuing higher levels of legal status through formal US citizenship. Temporary visitors occupy a stronger legal position than undocumented immigrants because they reside in the country with the permission of the government. Yet the legal standing of a high-skilled worker is highly conditional. There is the possibility of a pathway to formal citizenship for temporary visa holders who obtain H-1B visas, but not for all temporary visa holders. US immigration policies that undermine foreign workers, for the protection of US citizen workers, cause temporary workers to feel uncertain about pursuing permanent residence. A significant finding from the interviews is that many H-1Bs want to obtain green cards and yet remain ambivalent about pursuing citizenship.[41] This hesitancy shows that their decision to settle in the United States is transactional. It turns on factors like administrative hassle, shifting immigration policy, social status, and economic opportunity. The departure of high-skilled temporary visa holders removes valuable potential citizens from the United States. An easier pathway to permanent status or citizenship and a more welcoming climate could prevent this transactional thinking that deprives the United States of talented citizens.

DACA, too, is far from complete. It provides only short-term legal protection from deportation. In 2017 President Trump rescinded the program such that no new DACA applications could be processed.[42] DACA nonetheless was extremely successful facilitating social and political incorporation, as the experience of seeking and claiming DACA benefits mobilized thousands of formerly undocumented immigrants to come out of the shadows, tell their stories, support one another, seek allies in collective actions, and contact Congress while fighting for the program's survival.[43] Still, this substantive integration eroded without a pathway to formal citizenship. The optimistic nature of many DREAMers and DACA recipients suffered under the protracted uncertainty of their undocumented status. The stress and anxiety associated with the uncertain future of the program hurt their social confidence, and the program's rescission injured DACA recipients' economic prospects, as academic and professional plans were interrupted by legal filings and injunctions. Moreover, the failed attempts to pass a DREAM Act as part of national immigration reform rendered some DACA recipients cynical about politics. A legal pathway, therefore, is needed to reinstate a sense of substantive belonging and prevent the loss of social, economic, and political gains. Still, compared with international students, an overwhelming proportion of DACA students would take a green card and then pursue a pathway to citizenship, if either became available.

Limits on Formal Citizenship Erode Equality

Temporary visa holders, undocumented immigrants, and DACA recipients are keenly aware of how limitations on their legal status interact with other markers of substantive equality to place them in a subordinate position vis-à-vis formal citizens. In a country where race is linked with inequality, the visible minorities in every legal category recognize the interlocking stereotypes of criminality with unlawful status (for Latinos), economic threat with foreigner

TABLE 5.1. Intersection of formal and substantive citizenship: temporary and undocumented immigrants.

		Formal	
		−	+
Substantive +		(4) DACA	(1)
Substantive −		(3B) (3A) F H-1B	(2)

status (for Asians), and national security threat with terrorism (for Muslims). Individuals within each group who can "pass" as US citizens because their skin color, language skills, or surname conforms to mainstream American culture feel that they are inoculated against such stereotypes.[44]

The erosion of substantive belonging for those lacking formal citizenship arises in different ways for temporary visa holders and undocumented immigrants that map onto the citizenship matrix presented in table 5.1.

Transactional Mindsets Inhibit Allegiance of Temporary Workers (Table 5.1, Box 3A)

Among temporary visa holders, the high-skilled workers experience a medium to low level of social belonging. Typically, their sense of belonging is lower than most permanent residents and yet they are higher than international students in social belonging. This middle position might be due to life stage and duration of residence: most of the workers are older than international students and have lived in the United States for longer periods of time. But it also stems from their more flexible legal options: workers on H-1B visas can register dual intent when coming to the United States to engage in temporary work and to remain once eligible for permanent residence. Immigration procedures facilitate this transition process, typically waiving the requirement of a US Citizenship and Immigration Services interview and relaxing the paperwork required to apply for a green card. As revealed by interviews and quantitative metrics, a high number of these workers proceed to obtain green cards when adjusting status. While there are certainly problems in the pathway from a temporary visa to a green card, the existence of a pathway is a promising sign.

Of the many Chinese and Indian technology workers interviewed, Dazhen exemplifies the straddling nature of a temporary visa. He lives in between two worlds, a transnational migrant with meaningful social and economic ties in his sending and receiving countries. He has good reasons to stay in the United States: his children are receiving a good education in the United States and his job here is going well.[45] He also has good reason to return to China, because his parents live in China and job prospects are strong there as well. So he is uncertain whether he will remain permanently in the United States. That sense of uncertainty inhibits his political engagement as well as his continuing legal integration, as he delays the pursuit of a green card for which he is eligible. Deepti, an Indian scholar on an H-1B, has lived in the United States for more than a decade since she came to the United States as a college student. She possesses an H-1B work visa that permits transition to legal permanent residence, but she is uncertain how long she will stay in the United States. She presumes that a green card will be enough, even if she plans to live here indefinitely. Whether she formalizes her legal status as a green card holder depends on her career, specifically what practical needs it presents in terms of travel, funding, and access to archives for her research.[46] Dazhen's and Deepti's uncertainties give rise to a transactional mindset about economic, social, and legal integration.

Living in one place while being tethered to another country can limit prospects for other aspects of substantive integration, too.[47] Temporary visa holders prioritize economic considerations and show no territorial loyalty when planning for the future: finding a good job, winning grants, obtaining security clearances required for promotions. This career-minded approach necessarily feeds their uncertainty about remaining in the United States.

The sense of uncertainty about future plans and continuing integration is compounded by the conditional nature of visa renewals in a volatile policy climate. This was especially true for technology work, the largest areas of interest for international students, scholars, and high-skilled workers. The Trump administration's adverse policies toward legal immigrants and high-skilled laborers have led to some anxiety about the continuing availability of J and H-1B visas. Ksenia, a postdoctoral fellow who may derive a visa from her spouse, said, "With the new administration, you don't know what to expect. And they have been changing a lot with H-1Bs, [though] they didn't do anything with research positions. They've been playing with tech, but I don't want to be in the position where my job is not dependent on my abilities but based on the discretion of someone from the government."[48] Substantive work involving sensitive information and requiring security clearances, such as aerospace engineering and defense work, makes these individuals vulnerable to restrictionist immigration policies and employment practices beyond the usual requirements for lawful employment. Chinese, Canadian, European, and Middle Eastern temporary visa holders all mentioned temptations to return and work in their home countries, which had booming economies and fewer limitations. As the Canadian scientist Bob said pointedly, "If you want to deport me, go ahead. I'll go back to Canada and it will be fine."[49] The current hostile climate in the United States weakens the allegiance of even longtime temporary workers, resulting in a thin conception of citizenship. A transactional mindset makes choosing to stay or go an economic calculus rather than a decision about membership and belonging. Migrants might choose to stay because of career or salary considerations, or because they can obtain rights that could be instrumentally beneficial—for example, the ability to obtain dual citizenship that can be passed down to a future child—and then only so long as the comparative advantage lasts. This is especially true for migrants from privileged backgrounds, where circumstances such as having a strong economy at home, being from a majority racial background, and originating from a liberal democracy all favor returning to their home country. Once eligible, people with these characteristics tend to naturalize at a lower rate. Presumably, they weigh the administrative hassle of clearing blocked or broken pathways against the expected benefits of pursuing formal citizenship.

Like the permanent residents who "stay green," those on temporary visas let instrumental considerations dictate when and whether they will leave, taking with them valuable skills, training, and investment. Unless they develop family ties to tether them in the United States, most feel little identification with America during their sojourn. Their future-oriented thinking is driven by practical rather than emotional or ideological considerations. The lawful permanent residents in chapter 4 were increasingly motivated to strengthen their formal status for defensive reasons in a hostile political climate. The critical difference here is that temporary migrants who lack the possibility of long-term residence—and then citizenship—simply leave rather than remain as guests.

International Students Lack Present Belonging, Forestall Future Planning (Table 5.1, Box 3B)

Compared with temporary workers, international students have a more extreme sense of isolation. Abishek, an undergraduate student from India, said, "I just feel like I'm a student here. I'm here to study and to experience a different culture and to gain as much as possible . . . before I go home."[50] While this "temporary" mindset accords with the official terms of their visas, which limit their stay to the duration of their studies, these students can spend years in the United States—long enough to develop ties. While a college student might migrate to the United States expecting to stay for just two to four years, in reality many F visa holders remain in the United States for six or more years as they transition between multiple degrees and multiple temporary visas. Consider the case of Mei, who came to the United States from China on an F visa for college as an eighteen-year-old. She has lived in the United States for ten years, first extending her F visa for a master's degree before working at an externship and then commencing law school on a third F visa that led to her securing a full-time job on an H-1B.[51]

This temporary mindset maintained throughout longer stays can inhibit social investments, leading to social isolation and compounding the problem of substantive integration. Sandra, a postdoctoral student from Lebanon on a J visa, which does not permit dual intent as a pathway to citizenship, described feeling "stuck" in the transition between the student visa for her doctoral coursework and the temporary work visa she needed for her postdoctoral research. Up against a visa renewal deadline, she took unpaid leave when her work permit was expiring. The university waited six months to initiate the application and the government processing took an additional eight months before she began to "prompt and poke" her supervisors to expedite the process. "I came to this country because there are good opportunities, and there isn't anything stopping me from leaving," she says. She points to "the fear of not knowing what's going to happen," which makes it hard for her to focus on the present during her time here. Feeling "stuck" prevents her from cultivating meaningful social ties.[52] In the case of Abishek, the Indian international student, home country loyalty held him back from integrating. He had a positive experience in the United States, yet he seemed reluctant to get involved in campus life or develop social politics while waiting to return: "If I stayed and became a citizen here, one of my biggest regrets is that I would not be able to contribute to my country or its development. . . . I will for sure go back to India."[53]

As a result of legal obstacles and administrative difficulties extending their stay in the United States, many international students have not spent much time thinking about whether they would pursue a pathway to citizenship if they someday were to become eligible. Explaining why he is not sure, a Saudi Arabian student said, "That's in the future. I am hopeful about the opportunities I can attain after completing my [master's] program, but I will eventually return to either Saudi Arabia or Dubai. . . . Why would I stay if I can gain better social status in my home country because of my education here [versus facing] a belief that the Middle East is linked to terrorism?"[54] These sentiments accord with national trends for international students. As reported in a 2017 Institute of International Education survey, the top two factors causing a decrease in new enrollment for international students were the visa application process and the political environment.[55] In a Snapshot survey, 52 percent of universities reported that their international students have cited the social or political climate as a deterrent to studying in the United States.[56]

Lacking longer-term perspectives for life in the United States, international students spend little time entertaining the possibility of becoming American. Many of their present-day decisions are shaped by their uncertainty about the future in a difficult climate.

DACA Recipients: Partial Social Belonging Spills Over into Economic Vulnerability and Political Alienation (Table 5.1, Box 4)

Reversing the low formal, low substantive citizenship pairing of temporary migrants, longtime undocumented immigrants register low in formal citizenship and yet high in substantive citizenship. DACA recipients who migrated to the United States at a young age and grew up in America enjoy a sense of belonging despite their lack of formal legal status. As in other studies, the DACA recipients in my study display strong social integration in their sense of belonging and stronger economic and educational success than other undocumented immigrants.[57] The DREAMer narrative of being American despite lacking legal status underscored their prevailing sense of inclusion: "With or without DACA, my sense of belonging does not depend on papers. So I feel like I just belong."[58] Most DACA recipients could not fathom living somewhere else. This sense of substantive belonging arises from the social ties, civic participation, and economic engagement that mark their long residence in the United States.

Still, my interview data reveals scholars have paid insufficient attention to the legal insecurity felt by DACA recipients as a result of their liminal legal status.[59] At its inception and implementation, DACA facilitated substantive belonging (economically, socially, politically, and somewhat legally) for a group that had until 2012 been undocumented. But their liminal legal status clashed with substantive belonging and therefore never permitted full integration. DACA recipients reported the jarring sense that their legal status and their substantive experience did not match. Shan, for example, overstayed her tourist visa at a young age and then tried to fit into her local community on the Western Slope of Colorado, where immigrants and racial minorities are scarce. She noted the disconnect between feeling American and having the papers to prove it: "We all say that we are American in every sense of the word. We attended the American school system, our friends are all Americans ... yet [I cannot live like an American] without papers."[60] DACA recipients' lack of formal citizenship puts downward pressure on their sense of belonging, eroding their social integration. Compared with the status of temporary visa holders, DACA recipients' less secure formal citizenship status, premised on executive discretion, sits uneasily alongside their strong sense of substantive belonging. This contradictory sense of belonging departs from the more expected alignment of formal and substantive citizenship.

A faltering sense of social belonging is heightened as shifting immigration policies constrict formal belonging. Policies for undocumented immigrants changed for the worse with President Trump's rescission of DACA. In the changed climate, Esen reported feeling "trapped in a birdcage," where she cannot go forward or back despite her longtime residence or significant achievements in the United States.[61] Many DACA recipients dare not open themselves up to the risk of deportation by returning to their home country and facing uncertain return.[62] Though the by-product of two cultures, they are more American than foreign. They consider themselves not transnational but instead full members of American society by virtue of their strong ties to their local communities and involvement in economic and political life.

While some DREAMers remain hopeful about their social standing in America, the interviews show others are becoming skeptical about their future, which adversely affects their social belonging, educational and economic prospects, and civic participation. Constantly questioning the basic presumption that one's life will continue in the United States erodes the pathway to integration. Many DACA recipients learned about and began to identify with their irregular citizenship status as they entered college. Hearing that DACA would be rescinded, many DREAMers remained optimistic that it would work out, since it somehow had before. Some, though, expressed uncertainty about whether the changes made it possible or worthwhile to stay in school. Their uncertainty was especially strong given their inability to afford tuition without legally sanctioned work or prospects for obtaining a good job following graduation if their status were revoked. Some DACA recipients said their focus turned to the present: gaining skills that would enable them to work in the United States or abroad in case their work permit expires or gets revoked. These immigrants spoke of being grateful for the chance to "tak[e] advantage of the moment" by getting job experience while possible, despite an uncertain pay-off.[63] Others spoke more negatively of "being in a holding zone" or facing "paralysis" about their educational and professional trajectory.[64] Gabrielle said, "It is really hard to think about the future. I try to live in the moment and work on myself rather than make big plans because if I don't meet those plans, then I'll just be disappointed."[65] Emelio shared this sentiment: "I'm not really scared or paranoid about being deported. But I know it's a possibility if DACA were to end. [Having a] permanent solution would help because I would know that my future would be here in this country, and I would know that having obtained a degree in this country would actually be worth it . . . because I would be able to stay."[66] Enforcement inhibited their social ties as well, with fear causing many DACA recipients to hide their status and other important aspects of their lives from friends and teachers. The climate of fear also causes DREAMers to prioritize family needs over friendships.[67] Jazmin said she would choose family over staying with friends in the United States: "I see here as home. But then I also know that the most important home to me is being with my whole family. So if it came down to it, I guess I would rather be with my family in Mexico than be here without them."[68]

While DREAMers were once grateful for DACA, many have realized its limitations. What was once tantalizing is now inadequate. DACA has always been discretionary, but the "fragility" of a discretionary status becomes much clearer once it is threatened.[69] The rescission of DACA made DREAMers at once more insistent about the value of DACA and more dismissive about it as a legal protection. More than one person noted that the prospect of losing

DACA was not hypothetical, even before the rescission.[70] Gabriela said that the DACA rescission heightened the legal insecurity for immigrants across legal statuses, building a sad sense of solidarity: "I used to think that I could be a DACA holder for the rest of my life, but seeing what's happened to [Temporary Protected Status] I realize nobody is secure anymore. DACA is not a guarantee. I think no immigrant feels like they belong, no matter if they have papers or not."[71]

This dawning realization of legal threat affects integration. Although DREAMers are notable for their optimism and resilience, when pressed to contemplate the post-rescission environment, some showed signs of discouragement and self-doubt about their belonging in America. Still, they remained engaged and extremely well informed about immigration-related news and DACA developments. Jazmin, a law student, was so well informed that she rattled off the diverging litigation outcomes in federal courts evaluating the rescission of DACA.[72] She expressed caution about the political situation and prospects for improvement given that DREAMers have come close but failed to obtain a path to citizenship over the course of a ten-year campaign. Others were more pessimistic, expressing outright dismay about having their future put to public debate and resting in the hands of "a man who does not care about you," underscoring the arbitrariness of the law and the futility of legal liminality.[73]

Their frustrations aside, the DACA recipients I interviewed resoundingly expressed the desire for a permanent legal status in the form of a pathway to citizenship. They would accept a green card or citizenship, if it were offered, albeit largely for defensive reasons similar to those of the green card holders in chapter 4.[74] Faced with the prospect that neither politics nor the courts would lead to a stable legal status, a few contemplated "returning" to shadow lives in the United States. A few imagined returning to their countries of origin, where they had few or no ties but could profit from the education and work experience they had gained in the United States. Esteban said, "With all the opportunities I have here [working as a receptionist at a law firm] under DACA, [if DACA ended] I could possibly do contract paralegal work, open my own LLC, and run my own business. There's a lot of DACA recipients who now have opportunities based on what they've been doing up until now—they have professions or knowledge that can help them with jobs."[75] Emelio is one such skilled DACA recipient who says he will use his bachelor's degree to be "ready for the workforce, whether here or abroad."[76]

These DACA interviews, conducted during the first term of the Trump presidency, present a different picture from those of prior DACA studies.[77] This portrait underscores the damaging effect of legal liminality for immigrants in three senses: incompleteness, contingency, and volatility. This unstable climate instilled the sense that the government is trying to take their protected status away. Previously, many were simply undocumented immigrants grateful to have a leg up. Feeling that their rights were threatened impressed upon the DREAMers the need to move from a liminal to a permanent solution. It seems substantive citizenship does not compensate for a lack of formal citizenship during heavy immigration enforcement.

Unblocking Pathways to Citizenship

Putting together the stories of immigrants in chapter 4 and the present chapter, the simple fact of being a noncitizen makes for a liminal existence marked by uncertainty about the future. This citizenship insecurity is the defining feature of lacking formal citizenship during an era of enforcement. Assuredly, the experience of legal liminality takes different forms and varies in intensity along the spectrum of semi-citizenship. The lawful permanent residents in chapter 4 felt vulnerable to the threat that their green card would not be renewed, that naturalization requirements would change, or that aggressive enforcement could lead to deportation for trivial offenses. The interviews in this chapter showed more intense citizenship insecurity for immigrants, pathways to citizenship.

This chapter shows that temporary migrants negotiate their liminal status through a series of applications, renewals, and other bureaucratic forms. Undocumented immigrants negotiate a patchwork of incomplete protections spread across a patchwork of federal, local, and nongovernmental or family support. Obtaining a limited legal status such as DACA improves their immediate situation, but it does not fundamentally alter this unstable existence. Citizenship security becomes more important as one's status becomes less stable during an enforcement era.

The inherent insecurities associated with being a noncitizen in a time of heavy immigration enforcement are more pronounced for temporary visa holders, such as Mei, or formerly undocumented immigrants who now hold DACA status, such as Natalia. As they scan the horizon in an ever-changing immigration landscape, their vision of the future falters. Existing approaches toward temporary visa holders and undocumented immigrants in limited legal statuses consider them beyond the reach of formal citizenship and discount their prospects for integration.

I contend that immigrants should not be presumptively excluded from belonging while living in the United States. During their stay, social, economic, political, and legal avenues should provide for their substantive integration. Consistent with my argument that formal citizenship is a prerequisite for equal membership in society, the federal government should implement practical reforms that smooth transitions to durable legal status. For example, more temporary visas should permit dual intent that can lead to lawful permanent residence. Noncitizens facing blocked pathways to citizenship, such as the undocumented immigrants with limited legal protection, require more ambitious institutional interventions to stabilize their position in society. The interviews with DREAMers show that blocked pathways to lawful permanent residence and naturalization impede substantive integration, and that the stakes of formal citizenship worsen in an enforcement climate.

The trajectory of citizenship policies in an enforcement era is clear: the federal government's limited avenues for outreach and service provision are infected with an enforcement bias. This enforcement bias heightens the need for formal citizenship. The result is that immigration enforcement exacerbates citizenship inequality. Correcting this bias requires redesigning institutions. For temporary visa holders like Mei, this means facilitating their transitions from international students cultivating skills and knowledge to workers who can use these skills and knowledge within the United States if they so choose. For DACA recipients, this means providing a means to regularize their status and eventually gain access to US citizenship. Beyond legal pathways to citizenship, institutional support is required to promote substantive integration so that citizenship is not only a formality. These ideas are more fully developed in chapter 6.

PART III

A WAY FORWARD

CHAPTER 6

Constructing Pathways to Full Citizenship

THE METICS OF ANCIENT GREECE lived and worked in the city of Athens, but they did not have political or economic rights. They were "resident aliens . . . who 'could not hope to become citizens.'"[1] Because the metics were not citizens, they were not able to pass the privilege of citizenship along to their children. The limited legal status of the metics subjected them to contempt and to persecution by citizens, who could use the law to limit metics' rights and to profit from their disenfranchisement. This worrisome portrait of inequality from the classical age extends to immigrants in modern times. Without government intervention to change their prospects for citizenship, immigrants are unequal to citizens. The close association between their formal status and their unstable economic, social, and political existence compounds their concern over unequal citizenship.

Compared with ancient Greece, the United States has a history of exclusion that is less stark, with dark periods giving way to occasional bursts of light. Optimists read history as an expanding progression of rights that bends toward equality for subordinated groups. Think of the saying "The arc of the moral universe is long, but it bends toward justice," famously pronounced by Martin Luther King Jr. and then rearticulated by President Barack Obama. Equality laws have been extended to some important groups who once lacked formal citizenship: women and African Americans gained legal personhood and consequently the right to vote, to work and own property, and to participate in arenas that were previously the province of white men. The problem with this upbeat view of history is that the march toward equality does not include all, especially not *noncitizens*.[2] Immigration law justifies the exceptional treatment of immigrants as outsiders with an exclusionary rationale. Distinguishing between those who are insiders and those who should remain outsiders is a precondition for citizenship law and even national security.[3] The Supreme Court announced 150 years ago in a case that remains good law, "The power of exclusion of foreigners is an incident of sovereignty belonging to the government of the United States, as a part of those sovereign powers delegated by the Constitution. . . . Jurisdiction over its own territory to that extent is an incident of every independent nation. It is a part of its independence. If it could not exclude aliens, it would be to that extent subject to the control of another power."[4] Under this view, the border excludes foreigners and citizenship inequality is inevitable. This viewpoint asserts the nation's right to define national boundaries, to forge a collective identity, and to protect the existing communities from economic, cultural, and political intrusion.[5] The argument rests on long-standing claims to national sovereignty and deference to the political branches within the nation-state. In this view, the claims of immigrants represent a threat to national security and public safety.

Not everyone agrees with this view. After all, the US Constitution contains equality provisions applicable to *all* persons within the territory, regardless of their legal status,[6] and iconic symbols such as the Statue of Liberty proclaim the cherished place of immigrants in America.[7] And despite the exclusionary actions and rhetoric that immigrants face, proponents of more immigrant-friendly policies advocate on their behalf and seek ways to welcome them. To liberals and progressives, it is inappropriate to use an external boundary to justify inequality toward someone living inside the country on the basis of their legal status.[8] Critical theorists, too, are skeptical of formal citizenship's power, but for different reasons. They distrust the federal government's normative claim to authority over conferring membership within its borders.[9] States and cities, nongovernmental community organizations, schools, churches, and unions stand in to integrate immigrants.[10] These critiques of the conventional view of borders provide building blocks for a national immigrant integration policy.

This concluding chapter revisits the opening dilemma of the book: How do immigrants pursue citizenship when immigration policy prioritizes enforcement? It recognizes that formal citizenship is ascendant in the current state of affairs, and that the federal government bears responsibility for integrating its citizens. Global citizenship is on the wane, with America First and Brexit chipping away at the notion of an international community. Local government, while vital and active, remains constrained by exclusionary federal immigration laws in many areas. As a result, citizenship regulated by the federal government is once again paramount. This state of affairs represents an opportunity as well as a challenge. Rather than subordinating immigrants to national interests, as it has done in the past, the United States can adopt a vision of national interest that includes integrating immigrants with the help of states, cities, and community organizations to deliver vital benefits and services.

A national plan for immigrant integration, with government initiatives at the hub and spokes running through other local and nongovernmental institutions, would extend immigrant access to formal citizenship and thicken the meaning of citizenship to include social, economic, and civic engagement. This vision easily applies to green card holders who are permanent residents of the United States and seeking naturalized citizenship, including refugees and veterans. It would also apply to temporary visa holders and undocumented migrants who live, work, and contribute substantively to their new country. Pathways to formal and substantive citizenship should be promoted where neglected and constructed where missing. On-roads and off-ramps should support formal paths and foster substantive citizenship. A measure of equity should be injected into enforcement. This vision of a national immigrant integration policy, a corrective to immigration law subsumed in enforcement, will improve individual lives and build a collective citizenry.[11]

Citizenship Insecurity Inhibiting Integration

Immigration law is binary: everyone who is not US-born or naturalized is a noncitizen alien.[12] This book uses the term *semi-citizen* to capture the spectrum of membership and belonging for noncitizens, from DACA recipients to temporary visa holders to permanent residents. A national immigrant integration policy challenges institutional assumptions about who is responsible for helping immigrants become part of American life. Expanding on immigration law's traditional assumptions of the citizen/alien dichotomy broadens the notion of membership beyond formal belonging. Official recognition of legal status is critical to belonging and integration. Yet my interviews show that legal status is only one component of how immigrants experience citizenship. While the relationship between formal citizenship and economic, social, and political integration varies for each immigrant category, full citizenship cannot be obtained without legal status: formal citizenship is necessary, if not sufficient, to level citizenship inequalities in conditions of strong immigration enforcement.

Gradients of formal citizenship such as a temporary visa or a green card become footholds for substantive belonging.[13] National polls show overwhelming support for the Deferred Action for Childhood Arrivals (DACA) program and expanded forms of protection from deportation.[14] DACA recipients want a visa, green card, and a path to citizenship.[15] Many of the temporary workers and visa holders in my interviews want a green card. Among the green card holders, feelings about naturalizing are more divided: some desire the protection and benefits of citizenship the moment they are eligible, while others doubt that a formal status will transform their social position or alter their sense of belonging. They correspondingly delay or decline to pursue formal citizenship. Refugees who possess a straightforward path to formal citizenship still long for greater social and economic belonging.[16] Military service members feel stronger social belonging than most green card holders, though the enforcement era has chipped away at those feelings.[17]

If formal status encourages integration, the converse is true, too: a lack of status can inhibit integration. Immigration law limits the possibility that substantive belonging can substitute for formal citizenship because so many social, economic, and political benefits are tied to legal status. DACA recipients whose protective status has been threatened by rescission demonstrated a sense that hard-won substantive belonging was eroding in a climate of legal uncertainty.[18] Temporary visitors withhold their investment in American life given uncertain returns. Formal legal status cannot be skipped on the road to citizenship equality.[19]

This book recognizes that citizenship status is legally defined and socially constructed. Becoming a citizen is a process mediated by formal and informal institutions. Citizenship is the by-product of a complex social process in which the law functions as both gatekeeper and facilitator of a more comprehensive form of citizenship with economic, social, political, and legal dimensions. This social process generates an unstable legal status that is incomplete, contingent, and temporary. In times of intensive enforcement, it is even more unstable and inhibits economic, social, civic, and further legal integration.

While the interviews exhibit considerable variety in the experiences of noncitizens, they show that immigrants all felt a sense of insecurity and partial integration. Though this sense of citizenship insecurity was the dominant experience reported in my interviews, some immigrants felt more optimistic about their possibilities for fitting in. Their optimism tended to focus on instances of state and local integration, primarily in locations with pro-immigrant integration policies.[20] While these stories inspire hope for undocumented immigrants, they are exceptional and inspiring precisely because the main characters demonstrate courage and maintain hope in the face of a dispiriting national immigration policy. In my study, the resilience of DACA activists stands out as remarkable as compared with the experiences of the everyday immigrants I encountered who struggle with the United States' middling commitment to their integration.[21]

How do other noncitizens feel? Certain categories of immigrants were not covered in this book's empirical research because of limited time and resources. Many have lesser forms of status than those I interviewed and would tell an amplified version of the same story of citizenship insecurity. Green card holders whose status is being stripped as a result of criminal or immoral conduct were not included in the broader category of green card holders, but they undoubtedly feel citizenship insecurity and confront structural barriers to integration.[22] Workers toiling away in low-wage, low-skilled jobs on H-2 visas were not included in the broader category of temporary workers, but they would feel the limitations of their liminal protection at least as starkly as the high-skilled workers on H-1B visas.[23] Undocumented immigrants who were statutorily ineligible for DACA and other forms of relief from deportation were not included, but they assuredly bristle at the threat of enforcement and wish for a more stable status.[24] Other groups were omitted because their particular experiences extend beyond the scope of a study of immigrants seeking to integrate in the contemporary enforcement climate.[25] These research omissions were made primarily for practicality. Further research on more groups would likely confirm or even magnify the core findings: whether refugee or service member, green card holder or visa holder, documented or undocumented, immigrants are struggling to integrate in an enforcement era.

Broadening the Pathways to Citizenship

How, then, should formal citizenship be obtained in a vast and multicultural society? The federal government dispenses the rights of formal citizenship and is the only institution that can level the uneven terrain for citizens and noncitizens. A logical extension of this institutionalist explanation for integration is that the federal government should enhance access to naturalized citizenship. This might include making technical fixes to the naturalization process and streamlining the process to reduce administrative burdens. It might include expanded eligibility for citizenship with reforms to temporary visas that facilitate adjustment of status. For example, for temporary visitors either an intent to remain, if eligible for dual intent, or accrual of significant lawful presence—say five years with visa extensions and renewals—could signal a desire to settle and merit adjusting status. These federal efforts should complement the informal and decentralized support for naturalization that is much needed but relied on too heavily. By delegating immigrant integration, the federal government neglects its responsibility and sends negative messages to immigrants about the value of integrating into society.

At the same time, the substantive dimensions of belonging do not automatically emerge from formal citizenship and should not be contingent on formal status. The pathway to semi-citizenship is paved by local support and voluntary institutions. Throughout my exploration of immigrant integration in Colorado, the names of city offices and community organizations came up again and again: the Boulder Public Library, the Denver Public Schools, the Aurora Immigrant and Refugee Commission, Catholic Charities, Lutheran Family Services, the International Refugee Assistance Program, Veterans for New Americans, Mi Familia Vota, the Asian Pacific Development Center, and the Colorado African Organization. These organizations collectively work to level barriers to economic opportunity, broaden access to public benefits, and enhance political participation. Their efforts to naturalize and integrate immigrants could be better coordinated with government efforts. Information about the benefits of naturalization could supplement resource directories of citizenship workshops, classes, and US Citizenship and Immigration Services (USCIS) preparation materials. Assistance with English-language and civics tests and naturalization applications could be supplemented with pretesting for USCIS interviews similar to the State Department's visa wizard, which helps visitors assess their visa options, or with web-based software like SimpleCitizen that is modeled on TurboTax.[26] Civics education could be paired with citizenship workshops and voter registration drives. Legal clinics providing free or low-fee legal assistance for immigrants resisting deportation could be broadened to support applications for green cards and naturalized citizenship.

On the federal level, the United States has carried out some initiatives on immigrant integration on a limited scale, though some of these initiatives have ended or eroded in the enforcement era. Agencies within the immigration bureaucracy and the Defense Department have a history of coordinating to provide military service members with a streamlined path to citizenship that involves fee waivers, shortened timelines, and high success rates.[27] To integrate refugees, the federal government allocates funding to state resettlement offices and nonprofit organizations to ensure basic economic survival in the early stages of settlement.[28] From there, federally funded case workers cooperate with communities and businesses to further integrate refugees so they can be self-sufficient and claim the mainstream protections afforded to all citizens.[29] On a national scale, 1995 Immigration and Naturalization Service (INS) commissioner Doris Meissner announced the Citizenship USA initiative with a goal of responding to increased interest in naturalization. Citizenship USA launched mass media campaigns in five districts with the largest naturalization backlogs.[30] The Citizenship USA effort increased filings but faltered after a report found that expanding the capacity had compromised the integrity of naturalization processing. Problems were immediately rectified, but the Citizenship USA program has not been pursued.

Outside of the naturalization context, the federal government advances immigrant integration in partnership with other government agencies and private charities. It works with local schools to ensure equal educational opportunity for nonnative English-speaking school children—adhering to the ruling in *Lau v. Nichols* (1974)[31] guaranteeing equal educational opportunity for all non-English-speaking students.[32] These principles have spurred additional programs facilitating immigrant integration: the expansion of adult language and civics education programs in libraries and community centers,[33] language access in health care and other federal programs,[34] and language rights in courts.[35] Another example of government incorporation of immigrants beyond naturalization occurs within federal workplace agencies. Workplace agencies such as the US Equal Employment Opportunity Commission protect immigrant workers by extending them the protection of employment and labor laws.[36]

These efforts represent some of the more promising ways that the federal government facilitates inclusion and citizenship equality. However, they are not widespread and the government's level of commitment to them is wavering in the era of enforcement.

Constructing Citizenship

Citizenship theory can improve immigrant integration. T. H. Marshall, Linda Bosniak, and Elizabeth Cohen have all written of citizenship as consisting of braided strands of rights, benefits, and identities.[37] These strands can be unbraided—so that one can have social belonging without legal status—and then recombined in various ways. Decoupling the substantive dimensions of belonging from legal status allows for immigrant integration during times of enforcement. A multilevel institutional approach works best for braiding together the strands of formal and substantive citizenship toward the end of full citizenship.

Facilitating Formal Citizenship

Promoting full citizenship reconceives the singular role of the federal government in immigrant integration and enforcement. The federal government needs to take the lead on protecting the threshold of constitutional and statutory rights of immigrants and adopt a coordinated approach toward integration with other agencies. Given the emphasis on formal citizenship in this book, a linchpin of the plan must be enhanced support for immigrants pursuing naturalized citizenship and the elimination of barriers that stymie it. Other than naturalization, the government should encourage transitions between statuses for temporary visa holders and undocumented immigrants. It should also coordinate and incentivize civics and language training, educational opportunities beyond K–12 schooling, economic support and job training, opportunities for civic engagement, and social ties.

Green Card Holders Enhancing outreach about citizenship eligibility may be key to changing the laissez-faire approach toward naturalization and integration. A 2019–20 bill introduced in Congress includes measures to bolster naturalized citizenship. The bill, titled "New Deal for New Americans Act of 2019," would eliminate roadblocks to citizenship for eligible residents, such as rising application fees and processing backlogs, and it would create a new federal office charged with immigrant integration.[38] An independent federal office of integration[39] or a cabinet-level interagency task force could foster leadership and facilitate efforts across the federal government.[40]

The successful implementation of any citizenship supports would require renewed commitment from the federal government agencies directly involved in immigration policy, including the existing US Citizenship and Immigration Service. USCIS adjudication of naturalization and other immigration benefits could also be improved.[41] The naturalization process is complex and the wait time is lengthy. In many parts of the country, the wait time for naturalization is ten to eighteen months, in excess of the statutory timeline of six months, as a result of inefficient processes, burdensome vetting requirements, and resource allocations that prioritize fraud and national security concerns over granting benefits.[42] Immigrants bear the burden of navigating this bureaucracy, and some never make it through because of denials or requests for more evidence. As former INS commissioner Doris Meissner put it in a 1996 report to Congress about the INS, the government needs to put the S, or "service," in the INS; the same needs to be done with USCIS.[43]

Beyond the USCIS's coordinated outreach, citizenship eligibility could be carried out by federal agencies that already provide services to immigrants, provided that the agencies can maintain fidelity to the purpose of immigrant integration. Some candidates for increased outreach include the Internal Revenue Service, the US Department of Education, the US Equal Employment Opportunity Commission, the Labor Department, the US Department of Health and Human Services, the State Department, or the Social Security Administration. Taking one example, the Internal Revenue Service maintains a trusting relationship with immigrants by offering protected Individual Taxpayer Identification Numbers to those who are not eligible for a social security number but have earned income in the United States on which they owe taxes, such as international students and undocumented immigrants.[44] The Internal Revenue Service could tap its database of Individual Taxpayer Identification Number users to dispense timely and relevant information about immigration benefits such as eligibility for adjustment of status and naturalization.[45] Studies show that immigrants respond positively to dispersal of information about citizenship eligibility when it occurs in schools, community centers, and libraries.[46] Involving the federal government could increase efficiency and enhance messaging about the national commitment to immigrants.

Tapping into state and local agencies already involved in integration could supplement federal efforts for naturalization; in effect, this would extend the inclusionary efforts of "new immigration federalism" to naturalization.[47] State departments of motor vehicles (DMVs) could promote naturalization in the manner that they promote voter registration under "motor voter" laws.[48] A new law could be enacted to facilitate naturalization through DMV offices, which serve immigrants of varying statuses and citizens alike. Adapting the motor voter laws in a new law that lets DMVs assist with naturalizations would require simplifying the naturalization process so that it could be administered by a DMV official. State health insurance registration could be similarly linked to naturalization.

To be effective, public agencies would need to limit the purposes for disclosure of citizenship status to promoting integration and find ways to protect the privacy of immigrants vulnerable to immigration enforcement. These safeguards, which could be enacted in legislation or regulations, are crucial for coordinated outreach to work. To see why, consider a 2019 executive order urging government agencies with information about citizenship status to share that information with the Census Bureau for their decennial count and reapportionment efforts.[49] The Department of Homeland Security subsequently offered to release administrative records revealing citizenship status to the Census Bureau.[50] While the use of this citizenship data remains to be seen, the potential for citizenship information to be broadly disclosed and then used for nonintegrative purposes—such as limiting apportionment to citizens, public benefit restriction, or immigration enforcement—could be destructive to integration.[51] One limitation is for the releasing agency to aggregate data without revealing personally identifiable information; this is the practice of the Census Bureau. Another limitation is to specify the permissible uses of citizenship data; the Internal Revenue Service authorizing statute might serve as an example. The Internal Revenue Service has historically taken privacy very seriously for immigrants and other tax filers and limited disclosures for non-tax related purposes. Still filing is not free of risk: the Internal Revenue Service is required to disclose information upon request of certain Treasury Department employees, and federal laws permit disclosure of tax information to other federal agencies for nontax criminal violations, terrorist activities, and emergency circumstances with court order.[52] State DMVs that extend driver's licenses to immigrants are calling for stricter standards for disclosure to law enforcement and stronger privacy protections amid revelations that immigration officials accessed their databases and used facial recognition software to identify enforcement targets in several states.[53] Guidelines for disclosure of citizenship status and limitations on the use of sensitive information would ensure that the agencies with information about immigration status use it to broaden access to citizenship, not to curtail it.

Agency oversight, whether through executive, legislative, or judicial means, would help prevent disclosure of immigration status or misuses of information for purposes that erode integration.

Beyond outreach, the government could reform citizenship laws by altering eligibility criteria in ways that cultivate legal residents' ability and desire to naturalize.[54] Currently, the basic criteria include five years as a green card holder; five years of continuous presence; basic understanding of the English language, US history, and civics; good moral character; attachment to the ideals of the US Constitution; and an application fee. The concept of immigrant intent to remain in the United States underlies these requirements, making duration and commitment into proxies for the desire to settle. The government could allow residents to identify their intent to naturalize at the time their green card is issued, and then follow up with them once their five-year residency requirement is met and as the ten-year timeline for renewal approaches.[55]

The application fee is another eligibility criterion that affects naturalization rates.[56] Current law makes naturalization more expensive than renewing a green card: $725 ($640 application and $85 biometrics) versus $540 ($455 application and $85 biometrics).[57] Proposals to raise fees appear routinely and preceding each fee increase, immigrant advocates stress the need to lower user fees or issue fee waivers for poorer immigrants.[58] They contend that maintaining affordability of fees and fee waivers at each level is needed to keep the pathway to citizenship accessible. Fee equalization would also encourage naturalization: I propose that the USCIS could charge equal amounts—say $500 for both types of applications—rather than tiering the prices. The equivalent fees would change the financial incentives that favor renewal over naturalization and ensure that decisions to naturalize are not based on financial cost.

Temporary Visa Holders Temporary visitors confront many obstacles to settling in the United States under existing immigration law. Under current law, international students and postdoctoral researchers on F-1 and J visas must express intent to return home at the conclusion of their educational programs; engaging in activities that indicate settlement subjects them to presumptions of immigration fraud.[59] International students are stymied by the inability to express a dual intention that signals a desire to stay in the United States once eligible, and changing their official intentions as their educational goals, career plans, and family circumstances change while living in the United

States can be a cumbersome process.[60] High-skilled workers on an H-1B visa do have the ability to express dual intention to temporarily visit and eventually settle, though reduced caps and strict standards on their adjustment process make the possibility of settling harder.[61] The intensified adjudication process makes the prospect of extending their visas or obtaining their green card and then naturalizing feel elusive.[62] The interviews with Chinese and Indian technology workers on H-1B visas, who are permitted to express a dual intent and adjust, demonstrate that feeling like a guest, rather than one who belongs, feeds the sense of uncertainty about the future and inhibits integration.

While supporters of current immigration laws may prefer that the terms of temporary visas limit settlement integration, the empirical reality shown in the New Immigrant Survey and other data is that many of those immigrants find ways to lawfully live in the United States. Their feelings of uncertainty would be eased by making it simpler for temporary visa holders to express an intention to remain, to extend their visas or transition between visas and green cards, or acknowledge significant time living lawfully in the United States. These changes would provide a way for temporary visa holders to indicate, without fear of visa denial or deportation, their hope to remain in the United States and to plan their lives accordingly. USCIS could improve its service delivery in this regard. The US government or another agency could inform temporary visitors once they become eligible to adjust to a green card using the channels described for outreach about naturalization eligibility. Collaboration with universities and employers would also help temporary visa holders navigate their status transitions. University offices for visiting scholars, postdoctoral researchers, and international students play a vital role in supporting this group by offering cultural orientation workshops and assistance in navigating procedures for students to enroll, stay enrolled, graduate, and transition to the workforce.[63] Corporate support for generous terms on high-skilled worker visas and employer-sponsored green cards should be continued and expanded.[64]

Feelings of ambivalence about the future might change if temporary visa holders felt valued as members of communities while living in the United States. Instead, temporary visa holders receive mixed messages about their belonging from the federal government, corporations, and universities. On the one hand, they are prized for their knowledge, skills, work ethic, and tuition payments in the government proposals for more merit-based immigration. On the other hand, they face indifference and even skepticism in the form of entry barriers and procedural hoops to stay in US schools and companies under the terms of their visas. Sometimes they are viewed as cultural or economic threats and treated with outright hostility or discrimination.

I acknowledge that affirmatively supporting transitions for temporary visitors would challenge the underlying assumption in immigration law that temporary visitors are sojourning rather than settling in the United States. Conditions of continuing affiliation could be set for adjusting from a visa to a green card, similar to what is required of immigrants who marry US citizens. And not all immigrants will avail themselves of dual intent and easier transition mechanisms. Still, even if not every temporary immigrant is eligible to remain or chooses to settle, the United States should not make visitors feel unwelcome, as many feel during intensive enforcement.

Undocumented Immigrants The needs of undocumented immigrants seeking citizenship are the gravest of all the legal statuses examined in this book. Institutional support for undocumented immigrants depends on the diverse circumstances of those within the category, but it must begin with basic eligibility for citizenship and forgiveness of prior ineligibility. A limited form of legal status such as DACA, which protects qualifying undocumented immigrants from removal, is a start. But it is not enough. The protection is limited in many ways, including its present and persistent instability.

A legislated form of DACA would stabilize the protections from political change, but it would not solve the problem of liminality without more. DACA stops short of providing a permanent legal status, and it does not provide a way to adjust to formal citizenship. Among longtime undocumented residents, including DACA recipients, the intention to settle is strong. Though some of those interviewed expressed curiosity about visiting their countries of birth, DACA recipients were flummoxed by the prospect of being legally compelled to return to a country they didn't feel was their own. Impermanence inhibits integration in other ways, too. Faced with Congress's repeated failures to enact a DREAM act or comprehensive immigration reform, DACA recipients have grown wary of the US government. They have jumped through hoops and then watched goalposts shift as they navigate their limited legal status. Their social and civic engagements are faltering as a result of the stress of citizenship insecurity: a feeling experienced by other noncitizens, though in a dramatized form.

The government should permit those who entered without inspection a way to adjust status to US citizenship—as it does for those who overstay a visa.[65] Moreover, a measure of equity in enforcement would reduce the risk of deportation. Case-by-case discretion in enforcement decisions and the provision of relief in some circumstances would be preferable to the harsh and inflexible mandatory measures being instituted by the Trump administration.[66] Additional voluntary measures could serve as the baseline for equitable relief until broader, federal changes are made.[67] Mass legalization, last enacted in the Immigration Reform and Control Act in 1986, for example, permits categories of immigrants to become citizens after a shortened period of temporary and permanent residency. Congress could come up with additional avenues toward citizenship in future legislation.[68]

Streamlined procedures and coordinated implementation of legal protections are needed for undocumented immigrants as well. President Obama's innovation with DACA was formalizing a process for granting it to a large group.[69] Coordination among multiple layers of government and across the public-private-nonprofit sectors is needed because overcoming the real risk of removal requires cooperation: between USCIS, the immigration benefit provider; Immigration and Customs Enforcement, the enforcement arm of the Department of Homeland Security; and other levels of government. Sanctuary networks have stepped in to aid undocumented groups, but it is incumbent upon the federal government to provide a meaningful and secure path forward.[70]

Supporting Substantive Citizenship

Amending an immigration law or procedure is not a self-executing path to full citizenship. The call for increased access to formal citizenship and fixes to immigration law should not lead to overreliance on black letter law that cannot by itself solve complex problems. Formal citizenship is embedded in a society that perceives legal status as essential to full and legitimate membership. Disrupting the view that legal status is a prerequisite to belonging requires more than a legal intervention. But it does require such legal intervention. Once that intervention is made, societal supports will be necessary to implement policies and transform the meaning of noncitizenship into something fluid and forward-minded. These require a revitalization of the meaning of political, economic, and social citizenship.

Political participation has long been considered the sine qua non of citizenship.[71] Semi-citizens, much like African Americans and women during prior periods of American history, cannot vote, serve on juries, work in government jobs, nor run for elected office.[72] They are unequal stakeholders in society, despite paying taxes and despite their shared interests in community membership.[73] Revitalizing political citizenship requires cultivating a national community deserving of allegiance and tolerant of differences.[74] We can look abroad for some models. European and Scandinavian countries stress a national identity rooted in commitment to national citizenship.[75] France's principle of *laïcité* stresses a secular society rather than ethno-religious or ethno-racial particularism.[76] Denmark requires immigrants to undergo mandatory instruction in Danish values, religious traditions, and language in order to obtain public benefits.[77] In the United States, federal programs including President George H. W. Bush's A Thousand Points of Light, President Bill Clinton's AmeriCorps Initiative of the Corporation for National and Community Service, and President Obama's RefugeeCorps would embed the concept of national service in immigrant integration.[78] Citizenship for Service proposals permit military and possibly civilian service to form the basis for legalization and integration.[79] The New Deal for New Americans would make automatic voter registration available on a voluntary basis immediately after the citizenship oath ceremony.[80]

These examples demonstrate the potential of using civic engagement and national identity to foster integration, but there are pitfalls as well. The history of US immigration policy includes Americanization movements that stir up excessive national pride that leads to exclusion. While patriotic programs can helpfully bridge differences and bind together a nation, compelling immigrants to commit to a specified set of ideals can threaten the diversity of views and cultures that migrants bring with them when they settle.[81]

The right to earn is also a foundation of citizenship.[82] Yet immigrants' right to work is restricted and eligibility for education and public benefits is limited due to fear that they will incentivize unwanted and undocumented migration. Landmark decisions such as *Graham v. Richardson* (1971)[83] and *Matthews v. Diaz* (1976)[84] suggest that lawful permanent residents have long been subject to restrictions on welfare and public benefits, with an ever-expanding trend toward exclusion. Undocumented immigrants have had it even worse, with eligibility for public benefits circumscribed apart from carve-outs for education under *Plyler v. Doe* (1982)[85] and a patchwork of state benefits.[86] They have additionally been restricted from certain kinds of work under the public function doctrine. Recent controversies over welfare eligibility include disputes over the scope of health-care coverage under the Affordable Care Act, which specifically omitted DACA recipients while covering other categories of immigrants,[87] and the new rule that would consider immigrants who have lawfully used public benefits as "public charges" who are economically dependent on the state and therefore ineligible to obtain a visa or naturalize.[88] Revitalizing economic citizenship would require an extension of benefits with greater alignment between federal requirements and the state safety net. Australia makes no public benefits distinction between immigrants and citizens.[89] While the United States is unlikely to eliminate the citizenship distinction vis-à-vis granting public benefits, history shows that the eligibility and exclusionary criteria can be tailored to either promote or stall integration.[90]

Social belonging is another aspect of substantive citizenship, albeit one with a weak tradition under the United States' equality laws.[91] Lawful permanent residents are purportedly protected from discrimination on the basis of national origin, race, and other markers.[92] Due process is owed to all persons, including protections against arbitrary government actions.[93] Yet the substantive reality often falls short of the formal promises. Taking inspiration from refugee and language programs in the United States, schools and universities can enhance integration for immigrants who fall between the cracks of the government's piecemeal approach. The award-winning Visiting Scholar and Postdoc Affairs Program at the University of California, Berkeley, offers international students cultural orientation workshops and counseling on successful classroom and workplace strategies; it is essentially a refugee resettlement program for the highly educated.[94] In response to the travel ban, universities launched a "You Are Welcome Here" campaign to reach out to international students,[95] and they have expanded their efforts since data emerged indicating that enrollment of new international students is declining in part because they do not feel welcome.[96] These *voluntary* approaches resemble the multicultural approach adopted by the Canadian government for immigrants, refugees, indigenous people, and racial minorities.[97] A more affirmative approach toward immigrant integration, with the federal government at the helm, would enhance formal and substantive citizenship in the United States.

Citizenship Equality as the End Game?

The federal government would need to take affirmative steps to integrate immigrants in each of these proposals. Once immigrants become eligible for citizenship, their pursuit of equality resembles the pathways available to other naturalized and US-born citizens. Just as racial minorities who confront inequality and segmented assimilation require the protections of civil rights, language rights, and multiculturalism policies, immigrants transitioning to citizenship would benefit from legal protections against discrimination without regard to their prior legal status as immigrants. In a truly integrative climate, green card holders should not be persistently worried about losing their eligibility for citizenship and naturalized citizens should not be threatened with denaturalization or expatriation. Further, legal immigrants permanently residing in the United States should enjoy the same treatment as citizens living in the same communities.

The proposition that society should encourage greater equality between citizens and noncitizens, and among different categories of noncitizens, is both simple and radical. It is simple insofar as it reaffirms a tenet of equality aspired to in many spheres of life. It is radical insofar as it works against principles of immigration law that differentiate citizens and noncitizens. The United States has attributed outsized importance to borders and to legal status during the era of expanding enforcement. If the citizen/alien dichotomy implies unbridgeable political differences, citizenship equality rests on the premise of a linked fate—economic, social, political, legal—along the spectrum of semi-citizenship. In this inclusionary conception, citizenship becomes a shared identity and a collective endeavor, not an arbitrary marker of legal difference.

Striving for citizenship equality raises difficult normative questions. What should be the scope of integration efforts for the full spectrum of immigrants, ranging from undocumented immigrants to temporary visitors to green card holders who are eligible to naturalize?[98] How do we ensure that encouragement to integrate does not prompt discrimination against immigrants who cannot naturalize or pressure to assimilate to a narrowly defined set of behaviors or beliefs, whether due to citizenship ineligibility or due to ongoing race, gender, and class barriers that persist independent of formal citizenship?[99] And how do we maintain a meaningful national identity in light of the racial, religious, and ideological diversity immigration brings to the United States?[100]

The answers to these normative questions require sustained consideration. Yet they belong to a different project. This book takes the pursuit of citizenship for immigrants already living in the United States as its premise and proceeds to consider empirically the corrosive effects of excessive enforcement on that normative ideal. Answering foundational questions requires reconciling values of inclusion and diversity, liberty and equality, regulation and experimentation—values that can be at odds in a liberal democracy—and it is a task too complex for the closing pages of this book. I refer the reader to theorists who have studied the struggles of women, racial minorities, and poor people who have fought to earn formal citizenship and yet whose efforts for equality continue centuries after gaining formal rights.[101]

After normative premises are established, operational difficulties associated with proposed solutions must be confronted. How should we protect immigrant integration plans from federal enforcement? How do we promote integration without compromising the integrity of the citizenship acquisition process and the meaning of becoming American? Can the federal government be trusted to facilitate immigrant integration in light of long histories of exclusion? Can politicians forge bipartisan support to enact integration proposals, given the intense polarization of federal immigration policies during the modern enforcement era?[102]

The operational difficulties relate to policy design and implementation. I have offered some operational detail about how the federal government could notify immigrants of their eligibility to naturalize or obtain a green card: a linchpin of integration for immigrants pursuing citizenship. I have also offered ideas to enhance the prospects for formally and substantively integrating temporary visitors and undocumented immigrants. Continued thinking needs to occur among diverse stakeholders to map out a national immigrant integration plan.[103] The plan would require rethinking structural arrangements to enhance the capacity of service-oriented agencies and to bolster the independence of service-oriented and enforcement-oriented immigration agencies, while also permitting broader partnerships between immigration agencies with other branches. It also would require following up legal and societal reforms with effective implementation: the classic dilemma of "making rights real" joined with the unique challenge of changing course on immigration policy after decades of intense immigration enforcement.[104]

Looking Forward: Immigration and Integration in the Enforcement Era

Integrating immigrants in an era of enforcement demands citizenship equality among immigrants who are fundamentally unequal under US immigration law. It is a pressing issue after years of expanding enforcement that reached an apex in the Trump administration. In nearly every imaginable way, the Trump administration sought to restrict the flourishing of immigrants, without regard to status or criminality, with its enforcement-first policy agenda and its obsession with legal status. The Trump administration stretched thin the shared bonds of national citizenship with divisive political rhetoric. That rhetoric declares "America First" at the same time that it advances a version of American identity that excludes immigrants, racial minorities, women, and other vulnerable groups in society.[105]

Going beyond rhetoric, policies raising "second walls" stymie immigrant integration.[106] Challenges to legal migration such as caps on temporary visas for high-skilled workers and restrictions on Chinese scientists and Muslims block their initial entry point to US society.[107] Intensified vetting both for green cards and during naturalization processes for refugees, veterans, and other permanent residents block their subsequent integration.[108] The rule proposed by the Department of Homeland Security to classify as public charges those who have claimed welfare benefits also blocks integration.[109] Proposals to denaturalize citizens and narrow or eliminate birthright citizenship for US citizens show the disavowal of integration in the enforcement era.[110] These policies negatively affect immigrants at every point on the spectrum of citizenship, from entry to settlement.

These citizenship-eroding policies negatively affect US citizens as well. Social cohesion, defined as the willingness of members of society to cooperate with each other, makes it possible for our nation to survive and prosper.[111] Diversity makes the need for social cohesion more acute. Some studies show that racial diversity can deplete mutual trust and social capital, making it more difficult to encourage voting and enact social welfare policies.[112] But diversity can also strengthen society when insiders and outsiders develop trusting relationships. More pointedly, diversity strengthens society when majority groups can learn to trust the newcomers who surround them in greater numbers.[113] Exclusionary immigration policies, and the defensive mindsets they produce for immigrant newcomers and citizens alike, do not facilitate intergroup trust.[114] To the contrary, exclusionary policies breed self-protection, cynicism, and even violence.[115] The damage adheres to vulnerable immigrants, and it attaches to all immigrants, even those who need not be afraid of immigration enforcement. Immigration enforcement has the tendency to unsettle social belonging even if one is not the direct target. By virtue of their proximity to the targeted groups, legal immigrants are shaken by the dangers faced by illegal immigrants, and Latino citizens are shaken by the experiences of immigrants from other contexts. As my interviews show, the disintegrative effects spill over to society.

Excessively exclusionary enforcement policies negatively affect the future of immigration policy and the institutions of citizenship, too. The immigration courts and agencies responsible for adjudicating immigration are stretched to the breaking point.[116] Congress's push for comprehensive immigration reform, which would include a DREAM act and other remedies for undocumented status, seems to have stalled indefinitely.[117] The inability of our democratic institutions to function properly erodes citizenship. Some of the same worries that emerged for noncitizens have found their way into mainstream public engagement. People cannot get along. Dissent is unwelcome. Protests erupt into violence or are stamped out in a retaliatory manner.[118] Court cases concerning immigrants are wielded as swords in a battle for rights and recognition.[119] Immigrants express mistrust of government and cynicism about its institutional capacity to restore goodwill that would bolster integration.[120] The mere fact of being a noncitizen has become grounds for unequal treatment, and even formal citizenship may not protect you. The need for citizenship is acute, and yet the institutions of citizenship are withering on the vine.

The threat of immigration enforcement to citizenship includes many policy examples from the Trump administration, yet this is not a book about the Trump administration—or at least not exclusively. Returning to the central dilemma, integration and exclusion are both vital forces in a bounded nation-state. Encouraging the pursuit of citizenship in an enforcement era is difficult. Present circumstances necessitate the search for solutions. This book has called for a transformation of the federal government's role in the regulation of membership that leads to full citizenship. Immigration lawyers, scholars, and policy makers concede too much when they give up on the notion that the federal government can act in a citizenship-enhancing manner. The examples of cities, states, corporations, churches, and campuses inspire new ways to temper federal enforcement and promote integration. There are models from other nations as well: Canada and Australia exposes a national commitment to integration and structure government institutions to serve that vision. I have suggested policy tools that can reform the United States' institutional design and enhance its capacity for integration. These efforts could be guides toward a more ambitious conception of immigrant integration, pointing the way for specific reforms as political conditions permit.

Still, we should not lose sight of the guiding ideal of full citizenship in America. The immigrants interviewed for this book resemble the metics in ancient Greece. They are sojourner citizens: visitors residing in a foreign land and yearning to feel at home. As Tatiana, a scientist from Bolivia, said, "When you're a foreigner in a new place, you think 'I have to be respectful and realize I'm a guest.'"[121] That feeling of distance does not always close up with time. Esen, a DACA student who has resided in America for most of her life, described feeling "stuck" because she could not go forward or back.[122] The interviews in this book show that immigrants in nearly every legal status feel like outsiders during times of excessive immigration enforcement. Many express uncertainty over their future in a country that does not want them. Studying citizenship from their viewpoint reveals weaknesses in the United States' institutional indifference toward immigrants who are already living their lives in the country. Constructing more promising pathways to citizenship, including increased access to formal citizenship and expanded support for substantive integration, would let immigrants become full citizens while they live, work, and study in the United States. It would also renew America's institutional commitment to immigrants pursuing citizenship.

Appendix

Research Methods and Data

Data Overview

Engaging in participant observation and conducting interviews with immigrants about their experiences living, working, and participating in a society where they are noncitizens and about their experience of seeking formal citizenship enabled me to procure a bottom-up perspective on citizenship. I spoke to immigrants within their citizenship status groupings in order to gain a sense of the institutional support they perceived and how it compared with that perceived by other groups in the interview sample.

Together with a group of student research assistants, I spent three years (from 2016 to 2019) conducting in-depth interviews and surveys with more than one hundred immigrants and attended numerous citizenship and naturalization workshops.

Site Selection: Colorado, 2016–2019

Most of these interviews were conducted in Colorado from 2016 to 2018, and follow-up surveys were conducted in 2019.[1] Nearly one in ten Colorado residents is an immigrant; the top countries of origin for immigrants are Mexico (43.3 percent of immigrants), India (4.4 percent), Vietnam (3.2 percent), Germany (3.2 percent), and China (3.1 percent).[2] Among immigrants, 38.7 percent had naturalized as of 2015. One in nine workers in Colorado is an immigrant, with the largest numbers in construction, accommodation, and food services. Immigrants are concentrated at both ends of the educational spectrum, with one in four adult immigrants holding a college degree and fewer than one in three having less than a high school diploma. A significant share of immigrants are refugees and veterans.[3] International students and scholars make up a growing share of students at the flagship public university.[4] Approximately two hundred thousand undocumented immigrants formed 37 percent of the immigrant population and 3.8 percent of the total state population in 2014. More than fifteen thousand Deferred Action for Childhood Arrivals (DACA) recipients live in Colorado. The state is considered a "reemerging immigrant destination" because its immigration rates rose in the early twentieth century, declined, and are rising once again.[5]

The time period from 2016 to 2019 was one of rising immigration enforcement in the national policy landscape. Colorado is known as a purple state with shifting views regarding immigrants and integration that leaned toward being inclusive of immigrants during the study period. In 2015, the University of California Los Angeles Blum Center ranked Colorado within the top five for inclusion of immigrants, taking into account state policies toward immigrants and public benefits, education, labor and employment, driver licensing, and sanctuary policies.[6] From 2016 to 2019, Colorado dedicated significant resources to immigrant integration. It extended in-state tuition and then state financial aid to undocumented students through the ASSET Bill.[7] It provided driver's licenses to undocumented immigrants.[8] It covered lawfully residing immigrant women and children through Medicaid and the Children's Health Insurance Program.[9] Governor John Hickenlooper supported resettling an increased number of Syrian refugees in 2016 and Colorado agreed to keep supporting refugees following the Executive Order permitting state input in 2020.[10] Colorado does not have an official statewide sanctuary policy, but it limits the holding of undocumented immigrants for immigration enforcement and many county and city policies have adopted sanctuary policies, earning it a reputation as a sanctuary state.[11] Colorado does not have a mandatory E-Verify policy.[12] Views on immigration within the state range from the more liberal ones in the Front Range cities of Denver and Boulder to the more conservative ones in Colorado Springs and the rural Western Slope.[13] The mixture of policies and political opinions on immigration makes Colorado a good place to study immigrant integration.

Participant Observation

My research team conducted two years of ongoing observations of US Citizenship and Immigration Services naturalization ceremonies, community-organized naturalization drives, and library-sponsored citizenship classes. This ethnographic work introduced me to gatekeepers to the immigrant community and helped me earn the trust of immigrants who were seeking formal citizenship. I also spent time at organizational meetings for international students, international scholars, and DACA recipients on two college campuses.

These field observations presented a tableau of the changing context of citizenship and naturalization that reinforced the message emerging from the interviews. We paired this ethnographic data with intensive documentary analysis of changing laws and policies regarding immigration and citizenship.

Interviews

The sampling strategy for interviews was adapted for each group of immigrants because each has access to a different level of institutional support for naturalization and integration.

Green Card Holders

To gain a deeper understanding of the factors influencing naturalization decisions, we conducted interviews with three categories of green card holders about their decisions to naturalize or to refrain from doing so ($n = 75$–80 total). These interviews with lawful permanent residents consisted of three immigration subgroups, according to their legal categories and pathway to citizenship: (1) lawful permanent residents eligible for citizenship as a result of employer-based or family-sponsored visas ($n = 40$); (2) refugees and asylum seekers ($n = 25$); and (3) noncitizens who became eligible to naturalize as a result of their military service, some of whom are additionally refugees ($n = 15$). Sampling within immigrant subgroups eligible for citizenship enabled structured comparisons across subgroups of permanent residents seeking citizenship through different pathways.

I solicited interviews through naturalization drives, citizenship classes, and non-profit organizations that serve immigrants. I sent inquiries on email list-serves, circulated flyers at organizational meetings, and called on various personal and professional networks. Incentives varied by group: green card holders were offered small gift cards to coffee shops and grocery stores, international students were offered the chance to be entered in a lottery for an iPad, and DACA recipients were offered cash awards of forty dollars. The large naturalization drives have the benefit of wide representation of immigration statuses, with immigrants' pathways to citizenship ranging from family-sponsored to employer-sponsored visas and to refugee and military green cards. The language classes have the benefit of including those immigrants who may be eligible for naturalization but ultimately choose not to pursue it. The nonprofit and professional networks bolstered trust with gatekeepers. The email list-serves and flyers broadened our reach. Additional targeted outreach and interview incentives were offered to high-skilled workers, refugees, and noncitizens who have served in the military for closer study of subgroups whose members do not frequent naturalization drives.

I asked interview respondents how they became lawful permanent residents and about the social, economic, and political dimensions of their lives. For example, I asked about friends, family, language, quality of life, and feelings of belonging in the United States. I then asked them to comment on their motivation for citizenship: Why were they pursuing citizenship? What did they hope to obtain? Finally, I asked how current policies affected their decisions to pursue citizenship and how they thought they differed from others who had decided not to pursue citizenship.

Temporary Visa Holders

I next conducted interviews with temporary visa holders ($n = 20$). About half of the twenty temporary visa holders were international students on F-1 visas. The other half were scholars, scientists, and engineers working on H-1B visas in the university and surrounding high-tech businesses. Many originated from China, India, and Middle

Eastern countries that fell within the travel ban or other rumored policies of restricted immigration.

I reached these interviewees primarily through outreach mediated by a university office that serves international students and scholars. I additionally used professional networks to generate interviews in the high-tech companies and laboratories in the community because members of this subgroup often use employer-based services or have private attorneys.

These interviews served a different purpose from the green card interviews. I wanted to learn about the meaning of citizenship from those who are not eligible to pursue it. I asked respondents to talk about their migration and initial entry to the United States and their social, economic, and political experiences residing in the United States. International students, scholars, and H-1B technology workers were additionally asked about their home country versus US affiliations and future intentions to adjust legal status: To what extent do you identify with the United States versus your home country? How do you feel your temporary status affects your experiences in America? Do you anticipate staying in the United States? If so, do you intend to apply for an H-1B visa, green card, or US citizenship if eligible? I also asked international students and scholars to talk about liminality, stability, wanting to stay or return home, avoiding enforcement, exclusion, the political climate, transnational lives, and the availability of dual citizenship.

Undocumented Immigrants and DACA Recipients

My final category of respondents also confronted blocked pathways to citizenship. They were primarily undocumented immigrants who had temporary relief under DACA ($n = 20$). In the second half of 2017 and in 2018, as President Donald Trump announced his plan to rescind DACA, I spoke with DACA recipients about their experiences living with limited legal statuses.[14]

I reached the DACA recipients through a combination of outreach efforts: university offices that administer to the needs of first-generation and undocumented students, student organizations that provide mutual support and resource sharing for undocumented students, and legal clinics that assist DACA students with filing applications and understanding the benefits and constraints of their limited legal status.

DACA recipients were asked about their formal belonging, substantive integration, the relationship between formal status and substantive belonging, and whether they desired a pathway to formal citizenship: How did receiving DACA affect you? How would losing DACA affect you? What are your thoughts on proposed legislation that would maintain DACA, permit a green card, or provide a pathway to citizenship? What is your perception of the current political climate for immigrants? Following the rescission of DACA, they were asked about how the change affected their sense of belonging, their economic integration, and their view of politics.

Surveys

Written surveys were administered to several categories of immigrants in 2019 to gauge changes in response to policy changes. For example, the Colorado Immigrant Rights Coalition and the Colorado African Organization administered surveys that included a few questions from the interviews at citizenship workshops. A statewide survey administered to DACA recipients in cooperation with researchers Aaron Malone and Edelina Burciaga incorporated a few questions from the interviews. Though these surveys were not as in-depth as interviews and were matched to prior interviews, they provide a sense of shifts in responses in a changing political climate.

Analytical Approach

This book leverages a comparative approach to uncover the distinct experiences of citizenship for various categories of immigrants. The comparative approach sought broad distinctions in citizenship experiences across categories and context on the causes for variation within groups.

The interview transcripts were entered into NVivo data analysis software and marked with background information about the interview subject's characteristics: national origin, date of entry, race, gender, age at time of entry, years lived in the United States, and citizenship status at time of entry and time of interview. The interview transcripts were then coded for factors that other studies have found influence both formal and substantive citizenship, such as institutional support and a sense of substantive belonging versus exclusion.

Queries in the NVivo data analysis software helped me probe relationships between the characteristics of immigrants (e.g., refugee, temporary visa, DACA) and factors related to institutional support (e.g., complexity, delays, fees, language barriers, public vs. private support). Querying status and dimensions of integration revealed themes about the challenges and opportunities facing each group: social themes of belonging and identity, interest in the United States, and exclusion or discrimination; economic themes concerning education, career opportunity, and public benefits in the United States or the home country; political themes of home-country politics, electoral and nonelectoral participation in the United States, patriotism, service, wanting to give back, and political climate; and legal themes concerning travel and family sponsorship benefits, uncertainty, volatility, delay, exclusion, and enforcement.

Isolating chunks of interview transcripts relating to themes and matrices enabled me to organize the narratives for the empirical studies in the book.

Extending the Research

The primary limitation of my qualitative methods and data collection relates to the amount of diversity within immigrant communities. The decision to categorize immigrants by legal status is intentional; it is designed to highlight the way that legal categories shape the institutional intervention and social meanings for varieties of immigrants. Each legal category contains immigrants from different countries of origin and different races, genders, ages, and social classes. But as the variation within each legal category is factored in and the one hundred interviews sliced and diced, there is not enough data to systematically investigate the interaction of each of these background characteristics with legal status. Nor does the interview sample capture every subgroup that forms the larger categories of lawful permanent resident, temporary visa holder, and undocumented immigrant. Given the interest in pathways to citizenship, interviews were not systematically conducted with groups who are less likely to be eligible for pathways to citizenship under existing law: lawful permanent residents with criminal convictions, temporary workers on H-2 visas, and undocumented immigrants statutorily ineligible for DACA. Still, the qualitative data supplements quantitative data from public sources that do not disaggregate legal categories of citizenship.

A limitation of the organization- and event-centered interview recruitment strategies is that interviews skewed toward those who opted to naturalize, or who were seriously considering it. While this positive inclination represented the majority of refugees and military vets, it constitutes only 50 percent of lawful permanent residents with employer-based and family-sponsored visas and understates those who choose not to naturalize. Consequently, I used snowball sampling from personal networks and referrals of immigrant and service providers to locate green card holders who were eligible and yet chose not to naturalize, or who waited longer than the usual time to commence naturalization. Also, the recruitment strategy yielded an overrepresentation of family-sponsored immigrants. Many employer-sponsored immigrants seek assistance with naturalization from private attorneys or complete the forms on their own. Private attorneys are prevented by client confidentiality rules from sharing the names of those with whom they worked. This underrepresentation matters because quantitative studies show employer-based immigrants are less likely to naturalize than family-sponsored immigrants. Still, the concentration of interviews with high-tech workers and the overlap between green card holders eligible for citizenship through their employer sponsors and by marriage to a US citizen provide insight into the latter group.

Further research into immigrant integration in Colorado could broaden the population of immigrants to include those with fewer opportunities for integration and those less motivated to take advantage of existing channels than the ones within recruiting networks. In all likelihood, the narratives emerging from these interviews would show an even greater need for institutional support and an even stronger negative relationship between enforcement and integration.

Respondent Characteristics

TABLE A.1. Lawful permanent residents.

	LPR–FS ($n=25$)	LPR–EB ($n=15$)	Refugee ($n=25$)	Military ($n=15$)
Country of origin	Mexico Central/ South America Philippines Canada	China/Taiwan Japan Canada Germany Ukraine Pakistan India Kenya	Burma Bhutan Iran Iraq Libya Sudan	Mexico Central/ South America Ireland Iraq
Race	Latino	Asian White	Asian African Middle Eastern	Latino Middle Eastern White

Notes: LPR-FS = Lawful Permanent Resident (family-sponsored); LPR-EB = Lawful Permanent Resident (employer-based).

TABLE A.2. Temporary visa holders and DACA recipients.

	International students/ H–1Bs ($n=20$)	DACA ($n=20$)
Country of origin	Asia (8) • China (5) • India (2) • Malaysia (1) Middle East (4) • Saudi Arabia (2) • Lebanon (1) • Iran (1) Europe (4) • Germany (1) • Italy (1) • Netherlands (1) • Russia (1)	Mexico (12) Central America (4) • El Salvador (2) • Venezuela (1) • Ecuador (1) Asia (4) • China (1) • Korea (1) • Mongolia (2)

(Continued)

TABLE A.2. (Continued)

	International students/ H–1Bs ($n=20$)	DACA ($n=20$)
Race	Canada (2)	
	Latin America— Bolivia (1)	
	Asian (8)	Latino (16)
	"Muslim" (4)	Asian (3)
	White (6) (European/ Canadian)	White (1)
	Latino (1)	
Other status	F-1	Entered without
	J-1	Inspection (9)
	H-1B	Visa overstay (11)
	LPR-FS	
	LPR-EB	
	LPR-FS	

Notes: LPR-FS = Lawful Permanent Resident (family-sponsored); LPR-EB = Lawful Permanent Resident (employer-based); EWI = Entry Without Inspection.

Sample Questions for Interviews and Written Surveys

Interview Questions for Green Card Holders

- Background information: country of origin, migration pathway, legal status
- Indicators of social, cultural, economic incorporation
  - Q: Tell me about your family, friends, and community involvement in the US.
  - Q: Tell me about the language you speak at home, the holidays you celebrate, the cultural traditions that you keep.
  - Q: How would you describe your quality of life? Do you have the economic opportunities that you want? What kinds of opportunities or institutional support would improve your quality of life?
  - Q: Tell me about your involvement with your community. Have you ever participated in a town hall, called or written a letter to a politician, signed a petition, participated in a protest, voted?
- Naturalization
  - Q: How did you become eligible to naturalize? Since when?
  - Q: What would you hope to obtain by becoming a citizen?
- Belonging/becoming American
  - Q: What do you fear losing or leaving behind?
  - Q: What is your perception of the current political climate regarding immigrants?

Interview Questions for Temporary Visa Holders

- Background information: country of origin, initial entry, changes in status since entry
- Pathway to citizenship available
- STEM fields impacting course of study and career potential
  - Q: To what extent do you identify with the US vs. your home country?
  - Q: Do you feel like your temporary status or your uncertainty about remaining in US impacts your feelings about America? How so?
  - Q: Do you anticipate staying in US? Applying for green card? Citizenship?
  - Q: Perception of current climate, recent policies, role of fed government?

Interview Questions for DACA Recipients

- Migration history
- Experiences in US

- Experiences with DACA
  - Q: When did you receive DACA? How did receiving DACA affect you? (education, work, travel, feeling more secure, substantive belonging)
  - Q: How would losing DACA affect you?
- Perceptions of the policy climate
  - Q: What is your perception of the current political climate for immigrants?
  - Q: What are your thoughts on the proposed DREAM Acts?

Follow-Up Survey with Refugees

University of Colorado Citizenship Survey
Professor Ming Chen, CU School of Law

Thank you for considering participating in a study of immigrant integration in the United States. This academic study is being conducted by Professor Ming Hsu Chen and students at the University of Colorado Law School. It consists of the following questions about your decision to pursue citizenship in the United States. **All identifying information will be kept confidential and participation is voluntary.** If you have questions about the study, **please contact Professor Chen** at ming.h.chen@colorado.edu or 303-492-8398.

Questions

1. **What made you decide to naturalize?**

   _____
   _____
   _____

2. **What goals or objectives do you hope to obtain after naturalization/ citizenship?**
   (Please mark an "X" next to at least 1 response, you can mark more than 1 response)
   1. Greater sense of belonging / the "feeling" of citizenship _____
   2. Security from changes to immigration laws and LPR status _____
   3. Voting rights or ability to participate politically _____
   4. Greater employment and career opportunities _____
   5. Ability to help other family members naturalize or obtain LPR status

      _____

   6. The ability to travel securely/US passport _____
   7. Other _____

Demographic Information

   1. Country of origin:
   2. Date of entry, LPR eligibility, citizenship eligibility:

   _____

Thank you for your participation! We appreciate your time and consideration. **Professor Ming Chen, University of Colorado School of Law**, ming.h.chen@colorado.edu or 303-492-8398.

Notes

Chapter 1: Pursuing Citizenship in the Enforcement Era

1. Mercedes, interview with the author, Denver, Colorado, September 9, 2017.

2. Official declarations of the Trump administration are collected on White House.gov and the Department of Homeland Security webpage "Executive Orders on Protecting the Homeland," accessed December 13, 2019, https://www.dhs.gov /executive-orders-protecting-homeland. Campaign statements and Twitter posts are collected in news media. Ron Nixon and Linda Qiu, "Trump's Evolving Words on the Wall," *New York Times*, January 18, 2018, https://www.nytimes.com/2018/01/18/us /politics/trump-border-wall-immigration.html.

3. The US Citizenship and Immigration Services (USCIS) describes six months as the desired timetable for processing: "Frequently Asked Questions," US Citizenship and Immigration Services, accessed December 13, 2019, https://www.uscis.gov/sites /default/files/files/article/chapter3.pdf.

4. Processing times can be found by searching the website by USCIS district and immigration benefit. A search for the Denver field office shows close to a one-year wait (July 2016–September 2016 applications for citizenship, adjustment of status, and certification of citizenship were being processed as of August 2017). For an analysis of these figures, see Diego Iñiguez-López, *Tearing Down the Second Wall: Ending USCIS's Backlog of Citizenship Applications and Expanding Access to Naturalization for Immigrants* (Chicago: National Partnership for New Americans, July 2, 2019); Colorado State Advisory Committee to the US Commission on Civil Rights, *Citizenship Delayed: Civil Rights and Voting Rights Implications of the Backlog in Citizenship and Naturalization Applications*," September 2019 (reprinted in *University of Colorado Law Review* Forum 91 (2019), http://lawreview.colorado.edu/citizenship-delayed-civil-rights-and-voting -rights-implications-of-the-backlog-in-citizenship-and-naturalization-applications/).

5. Ruth, interview with the author, Denver, Colorado, May 8, 2017.

6. Esen, interview with the author, Boulder, Colorado, February 27, 2018.

7. Amanda Holpuch, "Trump's War on Refugees Is Tearing Down US' Life-Changing Resettlement Program," *Guardian*, June 26, 2019. The State Department and Department of Health and Human Service budgets related to refugees show

significant decreases from 2016 to 2017, 2018, and 2019, and an executive order permits states to veto refugee resettlement.

8. Miriam Jordan, "New Scrutiny Coming for Refugees from 11 'High-Risk' Nations," *New York Times*, January 29, 2018.

9. Philip Marcelo, "Gang Database Made Up Mostly of Young Black, Latino Men," AP News, July 30, 2019. President Trump warned of the dangers of the MS-13 gang in his 2018 State of the Union Address.

10. "About Us," US Citizenship and Immigration Services, last updated March 3, 2018, https://www.uscis.gov/aboutus; Richard Gonzales, "America No Longer a 'Nation of Immigrants,' USCIS Says," NPR, February 22, 2018, https://www.npr.org/sections/thetwo-way/2018/02/22/588097749/america-no-longer-a-nation-of-immigrants-uscis-says.

11. The Commerce Department, which sought to include a citizenship question on the census, lost its bid in the U.S. Supreme Court. Dept of Commerce v. N.Y., 588 U.S._(2019). Soon after, President Trump issued an executive order requiring that agencies with citizenship information share it with the Census Bureau and other agencies. Donald J. Trump, "Executive Order on Collecting Information about Citizenship Status in Connection with the Decennial Census," July 11, 2010, https://www.whitehouse.gov/presidential-actions/executive-order-collecting-information-citizenship-status-connection-decennial-census/.

12. John F. Kelly, "Memorandum on Enforcement of the Immigration Laws to Serve the National Interest," US Department of Homeland Security, January 20, 2017, https://www.dhs.gov/sites/default/files/publications/17_0220_S1_Enforcement-of-the-Immigration-Laws-to-Serve-the-National-Interest.pdf; "Attorney General Announces Zero-Tolerance Policy for Criminal Illegal Entry" (US Department of Justice, April 6, 2018), https://www.justice.gov/opa/pr/attorney-general-announces-zero-tolerance-policy-criminal-illegal-entry.

13. "DOJ Creates Section Dedicated to Denaturalization Cases," US Department of Justice, February 26, 2020, https://www.justice.gov/opa/pr/department-justice-creates-section-dedicated-denaturalization-cases.

14. Immigration and Nationality Act, § 101(a)(15).

15. The conceptual distinction between formal and substantive citizenship is made by a number of scholars. See, e.g., Evelyn Nakano Glenn, "Constructing Citizenship: Exclusion, Subordination, and Resistance," *American Sociological Review* 76, no. 1 (2011): 1; D. Carolina Núñez, "Mapping Citizenship Status, Membership, and the Path in Between," *Utah Law Review* 2016, no. 3 (2016): 477. Empirically, the significance of citizenship is demonstrable, albeit modest, with the most significant effects for racial minorities and immigrants from poor countries.

16. The meaning of formal citizenship is further defined in chapter 2.

17. Substantive citizenship is further defined in chapter 2. The unbundling of citizenship can be traced to T. H. Marshall, with specific dimensions varying among citizenship theorists and social scientists. T. H. Marshall, "Citizenship and Social Class," in *Citizenship and Social Class: And Other Essays* (New York: Cambridge University

Press, 1950), 30–39. While legal status can be equivalent to formal citizenship, its inclusion here indicates that some of these substantive benefits necessarily follow from government-conferred legal status and that legal incorporation and political incorporation are distinct, even if overlapping. Hannah Arendt famously said that citizenship is the "right to have rights." Hannah Arendt, *The Origins of Totalitarianism* (New York: Schocken Books, 1951).

18. Some scholars are skeptical of this view, eyeing state-dominated institutions such as citizenship with suspicion or indifference or pointing out their declining control over membership as supranational, subnational, and transnational communities emerge. See, e.g., Linda Bosniak, "Citizenship Denationalized," *Indiana Journal Global Law Studies* 7 (2000): 447–509; Yasemin Soysal, *Limits of Citizenship: Migrants and Postnational Membership in Europe* (Chicago: University of Chicago Press, 1995); and Peter Spiro, *Beyond Citizenship* (New York: Oxford University Press, 2008).

19. Linda Bosniak, *The Citizen and the Alien* (Princeton, NJ: Princeton University Press, 2006).

20. Bosniak, "Citizenship Denationalized."

21. Irene Bloemraad and Alicia Sheares, "Understanding Membership in a World of Global Migration: (How) Does Citizenship Matter?," *International Migration Review* 51 (2017): 823–67.

22. These claims may be descriptive or prescriptive in nature. For one example, see Joanna Weber-Shirk, "Deviant Citizenship: DREAMer Activism in the United States and Transnational Belonging," *Social Sciences* 4 (2015): 583–97.

23. Jose Antonio Vargas, a prominent journalist who revealed himself to be an undocumented immigrant, fostered a campaign called Define American that used "We are Americans. Just not legally" as its slogan and procured national media coverage on the cover of *Time* (June 25, 2012).

24. Irene Bloemraad, "Theorising the Power of Citizenship as Claims-Making," *Journal of Ethnic and Migration Studies* 44 (2017): 4–26.

25. Elizabeth F. Cohen, *Semi-Citizenship in Democratic Politics* (New York: Cambridge University Press 2009); Linda S. Bosniak, "Status Non-citizens," in *The Oxford Handbook of Citizenship*, ed. Ayelet Shachar et al. (New York: Oxford University Press, 2017), 314–36; Cecilia Menjívar, "Liminal Legality: Salvadoran and Guatemalan Immigrants' Lives in the United States," *American Journal of Sociology* 111, no. 4 (2006): 999–1037; Jennifer Chacon, "Producing Liminal Legality," *Denver University Law Review* 92 (2015): 709; Roberto G. Gonzales, Veronica Terriquez, and Stephen P. Ruszczyk, "Becoming DACAmented Assessing the Short-Term Benefits of Deferred Action for Childhood Arrivals (DACA)," *American Behavioral Scientist* 58 (2014): 1852.

26. Bloemraad and Sheares, "Understanding Membership."

27. Mary Waters and Marisa Gerstein Pineau, eds., *The Integration of Immigrants into American Society* (Washington, DC: National Academies Press, 2015).

28. Waters and Pineau.

29. See, e.g., Cecilia Menjívar and Daniel Kanstroom, *Constructing Immigrant "Illegality": Critiques, Experiences, and Responses* (New York: Cambridge University Press, 2013) (with contributions from Leisy Abrego, Leo Chavez, Nicholas de Genova, Roberto Gonzales, and Doris Marie Provine).

30. An institutional explanation for political integration of immigrants is modeled in Irene Bloemraad, *Becoming a Citizen* (Berkeley: University of California Press, 2006).

31. Waters and Pineau, *Integration of Immigrants*, 61, 66–71.

32. Waters and Pineau, 61, 66–71; Nadwa Mosaad, Jeremy Ferwerda, Duncan Lawrence, Jeremy M. Weinstein, and Jens Hainmueller, "Determinants of Refugee Naturalization in the United States," *Proceedings of the National Academy of Science* 115 (2018): 9175–80.

33. Zachary New, "Ending Citizenship for Service in the Forever Wars," *Yale Law Journal Forum* 129 (2020): 552–66; Ming H. Chen, "Citizenship Denied: Implications of the Naturalization Backlog for Noncitizens in the Military," *Denver University Law Review* 97 (forthcoming 2020).

34. For example, the works of Mary Waters, Irene Bloemraad, Tomás Jiménez, and Helen Marrow exemplify this view.

35. Tomás R. Jiménez, *Immigrants in the United States: How Well Are They Integrating into Society?* (Washington, DC: Migration Policy Institute, Summer 2011).

36. Bosniak, *The Citizen and the Alien* (acknowledging the importance of formal immigration status). Conceptions of citizenship in immigration law define it in terms of formal membership in a geopolitically bounded community. Admittedly, enlistment of local law enforcement to assist federal enforcement blurs the line. Some of this blurring, though, is subject to legal challenge.

37. Irene Bloemraad and Els de Graauw, "Immigrant Integration and Policy in the United States: A Loosely Stitched Patchwork," in *International Perspectives: Integration and Inclusion*, ed. James Frideres and John Biles (Montreal: McGill–Queen's University Press, 2012), 205–34.

38. Alejandro Portes and Min Zhou, "The New Second Generation: Segmented Assimilation and Its Variants," *Annals of American Academy of Political and Social Science* 530 (1993): 74–96.

39. Min Zhou, "Segmented Assimilation: Issues, Controversies, and Recent Research," *International Migration Review* 31 (1997): 975–1008.

40. Daniel Tichenor, *Dividing Lines: The Politics of Immigration Control in America* (Princeton, NJ: Princeton University Press, 2002).

41. For examples of varying state policies, see Pratheepan Gulasekaram and S. Karthick Ramakrishnan, *The New Immigration Federalism* (New York: Cambridge University Press, 2015); Edelina Burciaga and Lisa Martinez, "Political Contexts and Undocumented Youth Movements," *Mobilization* 22 (2017): 451–71.

42. Arizona's SB 1070 was substantially overturned in Arizona v. United States, 567 U.S. 387 (2012). This represented a critical turning point in state incursions into immigration federalism, with subsequent policies being more inclusionary at both the federal executive and state legislative levels.

43. Shoba Wadhia, *Banned: Immigration Enforcement in the Time of Trump* (New York: New York University Press, 2019).

44. Gulasekaram and Ramakrishnan, *New Immigration Federalism*. For a general source summarizing state laws, see the National Conference of State Legislators Immigration Reports (www.ncsl.org/research/immigration) or Welcoming America (welcomingamerica.org).

45. Rogers Brubaker, "Citizenship as Social Closure," in *Citizenship and Nationhood in France and Germany* (Cambridge, MA: Harvard University Press, 1992), 21–34.

46. Michael Walzer, *Spheres of Justice: A Defense of Pluralism and Equality* (New York: Basic Books, 1984).

47. Politicians and policy analysts invoking the brokenness of immigration range from President Trump to President Obama and from the Heritage Foundation to the Cato Institute to the Brookings Institution. Media references range from Fox News and *National Review* to the *Atlantic* and the *Nation*.

48. The foundation of these case studies is original ethnographic research and interviews conducted under University of Colorado research grants and an IRB protocol 16-0668.

Chapter 2: Unequal Citizenship

1. These four dimensions—social/cultural, economic, political, and legal—are referred to as substantive citizenship. Similar terms are used by theorists and sociologists of immigration. T. H. Marshall somewhat tautologically labeled "social citizenship" as expanding from civil, to political, to social in the context of the United Kingdom. T. H. Marshall, "Citizenship and Social Class," in *Citizenship and Social Class: And Other Essays* (New York: Cambridge University Press, 1950), 30–39. Evelyn Nakano Glenn uses "social citizenship" for a similarly multifaceted concept. Evelyn Nakano Glenn, *Unequal Freedom* (Cambridge, MA: Harvard University Press, 2002); Evelyn Nakano Glenn, "Constructing Citizenship: Exclusion, Subordination, and Resistance," *American Sociological Review* 76, no. 1 (2011): 1. Sociologists of immigration, social stratification, and demography use similar measures to study integration.

2. Positive progress is shown across nearly all integration measures. Economic progress is seen in educational attainment, income, occupational distribution, and living above the poverty line. Social progress is seen in intermarriage, residential integration, and language ability. Political integration is shown by naturalization and engagement with either civic affairs or formal politics, if eligible. Only health, crime, and the percentage of children growing up with two parents decline as immigrants and their descendants converge with native-born Americans. Mary Waters and Marisa Gerstein Pineau, eds., *The Integration of Immigrants into American Society* (Washington, DC: National Academies Press, 2015), 3.

3. While more than a quarter of the foreign-born immigrants today are highly educated and highly skilled, Mexicans and Central Americans, who constitute some of the largest groups of immigrants, start with low levels of education that reverberate through integration outcomes. Waters and Pineau, 3. The difficulties that Lati-

nos and Blacks encounter in integrating indicate segmented assimilation. Min Zhou, "Segmented Assimilation: Issues, Controversies, and Recent Research," *International Migration Review* 31 (1997): 975–1008. Post-1965 immigration to the United States has given rise to a literature focused on adult immigrants as well as a growing new second generation whose prospects of adaptation cannot be gleaned from the experience of their parents or prior generations of European immigrants. Alejandro Portes and Min Zhou, "The New Second Generation: Segmented Assimilation and Its Variants," *Annals of the American Academy of Political and Social Science* 530 (1993): 74–96.

4. Douglas Massey, *Categorically Unequal: The American Stratification System* (New York: Russell Sage Foundation, 2007). *Categorically Unequal* discusses differences in legal, regulatory, and instrumental benefits of citizenship. Also see Audrey Macklin, "Who Is the Citizen's Other? Considering the Heft of Citizenship," *Theoretical Inquiries in Law* 8 (2007): 333–66.

5. Marshall disaggregates citizenship by focusing on the partial membership of noncitizens. Marshall, "Citizenship and Social Class." Elizabeth Cohen, in *Semi-Citizenship in Democratic Politics*, says, "In fact the distinction between substantive and formal citizenship is applicable for *all* citizens, as established by a long tradition of political theory on this subject stretching from civic republican ideals to rights-based theorists to critical theorists unsatisfied with the presumed equality of formal rights." Elizabeth F. Cohen, *Semi-Citizenship in Democratic Politics* (New York: Cambridge University Press, 2009), 36.

6. Cohen and others disaggregate citizenship by focusing on the partial membership of noncitizens. While Cohen uses the term *semi-citizen* to distinguish between the autonomous and relative rights of partial citizens, the term is nevertheless useful for considering the varying levels of integration among immigrant subcategories. Cohen, *Semi-Citizenship*.

7. Sociological scholarship on undocumented immigrants and Deferred Action for Childhood Arrivals (DACA) recipients includes work by Leisy Abrego, Edelina Burciaga, Roberto Gonzales, Lisa Martinez, Shannon Gleeson, and Els de Graauw, among others.

8. The experience of women and African Americans possessing formal citizenship without equality of economic, political, or social circumstances illustrates the point. Critical race theorists speak of African Americans as existing as second-class citizens because, despite possessing formal status, they have been denied equality and basic entitlements to economic incorporation, as seen through differences in employment, public schools, or housing. This usage of the term *second-class citizenship* for formal citizens lacking substantive belonging extends to scholars of gender, sexuality, disability, class, and criminal justice.

9. Dredd Scott v. Sandford, 60 U.S. 393 (1857).

10. U.S. Const. amend. XIV.

11. Lucy Salyer, "Wong Kim Ark: The Contest over Birthright Citizenship," in *Immigration Law Stories*, ed. David Martin and Peter Schuck (New York: Foundation, 2005), 7.

12. United States v. Wong Kim Ark, 169 U.S. 649 (1898).

13. Ian Haney Lopez, *White by Law* (New York: New York University Press, 1996), 7.

14. Gabriel Jack Chin, "The Plessy Myth: Justice Harlan and the Chinese Cases," *Iowa Law Review* 82 (1996): 151–82; Leti Volpp, "Obnoxious to Their Very Nature: Asian Americans and Constitutional Citizenship," *Citizenship Studies* 5 (2001): 57–71; Mae Ngai, *Impossible Subjects: Illegal Aliens and the Making of Modern America* (Princeton, NJ: Princeton University Press, 2004); Leti Volpp, "The Citizen and the Terrorist," *UCLA Law Review* 49 (2002): 1575–600; Eric K. Yamamoto, Maria Amparo Vanaclocha Berti, and Jaime Tokioka, "Loaded Weapon Revisited: The Trump Era Import of Justice Jackson's Warning in Korematsu," *Asian American Law Journal* 24 (2017): 5–47; Robert S. Chang, "Whitewashing Precedent: From the Chinese Exclusion Case to Korematsu to the Muslim Travel Ban Cases," *Case Western Law Review* 68 (2018): 1183–222.

15. Detailed histories of immigration and history appear in Rogers Smith, *Civic Ideals: Conflicting Visions of Citizenship in U.S. History* (New Haven, CT: Yale University Press, 1997); Desmond King, *Making Americans: Immigration, Race, and the Origins of the Diverse Democracy* (Cambridge, MA: Harvard University Press, 2000); David Scott Fitzgerald and David Cook-Martin, *Culling the Masses: The Democratic Origins of Racist Immigration Policy in the Americas* (Cambridge, MA: Harvard University Press, 2014); Kunal Parker, *Making Foreigners: Immigration and Citizenship Law in America, 1600–2000* (New York: Cambridge University Press, 2015).

16. A handful of scholars have written seminal works that are a cross between Latcrit and critical immigration theory. Broader discussions of race and immigration include Robin Lenhardt and Jennifer Gordon, "Citizenship Talk: Bridging the Gap between Immigration and Race Perspectives," *Fordham Law Review* 75 (2006): 2493–520; and Kevin Johnson, "Race Matters: Immigration Law and Policy Scholarship, Law in the Ivory Tower, and the Legal Indifference of the Race Critique," *University of Illinois Law Review* (2000): 525–57.

17. The National Academies Press study and sociological studies of the children of immigrants show a narrowing trend, though there are still troubling differences across subgroups of immigrants, especially along racial groupings (segmented assimilation). Waters and Pineau, *Integration of Immigrants*.

18. Irene Bloemraad and comparative immigration scholars point to evidence that the citizenship premium for disadvantaged groups in the United States is particularly stark, with evidence suggesting that rights or instrumental benefits do not seeming to be the driving force in other countries. Comparative immigration scholars and sociologists say citizenship matters modestly and mostly to "vulnerable" immigrants in Western democracies. Irene Bloemraad, "Does Citizenship Matter?," in *The Oxford Handbook of Citizenship*, ed. Ayelet Shachar et al. (New York: Oxford University Press, 2017), 524–50.

19. On the normative challenges, see political theorists Joseph Carens and Linda Bosniak on "equal citizenship." Joseph Carens, *The Ethics of Immigration* (Oxford:

Oxford University Press, 2013); Linda Bosniak, *The Citizen and the Alien* (Princeton, NJ: Princeton University Press, 2006).

20. J. G. A. Pocock, "The Ideal of Citizenship since Classical Times," in *Theorizing Citizenship*, ed. Ronald Beiner (Albany: State University of New York Press, 1995), 29–52.

21. Marshall, "Citizenship and Social Class."

22. Judith Shklar, *American Citizenship: The Quest for Inclusion* (Cambridge, MA: Harvard University Press, 1991).

23. Michael Walzer, *Spheres of Justice: A Defense of Pluralism and Equality* (New York: Basic Books, 1984).

24. These measures are adapted from the Waters and Pineau, *Integration of Immigrants* and Ager and Strang's integration measures for refugees: means and markers, social connections, facilitators, and foundations. Alastair Ager and Alison Strang, *Indicators of Integration: Final Report*, Home Office Development and Practice Report 28 (London: Home Office, 2010). See also Colorado Department of Human Services, Refugee Services Program, *The Refugee Integration Survey and Evaluation (RISE) Year Five: Final Report: A Study of Refugee Integration in Colorado* (Colorado Department of Human Services, Refugee Services Program, 2016), https://drive.google.com/file/d/10S9Xp9Hw2PGOT-3C3is6pnPPrwtyxolf/view.

25. Mary Waters and Tomás Jiménez's overview of assimilation and integration explains that integration is meant to be a two-way process of convergence among native-born and immigrant members of society, not a one-way insistence on change in the immigrant community. Mary Waters and Tomás Jiménez, "Assessing Immigrant Assimilation: New Empirical and Theoretical Challenges," *Annual Review of Sociology* 31 (2005): 105–25.

26. For thoughtful discussion of the rhetorical force of illegality, see Cecilia Menjívar and Daniel Kanstroom, eds., *Constructing Immigrant "Illegality": Critiques, Experiences, and Responses* (New York: Cambridge University Press, 2013) (with contributions from Leisy Abrego, Leo Chavez, Nicholas de Genova, Roberto Gonzales, and Doris Marie Provine); Michael Jones-Correa and Els de Graauw, "The Illegality Trap: The Politics of Immigration and the Lens of Illegality," *Daedalus* 142 (2013): 185–98.

27. Legal terminology is in several respects out of step with common usage. *Illegal alien* refers to noncitizens out of compliance with the terms of citizenship status. It includes those who enter without inspection, those who overstay visas, and those who commit deportable crimes. In common usage, the term refers only to those who enter without inspection. Also, *noncitizen* is a broader category than *immigrant*; it includes lawful permanent residents as well as temporary visa holders who are technically nonimmigrants. Rare is the informal reference to a visa holder as a nonimmigrant.

28. Cohen, in *Semi-Citizenship*, usefully explains the *differences in kind* that attend these categories. Status matters differently among officially recognized groups for their realization of full citizenship. Cohen, *Semi-Citizenship*. Macklin has referred to these graduations as the "heft" of citizenship. Macklin, "Who Is the Citizen's Other?"

29. Hiroshi Motomura, *Immigration Outside the Law* (New York: Oxford University Press, 2014), 21.

30. Ngai, *Impossible Subjects*, describes the transition of US immigration law from a fluid US-Mexico border to a restricted one in the 1920s and then again in the modern liberal legal regime of 1965—with further restrictions in 1986, 1996, and 2001—as "creating" illegal aliens.

31. Jones-Correa and de Graauw, "Illegality Trap."

32. Linda Bosniak has since switched from the word *aliens* to *noncitizens* in her more recent scholarship. Linda Bosniak, "Status Non-citizens," in Shachar et al., *Oxford Handbook of Citizenship*, 314–36.

33. Hannah Arendt and Chief Justice Earl Warren have called citizenship the right to have rights for these reasons. Hannah Arendt, *The Origins of Totalitarianism* (New York: Schocken Books, 1951); Perez v. Brownell, 356 U.S. 44 (1958) (Warren, J. dissenting) ("Citizenship is man's basic right for it is nothing less than the right to have rights. Remove this priceless possession and there remains a stateless person, disgraced and degraded in the eyes of his countrymen.").

34. Bosniak, among others, refers to the protection from deportation as "territorial security" and consider it a defining characteristic of citizenship. The associated right stems from the Immigration and Nationality Act and international human rights instruments. Bosniak, "Status Non-citizens."

35. Cohen, *Semi-Citizenship.*

36. Bosniak, "Status Non-citizens," 333.

37. Rogers Brubaker speaks about citizenship as social closure in this fashion. Rogers Brubaker, *Citizenship and Nationhood in France and Germany* (Cambridge, MA: Harvard University Press, 1992).

38. A prominent example arises in Roberto Gonzales's *Lives in Limbo.* Gonzalez speaks of undocumented immigrant status as a master narrative that emerges for DREAMers as they transition from the protected legal status of childhood to adulthood. For instance, he compares two undocumented workers who came from different circumstances but who ended up in the same place. Both lives were circumscribed by the constraints of legal status—more like their parents than their native-born or citizen peers. Roberto Gonzales, *Lives in Limbo* (Berkeley: University of California Press, 2015), 179.

39. These laws included the Illegal Immigration Reform and Immigrant Responsibility Act of 1996, the Personal Responsibility and Work Opportunity Reconciliation Act of 1996, and the Antiterrorism and Effective Death Penalty Act of 1996. Some of these laws use "persons residing under color of law" or the abbreviation PRUCOL.

40. As one of many examples, Carens relies on time and residence as membership criteria. Carens, *Ethics of Immigration.*

41. Juliet Stumpf, "The Crimmigration Crisis: Immigrants, Crime, and Sovereign Power," *American University Law Review* 56 (2006): 367–419; Cesar Garcia Hernandez, *Crimmigration Law* (Chicago: American Bar Association, 2015).

42. Douglas Massey, Jorge Durand, and Nolan J. Malone, *Beyond Smoke and Mirrors: Mexican Immigration in an Era of Economic Integration* (New York: Russell Sage Foundation, 2003).

43. Volpp, "The Citizen and the Terrorist."

44. As Lenhardt and Gordon say, "The failure of citizenship status to ensure equality and certain basic benefits to racial minorities has not led CRT (critical race theory) scholars to reject formal citizenship status or legal rights as mechanisms for achieving racial justice." Lenhardt and Gordon, "Citizenship Talk," 2504n37.

45. A 2018 Current Population Survey Annual Social and Economic Supplement shows that citizenship narrows economic gaps in wages, poverty levels, and education levels. "Current Population Survey Table Packages Now Available by Sex for Race, Hispanic Origin and Foreign-Born Population," United States Census Bureau, August 19, 2019, https://www.census.gov/newsroom/press-releases/2019/cps-foreign-born.html.

46. This worry about immigrants becoming an underclass is seen in Plyler v. Doe, 452 U.S. 202 (1982) and referred to as an ethos by Hiroshi Motomura, Michael Olivas, and others who study undocumented immigrants.

47. Nancy Ettlinger, "Precarity Unbound," *Alternatives* 32, no. 3 (2007): 319–40 (extends economic insecurity to broader forms of uncertainty and unpredictability, especially terror); Judith Butler, *Precarious Life* (New York: Verso, 2004) (same, perhaps even broader by highlighting insecurity as a feature of post-9/11 counterterrorist governmentality that renders all of us vulnerable to losing our attachments and being exposed to violence).

48. Cecilia Menjívar, "Liminal Legality: Salvadoran and Guatemalan Immigrants' Lives in the United States," *American Journal of Sociology* 111, no. 4 (2006): 999–1037; Marcel Paret and Shannon Gleeson, "Precarity and Agency through a Migrant Lens," *Citizenship Studies* 20 (2016): 277–94; Kubal Agnieszka, "Conceptualizing Semilegality in Migration Research," *Law and Society Review* 47 (2013): 555–87; Susan Bibler Coutin, "Denationalization, Inclusion, and Exclusion: Negotiating the Boundaries of Belonging," *Indiana Journal of Global Legal Studies* 7 (2000): 585–91.

49. Menjívar, "Liminal Legality." Menjívar focuses on the liminality of immigrants with Temporary Protected Status, who hover between undocumented status and lawful status by virtue of their limited legal protection.

50. Menjívar, 1000.

51. Carens, *Ethics of Immigration*, 63.

52. The forms of disintegration are discussed more in chapters 4 and 5.

53. Robert D. Putnam, "E Pluribus Unum: Diversity and Community in the Twenty-First Century: The 2006 Johan Skytte Prize Lecture," *Scandinavian Political Studies* 30 (2007): 137–74.

54. Asad Asad and Matthew Clair, "Racialized Legal Status as a Social Determinant of Health," *Social Science and Medicine* 199 (2018): 19–28.

55. Linda Bosniak in numerous writings and Jacqueline Stevens in *States without Nations* question the presumed desirability of formal citizenship. Jacqueline Ste-

vens, *States without Nations: Citizenship for Mortals* (New York: Columbia University Press, 2009). The Not1More Deportation campaign that sought to end deportations and procure legal protections for undocumented adults, not merely DREAMers, also exhibits the belief that citizenship should not be contingent on legal status. Kathryn Abrams, "Contentious Citizenship: Undocumented Activism in the Not1More Deportation Campaign," *Berkeley La Raza Law Journal* 26 (2016): 46–69.

56. Michael Omi and Howard Winant, *Racial Formation in the United States* (New York: Routledge, 1986).

57. Haney Lopez, *White by Law*.

58. Statement from presidential candidate Donald J. Trump during the final debate of the 2016 election.

59. Performative citizenship is a tactic that de-emphasizes formal citizenship and instead contests the legal meaning of citizenship by offering new meanings based on civic engagement, among others. Kathryn Abrams, "Performative Citizenship in the Civil Rights and Immigrants' Rights Movements," in *A Nation of Widening Opportunities: The Civil Rights Act at 50*, ed. Ellen D. Katz and Samuel R. Bagenstos (Ann Arbor: Michigan Publishing Services, 2015): 1–28.

60. Omi and Winant, *Racial Formation*.

61. Critical race scholars have long cited Asian Americans and Latinos as examples of "perpetual foreigners" who then become subject to exclusion from naturalized citizenship. Claire Jean Kim, "The Racial Triangulation of Asian Americans," *Politics and Society* 27 (1999): 105–38; Leti Volpp, "Excesses of Culture: On Asian American Citizenship and Identity," *Asian American Law Journal* 17 (2010): 63–81.

62. Motomura, *Immigration outside the Law*.

Chapter 3: Winding Pathways to Citizenship

1. Esteban, interview with the author, Denver, Colorado, June 13, 2018.

2. Guy, telephone interview with the author, October 16, 2017.

3. Luis, interview with the author, Boulder, Colorado, October 23, 2017.

4. Carmen, interview with the author, Denver, Colorado, October 25, 2017.

5. Rogers Brubaker, "Citizenship as Social Closure," in *Citizenship and Nationhood in France and Germany* (Cambridge, MA: Harvard University Press, 1992), 21–34.

6. The Center for Immigration Studies and Federation for American Immigration Reform are think tanks dedicated to achieving lower levels of immigration. Samuel Huntington, *Who Are We? The Challenges to America's National Identity* (New York: Simon and Schuster, 2004), describes Latino immigration as a cultural threat to American national identity.

7. George Borjas, *Immigration Economics* (Cambridge, MA: Harvard University Press, 2014); George Borjas, *Heaven's Door: Immigration Policy and the American Economy* (Princeton, NJ: Princeton University Press, 2011).

8. Brubaker, *Citizenship and Nationhood*; Sarah Song, "The Boundary Problem in Democratic Theory: Why the Demos Should Be Bounded by the State," *International Theory* 4, no. 1 (2012): 39–68.

9. Hiroshi Motomura, *Americans in Waiting* (New York: Oxford University Press, 2007), 9–10, 15–62.

10. Motomura, 11, 80–114.

11. Motomura, 114–35.

12. Motomura, 136–67.

13. A variation of the intent argument highlights the passage of time as a justification for citizenship. Fewer theorists call for the full inclusion of temporary visitors, with the loudest chorus being for guest workers whose cyclical migration patterns refashion their short-term stays into longer periods of time in the United States. Cristina M. Rodriguez, "Guest Workers and Integration: Toward a Theory of What Immigrants and Americans Owe One Another," *University of Chicago Legal Forum* (2007): 219–88. Max Frisch, a Swiss author, succinctly captured this sentiment for European guest workers in his book, noting, "We asked for workers; but people came." Max Frisch, *Überfremdung I, in Schweiz als Heimat? Versuche über 50 Jahre* [*Switzerland as Home? Attempts over 50 Years*] (Frankfurt: Suhrkamp Verlag 1991), 219.

14. Rodriguez, "Guest Workers and Integration."

15. The concern is reflected in Plyler v. Doe, 452 U.S. 202 (1982). It recalls Michael Walzer's description in *Spheres of Justice* of the metics of ancient Athens, who were "resident aliens . . . who 'could not hope to become citizens.'" Michael Walzer, *Spheres of Justice: A Defense of Pluralism and Equality* (New York: Basic Books, 1984), 53. It is also echoed in writings on the need for a *Plyler* ethos for DREAMers. Hiroshi Motomura, *Immigration outside the Law* (New York: Oxford University Press, 2014); Michael Olivas, *No Undocumented Child Left Behind: "Plyler v. Doe" and the Education of Undocumented Children* (New York: New York University Press, 2012).

16. Dazhen, interview with the author, Boulder, Colorado, October 5, 2017.

17. Deepti, interview with the author, Boulder, Colorado, October 10, 2017.

18. Among the few theorists writing on temporary visas, see David Miller, "Irregular Migrants: An Alternative Perspective," *Ethics and International Affairs* 22, no. 2 (2008): 193–97; Elizabeth F. Cohen, *The Political Value of Time* (Cambridge: Cambridge University Press, 2018); and David Cook-Martin, "Temp Nations? A Research Agenda on Migration, Temporariness, and Membership," *American Behavioral Scientist* 63, no. 9 (2019): 1–15.

19. Miller, "Irregular Migrants," 196.

20. Motomura, *Americans in Waiting*, 155 ("Taking transition seriously means that equality is presumed and that LPRs should be treated like citizens until they have been here long enough to naturalize.").

21. INA § 101(a)(15)(B)(H)(i)(B).

22. INA § 101(a)(15)(B)(F)(i).

23. Charles Tilley, "Citizenship, Identity, and Social History," *International Review of Social History* 40, no. 53 (1995): 1–17 (describing thin citizenship as entailing few transactions, rights, and obligations).

24. Tilley (describing thick citizenship as occupying a significant share of all transactions, rights, and obligations sustained by state agents and people living in the jurisdiction).

25. U.S. Const. art I, § 8, cl. 4: "to establish a uniform rule of naturalization"; Naturalization Act of 1790.

26. The Fourteenth Amendment says that "all persons born or naturalized in the United States, and subject to the jurisdiction thereof, are citizens in the United States and the State wherein they reside." U.S. Const. amend. XIV, § 1, cl. 1. In addition to birthright citizenship and naturalization, family members may obtain citizenship as derivatives of the primary applicant.

27. American Immigration Lawyers Association, *AILA's Guide to U.S. Citizenship and Naturalization Law* (Washington, DC: American Immigration Lawyers Association, 2014); INA § 334(b). While the statutory framework for citizenship remains largely unchanged, agency regulations and bureaucratic processing have undergone changes in the Barack Obama and Donald Trump administrations. The effect of these changes remains to be seen.

28. Refugees are not part of Congress's general caps on immigrant admissions. Instead, INA § 207(a) permits the president to recommend a number for each fiscal year. The refugee cap has ranged from 200,000, when the Refugee Act of 1980 was enacted to the 30,000 proposed by the Trump administration for 2019.

29. INA § 207. Refugee adjustment to lawful permanent resident status within one year is mandatory, and their naturalization is voluntary. "Refugees," US Citizenship and Immigration Services, last updated October 24, 2017, https://www.uscis.gov/humanitarian/refugees-asylum/refugees.

30. INA § 207.

31. Mary Waters and Marisa Gerstein Pineau, eds., *The Integration of Immigrants into American Society* (Washington, DC: National Academies Press, 2015), 194–30.

32. INA § 328 describes naturalization through the military in peacetime.

33. INA § 328 describes naturalization through the military in periods of hostilities.

34. Naturalization at basic training began in the army in 2009 and subsequently expanded to the navy, air force, and marine corps. "Naturalization through Military Service," US Citizenship and Immigration Services, last updated September 30, 2019, https://www.uscis.gov/military/naturalization-through-military-service.

35. Statistics for military naturalizations are maintained by the USCIS and show roughly nine thousand naturalizations in the United States or abroad from 2012 to 2017 with three hundred additional for military spouses and children. "Military Naturalization Statistics," US Citizenship and Immigration Services, last updated December 6, 2018, https://www.uscis.gov/military/military-naturalization-statistics.

36. *Nonimmigrant* is defined by the USCIS as "a foreign national who is admitted to the United States for a specific temporary period of time" in a specified class of visa, and who does not intend to remain permanently. INA § 101(a)(15) (B)–(V).

37. INA § 275 uses the term *improper entry* to describe immigrants who enter the country outside approved checkpoints, elude examination of immigration officers,

or obtain entry with false documents. Immigrants who overstay their visa are un-authorized as well. INA § 245 permits adjustment of status to a green card for some categories for immigrants, but the requirements often elude immigrants who entered without inspections.

38. Princeton University, "The New Immigrant Survey," accessed December 13, 2019, http://nis.princeton.edu/project.html.

39. Numerical caps for immigrant admissions are set by Congress. In fiscal year 2013, 100,000 immigrants became lawful permanent residents, with the largest category being immediate relatives of US citizens. Thereafter, approximately 200,000 adjusted under family-sponsored categories (INA § 201(c)), and 140,000 adjusted under employer-sponsored categories (INA § 203(b)).

40. A report from the think tank New America recommends increasing the 3Rs, or "regularity, relevance, and reach of messaging," around the benefits of naturalized citizenship. Raph Majma, Lindsey Wagner, and Sabrina Fonseca, *Understanding the Catalysts for Citizenship Application: User Research on Those Eligible to Naturalize* (Washington, DC: New America Foundation, May 2019).

41. The cap on refugee admissions has been drastically reduced, and vetting requirements for refugees are stricter under the 2016 State Department guidance that accompanied President Trump's travel ban.

42. In October 2017, the Defense Department implemented two key policy changes to the expedited naturalization process for military members. The first change establishes additional background screening requirements that often result in longer waiting periods for approval that may extend beyond the duration of the applicant's legal status visa period. The second change requires completion of 180 consecutive days of service and the personal signature from the secretary of the relevant military branch, but there is currently no procedure in place to obtain that signature. After the implementation of these policy changes, military naturalization dropped almost 65 percent in the first quarter of fiscal year 2018 compared with the fourth quarter of fiscal year 2017. During that same time period, the denial rate of military naturalizations increased from 10 percent to 25 percent, and this trend appears unlikely to abate. These changes have led to an effective end to the military's expedited track to citizenship under the Immigration and Nationality Act. US Government Accountability Office, *Immigration Enforcement: Actions Needed to Better Handle, Identify, and Track Cases Involving Veterans* (Washington, DC: US Government Accountability Office, June 2009), https://www.gao.gov/assets/700/699549.pdf; Ming H. Chen, "Citizenship Denied," *Denver University Law Review* 97 (forthcoming).

43. Nonimmigrant intent is incompatible with establishing permanent residence in most instances under the Immigration and Nationality Act, unless the temporary visa specifically permits a dual intention to come for a temporary purpose and then remain.

44. Immigrants who enter without inspection face significant barriers to reentry and adjustment of status. Federal laws since the 1996 welfare reform render them ineligible for most social welfare benefits as well.

45. Princeton University, "New Immigrant Survey."

46. Princeton University.

47. Waters and Pineau, *Integration of Immigrants*; Tomás Jiménez, *Immigrants in the United States: How Well Are They Integrating into Society?* (Washington, DC: Migration Policy Institute, Summer 2011) (Jiménez uses five indicators of integration and finds progress along most dimensions, with significant variation across ethnic groups and notable lags for Latino immigrants relative to other immigrant groups); Irene Bloemraad, *Becoming a Citizen* (Berkeley: University of California Press, 2006).

48. Margie McHugh and Madeleine Morawksi, *Immigrants and WIOA Services: Comparisons of Sociodemographic Characteristics of Native- and Foreign-Born Adults in the United States* (Washington, DC: Migration Policy Institute, April 2016), http://www.migrationpolicy.org/research/immigrants-and-wioa-services-comparison-sociodemographic-characteristics-native-and-foreign.

49. See, e.g., Waters and Pineau, *Integration of Immigrants*; and Mary Waters and Tomás Jiménez, "Assessing Immigrant Assimilation: New Empirical and Theoretical Challenges," *American Review of Sociology* 31 (2005): 105–25.

50. Obtaining a visa has become even more difficult for certain groups subject to travel restrictions, such as the families of migrants from Muslim-majority countries affected by the Trump administration's travel ban.

51. In the interviews, Mei, Bob, and Rob explained that they came to the United States for college and then stayed for graduate school. They described their transition from F to H-1B as relatively smooth. However, Ksenia, a postdoctoral fellow from Russia, described a more difficult transition from her J visa to an H-1B. Interviews with the author, October 7, 2017, September 22, 2017, April 17, 2017, November 13, 2017.

52. In my interview sample, Latino immigrants and technology workers on or eligible for employer-based visas were the ones who often stalled at the green card stage or significantly delayed naturalizing to US citizenship. Their reasons varied from lack of institutional support to relative comfort with their existing status.

53. T. Alexander Aleinikoff et al., *Immigration and Citizenship*, 8th ed. (St. Paul, MN: West Academic, 2016) offers this for consideration: in fiscal year 2013, about 460,000 of the nearly 1 million new lawful permanent residents were new arrivals in the United States. In contrast, about 530,000 noncitizens became lawful permanent residents through adjustment of status, so by definition they were already in the United States. The percentage of noncitizens who became lawful permanent residents through adjustment was dramatically higher in the employment-based categories, where about 140,000 were adjustments and only 21,000 were new arrivals. Although some of these adjustments involved noncitizens who lacked lawful immigration status, these new immigrants generally had valid nonimmigrant status when they became lawful permanent residents. This pattern reflects a growing trend: the practical blurring of the line between immigrant and nonimmigrant status. Compare with the New Immigrant Survey data reports that say upwards of 60 percent transitioned from another status. Princeton University, New Immigrant Survey.

54. The White House Task Force on New Americans, One-Year Progress Report (2015), https://obamawhitehouse.archives.gov/issues/immigration/new-americans, and

numerous publications of the Center for the Study of Immigrant Integration speak about fees, complex forms, and delays as barriers to naturalization as well. See, e.g., Manuel Pastor and Jared Sanchez, *Promoting Citizenship: Assessing the Impacts of the Partial Fee Waiver* (Los Angeles: Center for the Study of Immigrant Integration, University of Southern California, Dornsife, 2016).

55. See, e.g., William S. Bernard, "Cultural Determinants of Naturalization," *American Sociological Review* 1 (1936): 943–53.

56. Bloemraad, *Becoming a Citizen*.

57. Bloemraad, 30.

58. Abishek, Naif, Basma, Hamid, and Hassan (Middle Eastern temporary visas and refugees), interviews with the author; Tatiana (Bolivia—temporary visa), Sandra (Lebanon—temporary visa), Shankini (Malaysia—temporary visa), Luz (Honduras—green card), and Mercedes (Mexico—green card), interviews with the author. See chapters 4 and 5 for discussion of these interviews.

59. David Cook-Martin, *The Scramble for Citizens: Dual Nationality and State Competition for Immigrants* (Palo Alto, CA: Stanford University Press, 2013), describes social disintegration.

60. Bob, Rob, and Stefan, interviews with the author, discussed in chapter 4.

61. Luz and Mercedes, interviews with the author, discussed in chapter 4.

62. Kyung Lah and Alberto Moya, "Motivated by Fear, Some Immigrants Are Turning to Citizenship," CNN, December 7, 2016, http://www.cnn.com/2016/12/07 /politics/citizenship-surge-after-donald-trump-election/index.html (reporting the story of Natalia, a longtime green card holder married to a US citizen, who applied for citizenship immediately after the presidential election, after many years of eligibility, as an "insurance policy" to protect herself and her family). See also David Cort, "Spurred to Action or Retreat? The Effects of Reception Contexts on Naturalization Decisions in Los Angeles," *International Migration Review* 46 (2012): 483–516 (explaining the increase in naturalization following Proposition 187 in California); and Cesar, telephone interview with the author, July 3, 2017 (told "you don't belong here" after serving in the military).

63. Min Zhou, "Segmented Assimilation: Issues, Controversies, and Recent Research," *International Migration Review* 31 (1997): 975–1008; Alejandro Portes and Min Zhou, "The New Second Generation: Segmented Assimilation and Its Variants," *Annals of the American Academy of Political and Social Science* 530 (1993): 74–96.

64. A similar finding emerges from a quantitative study of factors influencing naturalization in Latino communities. Maria Abascal, "Tu Casa, Mi Casa: Naturalization and Belonging among Latino Immigrants," *International Migration Review* 51 (2015): 291–322.

65. Language ability is consistently found to be associated with propensity to naturalize in quantitative studies. Thai V. Le et al., *Paths to Citizenship: Using Data to Understand and Promote Naturalization* (Los Angeles: Center for the Study of Immigrant Integration, University of Southern California, Dornsife, 2019), 4.

66. Rob, interview with the author, Boulder, Colorado, April 7, 2017; Stefan, telephone interview with the author, October 12, 2017.

67. Le et al., *Paths to Citizenship*, 2, 8; Philip Q. Yang, "Explaining Immigrant Naturalization," *International Migration Review* 28, no. 3 (1994): 449–77.

68. Hamid, telephone interview with the author, July 26, 2017; Adam, telephone interview with the author, August 25, 2017.

69. Mary, telephone interview with the author, June 18, 2017.

70. Catherine N. Barry, "Moving on Up? U.S. Military Service, Education, and Labor Market Mobility among Children of Immigrants" (PhD diss., University of California, Berkeley, 2013); Molly F. McIntosh, Seema Sayala, and David Gregory, *Non-citizens in the Enlisted U.S. Military* (Alexandria, VA: Center for Naval Analysis, 2011).

71. Francisco, telephone interview with the author, August 9, 2017.

72. US Government Accountability Office, *Immigration Enforcement*, 20.

73. INA § 101(a)(15); see note 35.

74. Sandra, interview with the author, November 27, 2017 (H-1B worker).

75. Shankini, interview with the author, November 21, 2017.

76. "Consideration of Deferred Action for Childhood Arrivals," US Citizenship and Immigration Services, 2012, https://www.uscis.gov/archive/consideration-deferred-action-childhood-arrivals-daca.

77. Shan, interview with the author, Boulder, Colorado, March 2, 2018.

78. Esun, interview with the author, Boulder, Colorado, February 27, 2018.

79. Josefina, interview with the author, Denver, Colorado, June 8, 2018 ("Yeah, I think that people see [DACA] sort of like a visa").

80. This complex relationship between enforcement and naturalization is discussed more in chapter 4.

81. Alejandro Portes and Jozsef Borocz, "Contemporary Immigration: Theoretical Perspectives on Its Determinants and Modes of Incorporation," *International Migration Review* 23 (1989): 606.

Chapter 4: Barriers to Formal Citizenship

1. While I do not mean to adopt this position reflexively, as the authors of some legal texts do, there is support for a claims-making approach toward citizenship that combines the relational aspects of citizenship with the state-administered aspects. Irene Bloemraad, "Theorising the Power of Citizenship as Claims-Making," *Journal of Ethnic and Migration Studies* 44 (2017): 4–26.

2. Mary Waters and Marisa Gerstein Pineau, eds., *The Integration of Immigrants into American Society* (Washington, DC: National Academies Press, 2015); Sofya Aptekar, *The Road to Citizenship: What Naturalization Means for Immigrants and the United States* (New Brunswick, NJ: Rutgers University Press, 2015). US citizenship also improves employment outcomes, wage growth, and access to better jobs. Bernt Bratsberg, James F. Ragan Jr., and Zafar M. Nasir, "The Effect of Naturalization on Wage Growth: A Panel Study of Young Male Immigrants," *Journal of Labor Economics* 20 (July 2002), 568–97; Organisation for Economic Co-operation and Development, *Naturalization: A Passport for the Better Integration of Immigrants?* (Paris: OECD, 2011).

3. Waters and Pineau, *Integration of Immigrants*, 125–30. There is significant variation in naturalization rates among subgroups. Naturalization rates are highest for refugees and noncitizens in the military. Latinos typically naturalize at lower rates than European, Asian, and African immigrants, and they wait for a longer period of time after eligibility. Those with more elite employer-based statuses naturalize at lower rates than those coming under a family-sponsored visa. The Department of Homeland Security Office of Immigration Statistics page "Profiles on Naturalized Citizens" includes petitions filed, approved, and denied for military and civilians by region and year. *Profiles on Naturalized Citizens,* US Citizenship and Immigration Services, https://www.dhs.gov/profiles-naturalized-citizens.

4. Figure 4.2 adapted from Waters and Pineau, *Integration of Immigrants*, fig. 4-3. See also Waters and Pineau, 125–30; and Paul Taylor et al., "II. Recent Trends in Naturalization, 2000–2011," Hispanic Trends, Pew Research Center, November 14, 2012, https://www.pewresearch.org/hispanic/2012/11/14/ii-recent-trends-in-naturalization-2000-2011/.

5. In general, elections boost naturalization numbers. In September 2016, application numbers were up by 26 percent and resulted in the highest number in a decade by the end of the fiscal year: nearly one million. U.S. Department of Homeland Security Office of Immigration Statistics, *Yearbook, Table 20 Petitions for Naturalization Filed, Persons Naturalized, and Petitions for Naturalization Denied: FY 1907 to 2018*, https://www.dhs.gov/immigration-statistics/yearbook/2017/table20.

6. Diego Iñiguez-López, *Tearing Down the Second Wall: Ending USCIS's Backlog of Citizenship Applications and Expanding Access to Naturalization for Immigrants* (Chicago: National Partnership for New Americans, July 2, 2018), https://www.immigrationresearch.org/system/files/Naturalization_Backlogs_Second_Wall.pdf; Diego Iñiguez-López, *Democracy Strangled: Second Wall of Barriers to Citizenship Risks Preventing Hundreds of Thousands of Immigrants from Naturalizing and Becoming Voters in Presidential Election of 2020* (Chicago: National Partnership for New Americans, March 2019), https://drive.google.com/file/d/1t1oWo6zc97qBpeXq93f5ycjFJfdBAlo6/view; Colorado State Advisory Committee to the US Commission on Civil Rights, "Citizenship Delayed: Civil Rights and Voting Rights Implications of the Backlog in Citizenship and Naturalization Applications," September 2019 (reprinted in *University of Colorado Law Review* Forum 91 [2019], http://lawreview.colorado.edu/citizenship-delayed-civil-rights-and-voting-rights-implications-of-the-backlog-in-citizenship-and-naturalization-applications/). See also USCIS Data Set: Form N-400 Application for Naturalization, Reports for Fiscal Year 2017, 1st Quarter, 2nd Quarter, 3rd Quarter (total applications range from 230,000 to 280,000); Fiscal Year 2016 (total applications range from 230,000 to 280,000); Fiscal Year 2015 (total applications range from 185,000 to 200,000). Many interview and media sources hypothesized a link between naturalization applications and the election. See, e.g., Hansi Lo Wang, "Green Card Holders Worry about Trump's Efforts to Curtail Immigration," NPR, February 21, 2017, https://www.npr.org/2017/02/21/516375460/green-card-holders-worry-about-trump-s-efforts-to-curtain-immigration ("We used to see two to three people

a week seeking citizenship services. Now we are seeing between 30 and 50 people a day," Jorge-Mario Cabrera, Coalition for Humane Immigrant Rights of Los Angeles's director of communications). Immigration attorneys report increased USCIS processing times, partly due to a citizenship backlog that is discernible through increased USCIS reporting times and backlog size. Check Case Processing Times, US Citizenship and Immigration Services, https://egov.uscis.gov/processing-times/.

7. Iñiguez-López, *Tearing Down the Second Wall.*

8. Early sociological studies of individual demographic attributes associate naturalization with time spent in the United States, language ability, and national origin. See, e.g., William S. Bernard, "Cultural Determinants of Naturalization," *American Sociological Review* 1 (1936): 943–53. Studying the influence of social context, including country of origin and destination, advances the field. See, e.g., Philip Q. Yang, "Explaining Immigrant Naturalization," *International Migration Review* 28, no. 3 (1994): 449–77. These frameworks are nuanced in subsequent studies of the "context of reception" that emphasize race and other characteristics that are especially salient in the United States. Alejandro Portes and Min Zhou, "The New Second Generation: Segmented Assimilation and Its Variants," *Annals of the American Academy of Political and Social Science* 530 (1993): 74–96; Min Zhou, "Segmented Assimilation: Issues, Controversies, and Recent Research," *International Migration Review* 31 (1997): 975–1008.

9. Irene Bloemraad, *Becoming a Citizen* (Berkeley: University of California Press, 2006).

10. The institutional support hypothesis suggests that institutional support and a welcoming context of reception positively affect integration outcomes. If cost, delay, and complex bureaucratic processes associated with attaining citizenship pose obstacles to naturalization, efforts should focus on lowering these barriers. Efforts to address these obstacles have had modest effects in the United States. Irene Bloemraad and Els de Graauw, "Immigrant Integration and Policy in the United States: A Loosely Stitched Patchwork," in *International Perspectives: Immigration and Inclusion*, ed. James Frideres and John Biles (Montreal: McGill–Queen's University Press, 2012), 205–34. More compelling are comparative immigration scholars pointing to the existence of citizenship and multiculturalism programs in Canada and Europe as a key factor for the divergence of naturalization rates among countries. Irene Bloemraad, "North American Naturalization Gap," *International Migration Review* 36 (2002): 193–228; Keith Banting, "Is There Really a Retreat from Multiculturalism? New Evidence from the Multiculturalism Policy Index," *European Comparative Politics* 11 (2013): 577–98.

11. Earlier periods in which defensive naturalization has been noted include the Japanese internment during World War II and Latino naturalization in California during the immigration reforms of the 1990s.

12. Donald J. Trump, "Presidential Executive Order on Buy American and Hire American," White House, April 18, 2017, https://www.whitehouse.gov/the-press-office/2017/04/18/presidential-executive-order-buy-american-and-hire-american.

13. Other works that discuss defensive naturalization include Aptekar, *Road to Citizenship*; Angela Banks, "The Curious Relationship between 'Self-Deportation' Policies and Naturalization Rates," *Lewis and Clark Law Review* 16 (2012): 1149–213; Michael Jones Correa, *Between Two Nations* (Ithaca, NY: Cornell University Press, 1998); Douglas Massey and Karen Pren, "Unintended Consequences of U.S. Immigration Policy: Explaining the Post-1965 Surge from Latin America," *Population and Development Review* 38, no. 1 (2012): 1–29; David Cort, "Spurred to Action or Retreat? The Effects of Reception Contexts on Naturalization Decisions in Los Angeles," *International Migration Review* 46 (2012): 483–516; Greta Gilbertson and Audrey Singer, "The Emergence of Protective Citizenship in the USA: Naturalization among Dominican Immigrants in the Post-1996 Welfare Reform Era," *Ethnic and Racial Studies* 26 (2003): 25–51; Yunju Nam and Wooksoo Kim, "Welfare Reform and Elderly Immigrants' Naturalization: Access to Public Benefits as an Incentive for Naturalization in the United States," *International Migration Review* 46 (2012): 656–79; Gary P. Freeman et al., "Explaining the Surge in Citizenship Applications in the 1990s: Lawful Permanent Residents in Texas," *Social Science Quarterly* 83 (2002): 1013–25. The trend is especially noted for Latinos, who have been mobilized by community groups against anti-immigrant initiatives. David Cort notes that Asian naturalization was more responsive to underlying economic conditions than policy shifts. But cf. Paul Ong, "Defensive Naturalization and Anti-immigrant Sentiment," *Asian American Policy Review* 22 (2011): 39–55.

14. Cort, "Spurred to Action or Retreat?" Cort's study of the effect of Proposition 187 on Latino naturalization in California found that the context of reception matters to naturalization because of resource mobilization theory, segmented assimilation, and social contexts related to the passage of Proposition 187 in the first place.

15. Ong, "Defensive Naturalization."

16. Nam and Kim, "Welfare Reform"; Freeman et al., "Explaining the Surge."

17. Raph Majma, Lindsey Wagner, and Sabrina Fonseca, *Understanding the Catalysts for Citizenship Application: User Research on Those Eligible to Naturalize* (Washington, DC: New America Foundation, May 2019).

18. Irene Bloemraad and Alicia Sheares, "Understanding Membership in a World of Global Migration: (How) Does Citizenship Matter?," *International Migration Review* 51 (2018): 823–67.

19. An exception is the *Paths to Citizenship* study, which provides state-by-state and contextual analysis of immigrants' likelihood of naturalizing. Thai V. Le et al., *Paths to Citizenship: Using Data to Understand and Promote Naturalization* (Center for the Study of Immigrant Integration, University of Southern California, Dornsife, 2019).

20. It is difficult to ascertain how enforcement and naturalization relate to one another. A New America report based on interviews states that fear of enforcement can either inhibit or enable motivations to naturalize and that stressful immigration interactions delay naturalization. Majma, Wagner, and Fonseca, *Understanding the Catalysts*. A paper by Mary J. Lopez and Catalina Amuedo-Dorantes, "Impeding or

Accelerating Assimilation? Immigration Enforcement and Its Impact on Naturalization Patterns" (Centre for Research and Analysis of Migration Discussion Paper Series, 2018), uses quantitative analysis of American Community Survey data to find that the effects of enforcement on naturalize differ for those living in mixed-status households and the general population of those eligible to naturalize. A later version of the same paper focuses more on the curtailment effects. Mary J. Lopez and Catalina Amuedo-Dorantes, "Impeding or Accelerating Assimilation? Immigration Enforcement and Its Impact on Naturalization Patterns" (Center for Growth and Opportunity Working Paper 2019.010, 2019).

21. Scholars work around this unfortunate gap in the quantitative data. For example, social scientists often use nation of origin as a proxy for legal status (i.e., Vietnamese or Cuban considered refugee, Chinese not). The Urban Institute uses Current Population Survey data to define a population of immigrants eligible to naturalize—in essence, subtracting from the overall immigrant population the subpopulation of undocumented and temporary migrants who are ineligible to obtain lawful permanent resident status and naturalization—but does not differentiate within the lawful permanent resident category. Michael Fix, Jeffrey S. Passel, and Kenneth Sucher, *Trends in Naturalization*, Urban Institute Immigration Studies Program Brief No. 3 (Washington, DC: Urban Institute Immigration Studies Program, 2003); Irene Bloemraad, email message to the author, July 17, 2017.

22. "Green Card for Refugees," US Citizenship and Immigration Services, last updated June 26, 2017, https://www.uscis.gov/greencard/refugees.

23. "Naturalization through Military Service," US Citizenship and Immigration Services, last updated September 30, 2019, https://www.uscis.gov/military/naturalization-through-military-service.

24. Multiple field interviews with the author, 2016–18; Aptekar, *Road to Citizenship* (similar top results).

25. See, e.g., Peggy Levitt, *The Transnational Villagers* (Berkeley: University of California Press, 2001).

26. Xiowen spoke of regular travel to China to see parents and expose her children to native culture; interview with the author, Boulder, Colorado, September 16, 2017.

27. Tanya, interview with the author, Denver, Colorado, September 9, 2017. She was turned away from a citizenship drive for lacking five years of continuous residence because she traveled so much to see her family in Nicaragua.

28. Eliud, interview with the author, Dallas, Texas, May 19, 2017.

29. Masaki, interview with the author, Boulder, Colorado, September 22, 2017.

30. Emir, telephone interview with the author, July 26, 2017; Hassan, interview with the author, Denver, Colorado, July 22, 2017; Adam, telephone interview with the author, August 25, 2017; Basma, interview with the author, Denver, Colorado, September 28, 2017; Berhani, interview with the author, Denver, Colorado, September 9, 2017; Fahima, interview with the author, Denver, Colorado, October 27, 2017; Jamal, interview with the author, Denver, Colorado, December 8, 2017; Sahar, interview with the author, Denver, Colorado, September 28, 2017.

31. The follow-up survey consisted of a brief questionnaire distributed by a non-profit refugee resettlement organization to its clients in Colorado in spring 2017. See appendix for more details.

32. Jose, interview with the author, Denver, Colorado, October 4, 2017; Guy, interview with the author, Denver, Colorado, October 16, 2017.

33. Kyung Lah and Alberto Moya, "Motivated by Fear, Some Immigrants Are Turning to Citizenship," CNN, December 7, 2016, http://www.cnn.com/2016/12/07/politics/citizenship-surge-after-donald-trump-election/index.html (reporting the story of Natalia, a longtime lawful permanent resident married to a US citizen, who applied for citizenship immediately after the presidential election, after many years of eligibility, as an "insurance policy" to protect herself and her family). See also Cort, "Spurred to Action or Retreat?"

34. Leigh Alpert (immigration attorney and coordinator of the American Immigration Lawyers Association's Colorado naturalization drives), interview with the author, Denver, Colorado, April 25, 2017.

35. Business immigration attorney Brad Hendrick relayed that his phone had been ringing off the hook, even from Canadian clients. Brad Hendrick, interview with the author, Denver, Colorado, February 16, 2017. The University of Colorado International Student and Scholars Office held full-capacity meetings with international students from India, China, and nonbanned countries wanting a legal check-up or assurances in January and February 2017.

36. Hassan, interview with the author, Denver, Colorado, July 22, 2017. A similar story about a Somali immigrant who naturalized one week before the travel ban is reported in David Montero, "Becoming a U.S. Citizen in the Time of Trump," *Los Angeles Times*, February 5, 2017, http://www.latimes.com/nation/la-na-naturalization-colorado-20170205-story.html.

37. Tanya, interview with the author, Denver, Colorado, September 9, 2017.

38. Chelsea, interview with the author, Boulder, Colorado, April 18, 2017.

39. Bob, interview with the author, Boulder, Colorado, September 22, 2017. The International Traffic in Arms Regulations limits access to high-tech data even within the United States to "US persons," which includes lawful permanent residents *and* US citizens. "Hiring Foreign Persons Export Compliance Update and Anti-discrimination Considerations," Hogan Lovells, November 1, 2016, https://www.hoganlovells.com/publications/hiring-foreign-persons-export-compliance-update-and-anti-discrimination-considerations. See also Edyael Casaperalta, "The New Atravesados: Tech Workers in the Digital Borderlands," *Rio Bravo: A Journal of the Borderlands* 24 (2019): 105–20.

40. See the "Noncitizens in the Military" section later in this chapter for more discussion of military motivations.

41. Mei, interview with the author, Boulder, Colorado, October 10, 2017; Deepti (H-1B faculty member seeking EB-1 or EB-2 visa), interview with the author, Boulder, Colorado, October 10, 2017.

42. Guadalupe, interview with the author, Denver, Colorado, September 9, 2017. See also Nam and Kim, "Welfare Reform."

43. The right to vote is the dominant right or benefit associated with citizenship in legal and political science literature. Judith Shklar, *American Citizenship: The Quest for Inclusion* (Cambridge, MA: Harvard University Press, 1991) (saying work and voting are cornerstones of citizenship); Jason Brennan, *The Ethics of Voting* (Princeton, NJ: Princeton University Press 2012). These assertions in the noncitizen context persist despite citizen voter turnout rates in the 50 percent range that persistently trail most developed countries in the world.

44. Bloemraad and Sheares, "Understanding Membership," 836.

45. Manuel Pastor and Jared Sanchez, *Rock the (Naturalized) Vote: The Size and Location of the Recently Naturalized Voting Age Citizen Population* (Center for the Study of Immigrant Integration, University of Southern California, Dornsife, 2012), https://dornsife.usc.edu/csii/rock-the-naturalized-vote/. Of course, the voter participation rate for all Americans, including US-born citizens, is low compared with other countries. Still, minority participation is even lower. Studies suggest that this, too, might be a result of insufficient institutional support such as party outreach to minority voters. Zoltan Hajnal and Taeku Lee, *Why Americans Don't Join the Party: Race, Immigration and the Failure (of Political Parties) to Engage the Electorate* (Princeton, NJ: Princeton University Press, 2011).

46. Studies of Latino mobilization following Proposition 187 in California exemplify this politicization. Cort, "Spurred to Action or Retreat?"

47. Survey questionnaire circulated by the author, Denver, Colorado, September 22, 2018.

48. Mercedes, interview with the author, Denver, Colorado, September 9, 2017

49. Luz, interview with the author, Denver, Colorado, September 9, 2017.

50. Hamid, telephone interview with the author, July 26, 2017.

51. Bob, interview with the author, Boulder, Colorado, August 5, 2017.

52. Rob, interview with the author, Boulder, Colorado, April 17, 2017.

53. University of Colorado Law School Immigration Law and Policy Society panel on refugee resettlement, April 20, 2017.

54. Ruth, interview with the author, Denver, Colorado, May 8, 2017.

55. Rob, interview with the author, Boulder, Colorado, April 7, 2017; Ruth, interview with the author, Denver, Colorado, May 8, 2017.

56. Rob, interview with the author, Boulder, Colorado, April 7, 2017.

57. Masako, interview with the author, Boulder, Colorado, September 22, 2017; Iryna, interview with the author, Boulder, Colorado, September 25, 2017. In the inverse, Rob and Bob felt limited in their ability to participate in politics, despite their strong feelings, because they felt it was not their place as noncitizens. Bob, interview with the author, Boulder, Colorado, September 22, 2017; Rob, interview with the author, Boulder, Colorado, April 7, 2017.

58. Luz, interview with the author, Denver, Colorado, September 9, 2017.

59. Carmen, interview with the author, Denver, Colorado, October 26, 2017.

60. Luz, interview with the author, Denver, Colorado, September 9, 2017.

61. Luis, interview with the author, Denver, Colorado, October 23, 2017.

62. Survey questionnaire circulated by the author, Denver, Colorado, September 22, 2018.

63. This was true at the numerous USCIS naturalization ceremonies I observed, in interviews with USCIS officials, and in interviews with service providers involved in the naturalization process. See also Cheryl Malkin, "New Citizens Celebrate with Tears, Smiles and Song," *Lancaster Eagle-Gazette*, April 3, 2017.

64. Rob, interview with the author, Boulder, Colorado, April 17, 2017; Bob, interview with the author, Boulder, Colorado, September 22, 2017.

65. Leigh Alpert, interview with the author, Denver, Colorado, April 25, 2017.

66. Blake Sifton, "In Pursuit of Asylum on the US-Canadian Border," Al Jazeera, September 18, 2017, https://www.aljazeera.com/indepth/features/2017/09/pursuit-asylum -canada-border-170911073915212.html; Michael D. Nicholson, "The Facts on Immigration Today: 2017 Edition," Center for American Progress, April 20, 2017, https:// www.americanprogress.org/issues/immigration/reports/2017/04/20/430736/facts -immigration-today-2017-edition/.

67. Amy Taxin, "Immigrants Are Rushing to Apply for Citizenship amid Trump's Immigration Moves," *Associated Press*, February 21, 2017. Studies from the 1990s show similar fears, but this was nevertheless a distinctive feature of current policy.

68. Luz, interview with the author, Denver, Colorado, September 9, 2017.

69. Luz, interview with the author.

70. Luz, interview with the author.

71. Guy, interview with the author, Denver, Colorado, October 16, 2017.

72. Luis, interview with the author, Denver, Colorado, December 23, 2017 ("it's happened with many people where because of the law, they have lost their [legal permanent resident status])."

73. For a similar interpretation, consider the view of Sam Steinberg, a US citizen with a lawful permanent resident wife: "We have someone who's shown himself to be unpredictable, who is about to take the Presidency," Steinberg said, stating that citizenship for his wife is simply protection. "He's making threats against me, and people like me, and people like my family. It would be silly not to be afraid. It would be irresponsible to not be afraid of what he could do or what he might do." Kyunh Lah and Alberto Moya, "Motivated by Fear, Some Immigrants Are Turning to Citizenship," CNN, December 7, 2016, https://www.cnn.com/2016/12/07/politics/citizenship-surge -after-donald-trump-election/index.html; Taxin, "Immigrants Are Rushing."

74. Jose, interview with the author, Denver, Colorado, October 4, 2017. Similar sentiments were expressed by Latino immigrants in Los Angeles in national media articles. Wang, "Green Card Holders Worry" (quoting Alondro Juarez, a Latina green card holder who has lived in California for twenty years and is now pursuing citizenship: "The Muslim ban was an eye-opener for Latinos with green cards, who will now tell you, 'Okay, first it was Muslims, and next, who's on the list? The Latinos, Hispanic population.'").

75. Stefan, telephone interview with the author, October 12, 2017.

76. Bob, a white Canadian technology worker, reported that his Middle Eastern colleague with similar credentials and legal status "went dark" during a recent project as a result of challenges in navigating the hostile climate. Bob, interview with the author, Boulder, Colorado, September 22, 2017. Phillip Kretsedemas, *Migrants and Race in the U.S.: Territorial Racism and the Alien/Outside* (New York: Routledge, 2014).

77. For the definitive socio-legal work on legal consciousness, see David Engel and Frank Munger, *Rights of Inclusion: Law and Identity in the Life Stories of Americans with Disabilities* (Chicago: University of Chicago Press, 2003). Similar work has arisen in the immigration context, focusing especially on undocumented immigrants or those with liminal statuses such as Temporary Protected Status or Deferred Action for Childhood Arrivals. Leisy Abrego, "Legal Consciousness of Undocumented Latinos," *Law and Society Review* 45 (2011): 337–69; Cecilia Menjívar, "The Power of the Law: Central Americans' Legality and Everyday Life in Phoenix, Arizona," *Latino Studies* 9 (2011): 377–95; Hiroshi Motomura, *Immigration Outside the Law* (New York: Oxford University Press, 2014).

78. Catherine N. Barry, "Moving on Up? U.S. Military Service, Education, and Labor Market Mobility among Children of Immigrants" (PhD diss., University of California, Berkeley, 2013). Compared with native-born service members, noncitizens cited patriotism more often as their reason for joining and were more likely to redeploy. In comparison, native-born citizens are more likely to enlist for instrumental reasons. Molly F. McIntosh, Seema Sayala, and David Gregory, *Non-citizens in the Enlisted U.S. Military* (Alexandria, VA: Center for Naval Analysis, 2011).

79. Adam, interview with the author, August 27, 2017.

80. A significant finding is that wanting to serve prevails over seeking citizenship benefits as a reason for enlistment. Most interview subjects were unaware or not thinking about any citizenship benefit when they enlisted. Even once they enlisted and became eligible for citizenship, most cited the desire for better jobs over other citizenship benefits. Cesar, telephone interview with the author, July 3, 2017; Jose, telephone interview with the author, June 11, 2017; Mario, telephone interview with the author, May 25, 2017.

81. Jose, telephone interview with the author, June 11, 2017.

82. Emir, telephone interview with the author, July 26, 2017.

83. Cesar, telephone interview with the author, July 3, 2017.

84. Francisco, telephone interview with the author, August 9, 2017.

85. Michael J. Sullivan, *Earned Citizenship* (Oxford: Oxford University Press, 2019); Zachary New, "Ending Citizenship for Service in the Forever Wars," *Yale Law Journal Forum* 129 (2020): 552–66.

86. Sofya Aptekar, "Citizenship in the Green Card Army," in *Immigration Policy in the Age of Punishment: Detention, Deportation and Border Control*, ed. David Brotherton and Philip Kretsedemas (New York: Columbia University Press, 2018), 257–75.

87. Cesar, telephone interview with the author, July 3, 2017.

88. New, "Ending Citizenship for Service in the Forever Wars."

89. For a more critical take on the experience of noncitizens in the military, see Sofya Aptekar, "Citizenship and Naturalization among Immigrant Members of the U.S. Military: Meanings and Mechanisms" (paper presented at the Law and Society Association Annual Meeting, May 30, 2017). Others have discussed the "poverty draft" and other exploitative practices in the military that interfere with meaningful integration. Adam McGlynn and Jessica Lavariega Monforti, "The Poverty Draft? Exploring the Role of Socioeconomic Status in U.S. Military Recruitment of Hispanic Students" (American Political Science Association Annual Meeting Paper, 2010).

90. Waters and Pineau, *Integration of Immigrants*, 125–30; Nadwa Mosaad et al., "Determinants of Refugee Naturalization in the United States," *Proceedings of the National Academy of Science* 115 (September 11, 2018): 9175–80.

91. Mary, telephone interview with the author, June 18, 2017.

92. For a more critical take on refugee resettlement, see Eric Tang, *Unsettled: Cambodian Refugees in the New York City Hyperghetto* (Philadelphia: Temple University Press, 2015).

93. Tang, *Unsettled*. Tang argues that resettlement in the United States is continuous with the refugee experience in the refugee camps, sharing many of the same characteristics.

94. Donald J. Trump, "Executive Order on Enhancing State and Local Involvement in Refugee Resettlement," September 26, 2019, https://www.whitehouse.gov /presidential-actions/executive-order-enhancing-state-local-involvement-refugee -resettlement/.

95. Hassan, interview with the author, Denver, Colorado, July 22, 2017. The point came up in interviews with many Latino green card holders as well. It reinforces findings from sociological studies such as Natasha Warikoo and Irene Bloemraad, "Economic Americanness and Defensive Inclusion," *Journal of Ethnic and Migration Studies* 44 (2018): 736–53.

96. In the Refugee Integration Survey and Evaluation study, 98 percent of refugees stated their wish to become a US citizen within the first five years of arrival (with slight decreases over time, from 99.4 percent in year one to 97.8 percent by year five). Every refugee interviewed for this chapter either planned to naturalize or had already done so. Colorado Department of Human Services, Refugee Services Program, *The Refugee Integration Survey and Evaluation (RISE) Year Five: Final Report: A Study of Refugee Integration in Colorado* (Colorado Department of Human Services, Refugee Services Program, 2016).

97. Adam, telephone interview with the author, August 25, 2017.

98. Hamid, telephone interview with the author, July 26, 2017.

99. Multiple refugees I interviewed spoke of economic pressure. Mary, telephone interview with the author, June 18, 2017; Hamid, telephone interview with the author, July 26, 2017; Hassan, telephone interview with the author, July 22, 2017.

100. On asking the government for help obtaining public benefits for which he qualified, he said, "Even compared to when I had a green card, I felt safer than now that I have citizenship." Hamid, telephone interview with the author, July 26, 2017.

101. Emir said migrating was literally the difference between life and death. Emir, telephone interview with the author, July 26, 2017. Mary discussed the hardships she faced as an ethnic minority in her home country of Burma (Myanmar). Mary, telephone interview with the author, June 18, 2017.

102. Hamid, the journalist and dissident from Iran, spoke the most specifically about current policy among immigrants themselves. Hamid, telephone interview with the author, July 26, 2017.

103. Harry Budisidharta, who works with South Asian youth at the Asian Pacific Development Center, said that gang activity is a problem in certain communities and can lead to enforcement actions and deportation. Harry Budisidharta, interview with the author, Denver, Colorado, May 1, 2017. The sense of threat from enforcement actions escalated under shifting policies to target longtime Vietnamese and Cambodian refugees. For more on the targeting of Asian refugee youth gangs, see Tang, *Unsettled*; and Charles Dunst and Krishnadev Calamur, "Trump Moves to Deport Vietnam War Refugees," *Atlantic*, December 12, 2018.

104. Under the travel ban, lawful permanent residents are exempt under Department of Homeland Security policy, and refugees who have obtained their determination are likely to be sufficiently connected to be permitted entry. The third travel ban, issued as "Presidential Proclamation Enhancing Vetting Capabilities and Processes for Detecting Attempted Entry into the United States by Terrorists or Other Public-Safety Threats," makes these exclusions permanent and applicable to more countries; issued September 24, 2017, https://www.whitehouse.gov/the-press-office/2017/09/24/enhancing-vetting-capabilities-and-processes-detecting-attempted-entry. This travel ban is being challenged in court.

105. Basma and Sahar, interview with the author, Denver, Colorado, September 28, 2017.

106. Kit Taintor, interview with the author, Denver, Colorado, April 24, 2017.

107. For example, Emir said that the reason he loves this country so much is that when he was a refugee, Americans he interacted with treated him fairly and well. He thinks that "if a refugee lives in a place that is hostile to them . . . those hostile people don't represent the rest of Americans," and he is optimistic that there are still plenty of places in this country where people will support, and welcome, refugees. He believes that as bad as the current climate is, it does not represent this country, its values, or most of its people, and that it is still better than the home country for most. Emir, telephone interview with the author, July 26, 2017. Warmth of welcome and threat environment constitute part of the "context of reception." Portes and Zhou, "New Second Generation."

108. Adam, telephone interview with the author, August 25, 2017.

109. Mary described being unsure how to proceed with her son's integration: "I don't want him to feel left out, but he does not understand his mother's accent and he may not learn his home language." Mary, telephone interview with the author, June 18, 2017.

110. Mary, telephone interview with the author, June 18, 17. The Karen people are a group of ethnic minorities who reside primarily in southern and southeastern Burma.

While they do not share a common language or culture, they have formed a pan-ethnic group in modern times.

111. A number of US studies indicate a rise in naturalization rates in the immediate aftermath of anti-immigrant initiatives in the 1990s among Latino, elderly, and nonwhite immigrants. Cort, "Spurred to Action or Retreat?"; Nam and Kim, "Welfare Reform"; John Logan, Sookhee Oh, and Jennifer Darrah, "The Political and Community Context of Immigrant Naturalization," *Journal of Ethnic and Migration Studies* 38 (2012): 535–54.

112. Catalina Amuedo-Dorantes and Mary J. Lopez, "Impeding or Accelerating Assimilation? Immigration Enforcement and Its Impact on Naturalization Patterns," Center for Growth and Opportunity at Utah State University, 2019, https://www.growthopportunity.org/research/working-papers/impeding-or-accelerating-assimilation.

113. Dani Carrillo, "Politics and Group Belonging: Predictors of Naturalisation Behaviour in France," *Journal of Ethnic and Migration Studies* 41 (2015): 1932–57; Floris Peters, Maarten Vink, and Hans Schmeets, "The Ecology of Immigrant Naturalisation: A Life Course Approach in the Context of Institutional Conditions," *Journal of Ethnic and Migration Studies* 42 (2016): 359–81; Martin Kahanec and Mehmet Serkan Tosun, "Political Economy of Immigration in Germany: Attitudes and Citizenship Aspirations," *International Migration Review* 43 (2009): 263–91.

114. Postnational and cosmopolitan theorists express the view that citizenship matters less in a global society such that the significance of formal nonaffiliation should not be overstated. See, e.g., Levitt, *Transnational Villagers*; Saskia Sassen, *The Global City* (Princeton, NJ: Princeton University Press, 2001).

115. Ruth, interview with the author, Denver, Colorado, May 8, 2017.

116. Emily Ryo, "Fostering Legal Cynicism Tthrough Immigration Detention," *Southern California Law Review* 90 (2017): 999–1053; Emily Ryo, "Legal Attitudes of Immigrant Detainees," *Law and Society Review* 51 (2017): 99–131. As Ryo and others have shown, legal cynicism can lead to breakdowns in social norms, lack of compliance, and the need for more top-down controls.

117. David S. Kirk et al., "The Paradox of Law Enforcement in Immigrant Communities," *Annals of the American Academy of Political and Social Science* 641, no. 1 (2012): 79–98. Similar findings are reported in the context of post–September 11 enforcement efforts that alienated Muslim, Middle Eastern, and immigrant communities.

118. Robert D. Putnam, "E Pluribus Unum: Diversity and Community in the Twenty-First Century: The 2006 Johan Skytte Prize Lecture," *Scandinavian Political Studies* 30 (2007): 137. But see Pauline Cheong et al, "Immigration, Social Cohesion, and Social Capital: A Critical Review," *Critical Social Policy* 27 (2007): 24–49.

119. Jennifer Stave et al., *Evaluation of the New York Immigrant Family Unity Project* (New York: Vera Institute of Justice, June 23, 2017) (documenting costs of mass removal on immigration courts); Jaya Ramji-Nogales, Andrew I. Schoenholtz, and Philip G. Schrag, *Refugee Roulette: Disparities in Asylum Adjudication* (New York: New York University Press, 2011); Ingrid Eagley, Steven Shafer, and Jana Whalley,

"Detaining Families: A Study of Asylum Adjudication in Family Detention," *California Law Review* 106 (2018): 785–868.

120. ACLU Southern California, "Muslims Need Not Apply: How USCIS Secretly Mandates the Discriminatory Delay and Denial of Citizenship and Immigration Benefits to Aspiring Americans," webinar, August 20, 2013, https://www.youtube.com/watch?v=Nqfzc6DW9EM (describing Controlled Application Review and Resolution Program); Felicia Schwartz, "In Vetting Refugees, U.S. Plans to Assess Ability to Assimilate," *Wall Street Journal*, September 29, 2017 (summarizing Trump administration report to Congress on refugees); Frances Robles, "Vetting Delays Snarl Path to Citizenship for Thousands in Military," *New York Times*, April 29, 2017; Marianna Sotomayor, "Naturalizations Backlog Could Keep Thousands of Immigrants from Voting," NBC News, October 16, 2016, https://www.nbcnews.com/politics/immigration/naturalizations-backlog-could-keep-thousands-immigrants-voting-n661951.

Chapter 5: Blocked Pathways to Full Citizenship

1. A *nonimmigrant* is defined in immigration law as "a foreign national who is admitted to the United States for a specific temporary period of time in a specified class of visa, and who does not intend to remain permanently." INA § 101(a)(15)(15)(B)–(V).

2. "Consideration of Deferred Action for Childhood Arrivals (DACA)," US Citizenship and Immigration Services, 2012, https://www.uscis.gov/archive/consideration-deferred-action-childhood-arrivals-daca.

3. Specific terms for each visa are detailed in the immigration statute (INA § 101(a)(15)(B)–(V)), agency regulations (C.F.R. § 214.1), and policy guidance. For example, see INA § 101(a)(15)(H)(i)(B) and USCIS and Department of Labor regulations for the work-related requirements for a "specialty occupation" high-skilled worker. "H-1B Specialty Occupations, DOD Cooperative Research and Development Project Workers, and Fashion Models," US Citizenship and Immigration Services, last updated January 16, 2020, https://www.uscis.gov/working-united-states/temporary-workers/h-1b-specialty-occupations-dod-cooperative-research-and-development-project-workers-and-fashion-models.

4. The Affordable Care Act and implementing regulations omit DACA recipients from health-care coverage. "Pre-Existing Condition Insurance Plan Program," US Department of Health and Human Services, 77 Fed. Reg. 52614, 52616 (Aug. 30, 2012), 45 C.F.R. § 152.2, https://www.govinfo.gov/content/pkg/FR-2012-08-30/pdf/2012-21519.pdf.

5. The USCIS guidance on DACA links to Form I-765 for the purpose of obtaining employment authorization. "Consideration of Deferred Action."

6. In the two years since Attorney General Jeff Sessions and Department of Homeland Security acting secretary Elaine Duke issued the "Memorandum on Rescission of DACA for USCIS, ICE, CBP" (September 5, 2017), multiple lawsuits have been filed to enjoin the rescission and also to challenge the injunctions. The injunctions will be ruled on by the US Supreme Court in 2019–20 (cert granted June 28, 2019). Department of Homeland Security v. Regents of the University of California, Case No. 18-587 (2019).

7. INA § 245. Adjustment of status permits a person to obtain a green card without departing the United States. Being able to adjust within the country provides a way to avoid re-entry bars in some instances where unlawful presence has accrued prior to becoming eligible for a green card.

8. INA § 245(i); 8 U.S.C. § 1255(i). "Adjustment of status of certain aliens physically present in the United States, Policy Manual, Adjustment of Status Policies and Procedures, Volume 7, Part A, Chapter 2: Eligibility Requirements," US Citizenship and Immigration Services, accessed December 17, 2019, https://www.uscis.gov/policy -manual/volume-7-part-a-chapter-2.

9. The rescission of DACA was preliminarily enjoined in several federal courts and reviewed in the Supreme Court. Department of Homeland Security v. Regents of the University of California, Case No. 18-587 (2019). See note 6.

10. "Open Doors: Research and Insights," Institute of International Education, 2017, https://www.iie.org/en/Why-IIE/Announcements/2017/11/2017-11-13-Open-Doors -Data; Elizabeth Redden, "International Student Numbers in U.S. Decline," Inside Higher Ed, April 23, 2019, https://www.insidehighered.com/quicktakes/2019/04/23 /international-student-numbers-us-decline.

11. INA § 101(a)(15)(F)(i); "Optional Practical Training for F-1 Students," US Citizenship and Immigration Services, last updated January 16, 2020, https://www .uscis.gov/working-united-states/students-and-exchange-visitors/students-and -employment.

12. Douglas Massey and Nolan Malone, "Pathways to Legal Immigration," *Population Research and Policy Review* 21, no. 6 (2002): 473–504 (relying on data from the New Immigrant Survey).

13. B. Lindsay Lowell, "H-1B Temporary Workers: Estimating the Population" (University of California–San Diego Working Paper No. 12, May 1, 2000), 9–12.

14. INA § 101(a)(15)(B)–(V).

15. Temporary protected status is provided by the USCIS under terms codified in INA § 244; 8 U.S.C. § 1245(a). It provides temporary relief from removal and work authorization to foreign nationals in the United States from countries experiencing armed conflict, natural disaster, or other extraordinary circumstances that prevent their safe return on a country-by-country basis. Temporary Protected Status designations for several countries are under challenge at this time. "Temporary Protected Status Alerts on Syria, Haiti, Nepal, Honduras, Nicaragua, El Salvador, and Sudan," US Citizenship and Immigration Services, last updated January 16, 2020, https://www .uscis.gov/humanitarian/temporary-protected-status.

16. One rare example is Kit Johnson, "Opportunities and Anxieties: A Study of International Students in the Trump Era," *Lewis and Clark Law Review* 22 (2018): 413–90 (predicting that the economic opportunities motivating international students to enroll in US universities will remain strong over indications of present anxieties). Another is David Cook-Martin, "Temp Nations? A Research Agenda on Migration, Temporariness, and Membership," *American Behavioral Scientist* 63 (2019): 1389–403.

17. Anna Lee Saxenian, "Silicon Valley's New Immigrant High-Growth Entrepreneurs," *Economic Development Quarterly* 16, no. 1 (2002): 20–31; Johnson, "Opportunities and Anxieties."

18. The travel ban restricted migration from Muslim-majority countries. Donald J. Trump, "Presidential Proclamation Enhancing Vetting Capabilities and Processes for Detecting Attempted Entry into the United States by Terrorists or Other Public-Safety Threats," White House, September 24, 2017, https://www.whitehouse.gov/the-press-office/2017/09/24/enhancing-vetting-capabilities-and-processes-detecting-attempted-entry; Donald J. Trump, "Presidential Proclamation on Improving Enhanced Vetting Capabilities and Processes for Detecting Attempted Entry," White House, January 30, 2020, https://www.whitehouse.gov/presidential-actions/proclamation-improving-enhanced-vetting-capabilities-processes-detecting-attempted-entry/. USCIS policies for employer-sponsored immigrants and H-1Bs have become more demanding, including mandatory interviews of green card holders where they were not previously required. Donald J. Trump, "Presidential Executive Order on Buy American and Hire American," White House, April 18, 2017, https://www.whitehouse.gov/the-press-office/2017/04/18/presidential-executive-order-buy-american-and-hire-american. On policies affecting Chinese scholars and students, see Patricia Zengerle and Matt Spetalnick, "Fearing Espionage, U.S. Weights Tighter Rules on Chinese Students," Reuters, November 29, 2018; Karin Fischer, "Trump Administration Suggested, Then Shelved, a Plan to Bar All Chinese Students," *Chronicle of Higher Education*, October 2, 2018.

19. "Immigration and Citizenship Data" on the USCIS website has a searchable field for DACA applications and receipts: https://www.uscis.gov/tools/reports-studies/immigration-forms-data, accessed December 18, 2019. Pew Research Center tabulates this kind of information as well. Gustavo Lopez and Jens Manuel Krogstad, "Key Facts about Unauthorized Immigrants Enrolled in DACA," Pew Research Center, September 25, 2017, https://www.pewresearch.org/fact-tank/2017/09/25/key-facts-about-unauthorized-immigrants-enrolled-in-daca/.

20. The USCIS statistics on DACA recipients are updated quarterly and posted to the agency website, "Immigration and Citizenship Data."

21. "Immigration and Citizenship Data."

22. "Immigration and Citizenship Data."

23. INA § 245(i).

24. See note 6.

25. Leisy Abrego and Sarah M. Lakhani, "Incomplete Inclusion: Legal Violence and Immigrants in Liminal Legal Statuses," *Law and Policy* 37 (2015): 265–93; Laura Enriquez, "Participating and Belonging without Papers: Theorizing the Tension between Incorporation and Exclusion for Undocumented Immigrant Young Adults" (PhD diss., University of California, Los Angeles, 2014); Caitlin Patler and Whitney Pirtle, "From Undocumented to Lawfully Present: Do Changes to Legal Status Impact Psychological Well-Being among Latino Immigrant Young Adults?," *Social Science and Medicine* 199 (2018): 39–48.

26. Define American uses the slogan "We are American, just not legally" to convey this message. See also Kathy Abrams, "Performative Citizenship in the Civil Rights and Immigrants' Rights Movements," in *A Nation of Widening Opportunities: The Civil Rights Act at 50*, ed. Ellen D. Katz and Samuel R. Bagenstos (Ann Arbor: Michigan Publishing Services, 2015), 1–28.

27. The National UnDACAmented Research Project national survey is the most comprehensive survey of the results of DACA. It has issued annual reports with findings about the effects of DACA on a national sample of survey respondents who received DACA. These findings are from a 2017 report containing statistics five years after DACA, Roberto G. Gonzales et al., *Taking Giant Leaps Forward: Experiences of a Range of DACA Beneficiaries at the 5-Year Mark* (Washington, DC: Center for American Progress, June 2017), https://www.americanprogress.org/issues/immigration/reports/2017/06/22/434822/taking-giant-leaps-forward/.

28. Gonzales et al.

29. Gonzales et al.

30. Gonzales et al.

31. Roberto G. Gonzales et al., "The Long-Term Impact of DACA: Forging Futures Despite DACA's Uncertainty, Findings from the National UnDACAmented Research Project," Immigration Initiative at Harvard, 2019, https://immigrationinitiative.harvard.edu/files/hii/files/final_daca_report.pdf.

32. Roberto G. Gonzales, *Lives in Limbo* (Berkeley: University of California Press, 2015).

33. Legal scholars writing about DACA acknowledge the need for continued legal reform to improve the lives of DREAMers. See, e.g., Michael Olivas, *Perchance to DREAM: A Legal and Political History of the DREAM Act and DACA* (New York: New Press, 2020); Hiroshi Motomura, *Immigration Outside the Law* (New York: Oxford University Press, 2014).

34. Cecilia Menjívar, "Liminal Legality: Salvadoran and Guatemalan Immigrants' Lives in the United States," *American Journal of Sociology* 111, no. 4 (2006): 999–1037.

35. Abrego and Lakhani, "Incomplete Inclusion"; Gonzales, *Lives in Limbo*.

36. Related ideas emerge in Susan Bibler Coutin et al., "Deferred Action and the Discretionary State: Migration, Precarity, and Resistance," *Citizenship Studies* 21, no. 8 (2017): 951–68; Jennifer Chacon et al., "Citizenship Matters: Conceptualizing Belonging in an Era of Fragile Inclusions," *UC Davis Law Review* 52 (2018): 1–80; and Shoba Wadhia, *Beyond Deportation: The Role of Prosecutorial Discretion in Immigration Cases* (New York: New York University Press, 2015).

37. The psychology literature refers to a related "sense of foreshortened future." Matthew Ratcliffe, Mark Ruddell, and Benedict Smith, "What Is a 'Sense of Foreshortened Future?' A Phenomenological Study of Trauma, Trust, and Time," *Frontiers in Psychology*, September 2014.

38. A similar concept of precarity appears in the essays in Marcel Paret and Shannon Gleeson, eds., "Building Citizenship from Below: Precarity, Migration, and Agency," special issue, *Citizenship Studies* 20, no. 3–4 (2016).

39. See chapter 2; Agniezka Kubal, "Conceptualizing Semi-legality in Migration Research," *Law and Society Review* 47 (2013): 555–87; Elizabeth F. Cohen, *Semi-Citizenship in Democratic Politics* (New York: Cambridge University Press, 2009).

40. Naif, interview with the author, Boulder, Colorado, November 21, 2017.

41. Dazhen, interview with the author, Boulder, Colorado, October 8, 2017; Deepti, interview with the author, Boulder, Colorado, October 7, 2017.

42. The injunctions on the DACA rescission will be ruled on by the US Supreme Court in the 2019–20 term (cert granted June 28, 2019). Department of Homeland Security v. Regents of the University of California, Case No. 18-587 (2019). See note 6.

43. Kathryn Abrams, "Ambivalent Citizenship: Assessing the Political Consciousness of Undocumented Activists," in Open Hand, Closed Fist: Undocumented Immigrants Mobilize in the Valley of the Sun (unpublished manuscript, December 2019).

44. These difficulties integrating across the color lines indicate segmented assimilation. Min Zhou, "Segmented Assimilation: Issues, Controversies, and Recent Research," *International Migration Review* 31 (1997): 975–1008; Alejandro Portes and Min Zhou, "The New Second Generation: Segmented Assimilation and Its Variants," *Annals of the American Academy of Political and Social Science* 530 (1993): 74–96.

45. Dazhen, interview with the author, Boulder, Colorado, October 8, 2017.

46. Deepti, interview with the author, Boulder, Colorado, October 7, 2017.

47. Scholars debate whether transnationals and dual citizens can be fully engaged in multiple places. Peggy Levitt, *The Transnational Villagers* (Berkeley: University of California Press, 2001); Peter Spiro, *At Home in Two Countries: The Past and Future of Dual Citizenship* (New York: New York University Press, 2016). There was little evidence of strong ties to both countries in my interview sample (e.g., Chinese and Saudi Arabian interviewees felt home country orientation).

48. Ksenia, interview with the author, Boulder, Colorado, November 13, 2017.

49. Bob, interview with the author, Boulder, Colorado, September 22, 2017.

50. Abishek, interview with the author, Boulder, Colorado, November 5, 2017.

51. Mei, interview with the author, Boulder, Colorado, October 7, 2017.

52. Sandra, interview with the author, Boulder, Colorado, November 27, 2017.

53. Abishek, interview with the author, Boulder, Colorado, November 5, 2017.

54. Waleed, interview with the author, Boulder, Colorado, November 5, 2017.

55. "Open Doors Survey."

56. "Fall International Enrollments Snapshot Reports," Institute of International Education, 2018, https://www.iie.org/en/Research-and-Insights/Open-Doors.

57. See the National UnDACAmented Research Project results in Gonzales et al., *Taking Giant Leaps Forward*.

58. Munk, interview with the author, Boulder, Colorado, March 4, 2018.

59. The finding that DACA boosts social belonging and well-being is qualified by the recognition that it is not a durable legal status because of the possibility of deportation for immigrants, and especially for their parents who are not covered. Gonzales et al., *Taking Giant Leaps Forward*; Roberto G. Gonzales and Angie Bautista-Chavez,

"Two Years and Counting: Assessing the Growing Power of DACA" (Washington, DC: American Immigration Council, 2014).

60. Shan, interview with the author, Boulder, Colorado, March 2, 2018.

61. Esen, interview with the author, Boulder, Colorado, February 27, 2018.

62. Gabriela, interview with the author, Boulder, Colorado, February 23, 2018 ("No, I would not return to my home country. I don't feel connected to it"); Isabella, interview with the author, Denver, Colorado, April 19, 2018 ("No, I would not belong").

63. Valentine, interview with the author, Boulder, Colorado, February 23, 2018 ("I assume [DACA] is not going to go for long so I'm trying to take advantage of my time. So I'm trying to get job experience now while I can because I never know what's going to happen. I'm very appreciative of it.")

64. Gabrielle, interview with the author, Boulder, Colorado, February 23, 2018.

65. Gabrielle, interview with the author.

66. Emelio, interview with the author, Boulder, Colorado, February 23, 2018.

67. Shan, interview with the author, Boulder, Colorado, March 2, 2018.

68. Jazmin, interview with the author, Boulder, Colorado, February 13, 2018.

69. Chacon et al., "Citizenship Matters."

70. Shan, interview with the author, Boulder, Colorado, March 2, 2018; Natalia, interview with the author, Boulder, Colorado, February 22, 2018.

71. Gabriela, interview with the author, Boulder, Colorado, April 19, 2018.

72. Jazmin, interview with the author, Boulder, Colorado, February 13, 2018.

73. Pedro, interview with the author, Denver, Colorado, June 7, 2018.

74. Esteban, interview with the author, Denver, Colorado, June 13, 2018; Jimena, interview with the author, Denver, Colorado, June 8, 2018.

75. Esteban, interview with the author, Denver, Colorado, June 13, 2018.

76. Emelio, interview with the author, Denver, Colorado, February 23, 2018.

77. The shift can be seen in the 2019 UnDACAmented Report as compared to earlier waves. Gonzales et al., *Forging Futures Despite DACA's Uncertainty.*

Chapter 6: Constructing Pathways to Full Citizenship

1. Michael Walzer, *Spheres of Justice: A Defense of Pluralism and Equality* (New York: Basic Books, 1984), 41.

2. Rogers Smith, *Civic Ideals: Conflicting Visions of Citizenship in U.S. History* (New Haven, CT: Yale University Press, 1997).

3. Linda Bosniak, "Status Non-citizens," in *The Oxford Handbook of Citizenship*, ed. Ayelet Shachar, Rainer Baubock, Irene Bloemraad, and Maarten Vink (New York: Oxford University Press, 2017), 314–36.

4. Chae Chan Ping v. United States, 130 U.S. 581 (1889).

5. An exemplar of these views may be Samuel Huntington, *Who Are We? The Challenges to America's National Identity* (New York: Simon and Schuster, 2004).

6. Yick Wo v. Hopkins, 118 U.S. 356 (1886).

7. A public dialogue about the ethos of the Statue of Liberty was touched off by a US Citizenship and Immigration Services (USCIS) official's rearticulation of the

Emma Lazarus poem in light of a rule change making immigrants who are receiving public benefits potentially ineligible for a green card and by another USCIS official's removal of "nation of immigrants" from the agency's mission statement. "Top Trump Official Ken Cuccinelli Faces Immediate Backlash for His 'Absurd' Rewrite of the Statue of Liberty Greeting," Rawstory, August 13, 2019, https://www.rawstory.com/2019/08/top-trump-official-ken-cuccinelli-faces-immediate-backlash-for-his-absurd-rewrite-of-the-statue-of-liberty-greeting/; Richard Gonzalez, "America No Longer a 'Nation of Immigrants,' USCIS Says," NPR, February 22, 2018.

8. Sarah Song, "The Boundary Problem in Democratic Theory: Why the Demos Should Be Bounded by the State," *International Theory* 4, no. 1 (2012): 39–68; William Kymlicka, *Multicultural Citizenship: A Liberal Theory of Minority Rights* (Oxford: Oxford University Press, 1995).

9. Jacqueline Stevens, *States without Nations: Citizenship for Mortals* (New York: Columbia University Press, 2009).

10. Pratheepan Gulasekaram and S. Karthick Ramakrishnan, *The New Immigration Federalism* (New York City: Cambridge University Press, 2015); S. Karthick Ramakrishnan and Irene Bloemraad, eds., *Civic Hopes and Political Realities: Immigrants, Community Organizations, and Political Engagement* (Santa Monica: Russell Sage Foundation, 2008); Shannon Gleeson, "From Rights to Claims: The Role of Civil Society in Making Rights Real for Vulnerable Workers," *Law and Society Review* 43, no. 3 (2009): 669–700; Els de Graauw, "Cities and the Politics of Immigrant Integration," *Journal of Ethnic and Migration Studies* 42, no. 6 (2016): 989–1012.

11. Jeff Chenoweth and Laura Burdick, *A More Perfect Union: A National Citizenship Plan* (Washington, DC: Catholic Legal Immigration Network, 2007), synthesizes many studies in favor of this idea.

12. INA § 101(a)(15).

13. Like critical race scholars, critical immigration scholars decouple belonging from status. They presume that substantive citizenship can be obtained from alternative sites of citizenship. See, e.g., Peter Markowitz, "Undocumented No More: The Power of State Citizenship," *Stanford Law Review* 67 (2015): 869–915; and Monica Varsanyi, "Interrogating Urban Citizenship vis-à-vis Undocumented Migration," *Citizenship Studies* 10 (2006): 229–49.

14. Mark Hugo Lopez, Ana Gonzalez-Barrera, and Jens Manuel Krogstad, "Hispanics and Their Views of Immigration Reform," Pew Research Center, 2018, https://www.pewresearch.org/hispanic/2018/10/25/views-of-immigration-policy/ (showing Latinos prioritize a pathway to citizenship for undocumented immigrants more than the US general public and that across Latino demographic subgroups, most prioritize a pathway to citizenship for undocumented immigrants).

15. Roberto G. Gonzales et al., "The Long-Term Impact of DACA: Forging Futures Despite DACA's Uncertainty, Findings from the National UnDACAmented Research Project," Immigration Initiative at Harvard, 2019, https://immigrationinitiative.harvard.edu/files/hii/files/final_daca_report.pdf; Roberto G. Gonzales et al., *Taking Giant*

Leaps Forward: Experiences of a Range of DACA Beneficiaries at the 5-Year Mark (Washington, DC: Center for American Progress, June 2017). This finding mirrored that of my interviews.

16. Mary, telephone interview with the author, June 18, 2017; Hasan, telephone interview with the author, July 22, 2017; Sahar, interview with the author, Denver, Colorado, September 8, 2017.

17. Adam, interview with the author, August 27, 2017; Cesar, telephone interview with the author, July 3, 2017; Jose, telephone interview with the author, June 11, 2017; Mario, telephone interview with the author, May 25, 2017; Emir, telephone interview with the author, July 26, 2017; Francisco, telephone interview with the author, August 9, 2017.

18. Cesar, telephone interview with the author, July 3, 2017; Francis, telephone interview with the author, August 9, 2017.

19. Dazhen, interview with the author, Boulder, Colorado, October 8, 2017; Deepti, interview with the author, Boulder, Colorado, October 7, 2017.

20. Leisy Abrego, "Legitimacy, Social Identity, and the Mobilization of Law: The Effects of Assembly Bill 540 on Undocumented Students in California," *Law and Social Inquiry* 33 (2008): 709–34; cf. Kathy Abrams, "Ambivalent Citizenship: Assessing the Political Consciousness of Undocumented Activists," in *Open Hand, Closed Fist: Undocumented Immigrants Mobilize in the Valley of the Sun* (unpublished manuscript, December 2019) (study of DACA activists in Arizona finding political authorization after SB 1070).

21. This resilience among everyday immigrants contrasts with resilience for activist immigrants, such as that found in Kathryn Abrams, "Open Hand, Closed Fist: Undocumented Immigrants Mobilize in the Valley of the Sun" (unpublished manuscript, December 2019).

22. For exemplary work on crime and immigration, see Juliet Stumpf, Jennifer Chacon, and Cesar Garcia Hernandez.

23. For exemplary work on undocumented workers, see Shannon Gleeson, Kate Griffith, and Jennifer Gordon.

24. Jose Antonio Vargas, *Dear America: The Story of an Undocumented Citizen* (New York: HarperCollins, 2019).

25. African Americans who were formerly slaves struggled to gain formal citizenship. Women and poor people earned formal citizenship centuries ago, but they continue to feel like second-class citizens struggling to fully belong. Latinos and the US-born children of undocumented immigrants worry that they will be the next targets of the enforcement regime. Yet despite the similarities, I was reluctant to speculate on these various and complex cases without carrying out the focused empirical research I conducted for my core subjects. The implications of this book for other semi-citizen groups are certainly worth considering in future research.

26. Carolyn Said, "SimpleCitizen Aims to Be the TurboTax for Getting a Green Card," *San Francisco Chronicle*, August 24, 2016, https://www.sfchronicle.com/business/article/SimpleCitizen-enables-DIY-green-card-applications-9182812.php.

27. "Naturalization through Military Service," US Citizenship and Immigration Services, accessed June 15, 2019, https://www.uscis.gov/military/naturalization -through-military-service. For a description of recent changes, see Zachary New, "Ending Citizenship for Service in the Forever Wars," *Yale Law Journal Forum* 129 (2020): 552–66.

28. The Office of Refugee Resettlement has benefited from federal grants to enhance technical assistance providers. A 2006 grant provided $200,000 for one year for a three-year project to bolster naturalization and civic participation activities ranging from English-language training, refugee outreach services, vocational training, job placement, and small business development to immigrant advocacy before state and federal agencies. Recent changes have been introduced in Donald J. Trump, "Executive Order on Enhancing State and Local Involvement in Refugee Resettlement," September 26, 2019, https://www.whitehouse.gov/presidential-actions/executive-order -enhancing-state-local-involvement-refugee-resettlement/.

29. "After a Green Card Is Granted," US Citizenship and Immigration Services, accessed June 15, 2019, https://www.uscis.gov/green-card/after-a-green-card-granted.

30. Citizenship USA is described in Chenoweth and Burdick, *More Perfect Union*, 102.

31. Lau v. Nichols, 414 U.S. 563 (1974).

32. *Lau v. Nichols* was extended under Title VI of the Civil Rights Act of 1964 to more agencies under Executive Order 13166 (2000) and included programs. Resistance to these changes can be seen in *Castaneda v. Pickard* (deferring to school choice on curriculum) and *Sandoval v. Alexander* (limiting public enforcement) in the public sphere. Rachel Moran, "Undone by Law: The Uncertain Legacy of *Lau v. Nichols*," *Berkeley La Raza Law Journal* 16 (2008): 1–10; Ming H. Chen, "Regulatory Rights: Civil Rights Agencies, Courts, and the Entrenchment of Language Rights," in *The Rights Revolution Revisited: Institutional Perspectives on the Private Enforcement of Civil Rights in the U.S.*, ed. Lynda Dodd (Cambridge: Cambridge University Press, 2018): 100–123.

33. The US Citizenship and Assimilation Grant Program awards funds to organizations that prepare lawful permanent residents for naturalization. Libraries are frequent recipients. A list of recent award winners is available here: "Citizenship and Assimilation Grant Program," US Citizenship and Immigration Services, accessed December 19, 2019, https://www.uscis.gov/about-us/citizenship-and-assimilation-grant-program.

34. US Government Accountability Office, *Language Access: Selected Agencies Can Improve Services to Limited English Proficient Persons* (Washington, DC: US Government Accountability Office, April 2010), http://www.gao.gov/assets/310/303599.pdf.

35. Jasmine Gonzalez-Rose has written about language rights in courts especially. Jasmine Gonzalez-Rose, "Language Disenfranchisement in Juries," *Hastings Law Journal* 65 (2014): 811–64; Jasmine Rose-Gonzalez, "The Exclusion of Non-English Speaking Jurors," *Harvard Civil Rights-Civil Liberties Law Review* 46 (2011): 497–549.

36. Ming H. Chen, "Where You Stand Depends on Where You Sit: Immigrant Incorporation in Federal Workplace Agencies," *Berkeley Journal of Employment and Labor Law* 33 (2012–13): 359–430.

37. T. H. Marshall, "Citizenship and Social Class," in *Citizenship and Social Class: And Other Essays* (New York: Cambridge University Press, 1950), 30–39; Linda Bosniak, "Citizenship Denationalized," *Indiana Journal of Global Legal Studies* 7 (2000): 447–509; Elizabeth F. Cohen, *Semi-Citizenship in Democratic Politics* (New York: Cambridge University Press 2009).

38. New Deal for New Americans, H.R. 4928, Session of 116th Congress (2019–20), https://www.congress.gov/bill/116th-congress/house-bill/4928; https://www.govtrack .us/congress/bills/116/hr4928; New Deal for New Americans, S. 3470, Session of 116th Congress (2020–21), https://www.markey.senate.gov/imo/media/doc/New%20Deal %20for%20New%20Americans%20Act.pdf.

39. President Obama established the White House Task Force on New Americans, and presidential candidates have proposed an office of immigrant affairs or an office of New Americans similar to that proposed in the New Deal for New Americans legislation that would focus on naturalization and integration efforts. See, e.g., "White House Task Force on New Americans: One-Year Progress Report," White House of President Barack Obama, 2015, https://obamawhitehouse.archives.gov/issues /immigration/new-americans. The Catholic Legal Immigration Network report (Chenoweth and Burdick, *More Perfect Union*) offered a similar recommendation a decade earlier.

40. Demetrios Papameditriou, Alexander Aleinikoff, and Deborah Meyers, *Reorganizing the Immigration Function: Toward a New Framework for Accountability* (Washington, DC: Carnegie Endowment International Migration Policy Program, 1998), reviews several proposals for reforming the INS and USCIS before recommending a cabinet-level agency, including an influential 1986 select commission that led to employer sanctions under the Immigration Reform and Control Act and recommended USCIS functions be moved to the State Department. Eventually, the creation of the Department of Homeland Security separated Immigration and Customs Enforcement and USCIS but kept them both within a single agency, with USCIS handling service and fraud investigation.

41. A US congressional hearing took up immigration benefit adjudication processing in 2019. Congress, House, Subcommittee on Immigration and Citizenship of the House Committee on the Judiciary, "Policy Changes and Processing Delays at U.S. Citizenship and Immigration Services," 116th Cong., 1st sess., 2019, https:// judiciary.house.gov/legislation/hearings/policy-changes-and-processing-delays-us -citizenship-and-immigration-services.

42. Diego Iñiguez-López, *Tearing Down the Second Wall: Ending USCIS's Backlog of Citizenship Applications and Expanding Access to Naturalization for Immigrants* (Chicago: National Partnership for New Americans, July 2, 2018).

43. Doris Meissner, "Statement of Doris Meissner, Commission, Immigration and Naturalization Service, U.S. Department of Justice," Hearing before the Subcommittee on Immigration of the Committee of the Judiciary U.S. Senate, 104th Cong., 2nd Session on Reviewing the Status of Operations at the Immigration and Naturalization Service, October 2, 1996, 9–18.

44. The "resident alien" designation used for tax purposes relies on a substantial presence test that determines the number of days an individual was present in the United States and earned income. Center for Economic Progress, *The IRS Individual Taxpayer Identification Number: An Operational Guide to the ITIN Program* (Chicago: Center for Economic Progress, 2014).

45. For more background on immigration and taxes, see Cynthia Blum, "Rethinking Tax Compliance of Unauthorized Workers after Immigration Reform," *Georgetown Immigration Law Journal* 21 (2007): 595–620.

46. The Citizenship Resource Center and Immigrant Integration Grants Program is a federal grant to support these partnerships, available here: "Grant Program," US Citizenship and Immigration Services, accessed December 19, 2019, https://www.uscis.gov/citizenship/organizations/grant-program.

47. Stella Burch Elias, "The New Immigration Federalism," *Ohio State Law Journal* 74 (2013): 703–52; Pratheepan Gulasekaram and S. Karthick Ramakrishnan, *The New Immigration Federalism* (New York: Cambridge University Press, 2015).

48. The National Voter Registration Act of 1993 was designed to reduce the cost of voting by incorporating registration into a transaction with a public agency such as the state DMV. State DMVs inquire about voter registration and proceed to register those individuals at the point of service. The program has increased voter registration and voter turnout. See Raymond W. Wolfinger and Jonathan Hoffman, "Registering and Voting with Motor Voter," *PSOnline* 34, no. 1 (2001): 85–92.

49. The executive order reads, "I am hereby ordering all agencies to share information requested by the Department to the maximum extent permissible under law." "Executive Order on Collecting Information about Citizenship Status in Connection with the Decennial Census," White House Presidential Actions, July 11, 2019, https://www.whitehouse.gov/presidential-actions/executive-order-collecting-information-citizenship-status-connection-decennial-census/. President Trump issued the executive order following protracted litigation over the inclusion of a citizenship question on the census and a Supreme Court ruling in *Department of Commerce v. New York* (2019) that the Commerce Department had provided insufficient justification for using the census to ask directly given the risk of an inaccurate count.

50. A *Time Magazine* article notes concerns about DHS and census collaboration that could bring enforcement into integration efforts. Mike Schneider, "Department of Homeland Security to Share Citizenship Data with Census Bureau," *Time Magazine*, January 6, 2020, https://time.com/5760108/homeland-security-citizenship-data-census-bureau/.

51. Whether the government's purpose for including a citizenship question on the census related to redistricting efforts was central to a Supreme Court lawsuit. Dep't of Commerce v. N.Y., 588 U.S. (2019). A lawsuit pending in Alabama would challenge the practice of counting all residents in the census for purposes of apportionment, regardless of their citizenship. Alabama v. U.S. Chamber of Commerce, Civil Action No. 2:18-cv-00772 (N.D. Alabama, August 2019).

52. Internal Revenue Code, 26 § 6103(h).

53. In July 2019, a public records request by the Center on Privacy and Technology at Georgetown Law School revealed that Immigration and Customs Enforcement used facial recognition software on DMV databases in at least three states that administer driver's licenses to undocumented immigrants. Congress, state governors, and cities are challenging the practice. "FBI, ICE Find State Driver's License Photos Are a Gold Mine for Facial Recognition Searches," *Washington Post*, July 8, 2019.

54. The Catholic Legal Immigration Network report, the New America Foundation report, and others suggest simplifications of eligibility criteria. Chenoweth and Burdick, *More Perfect Union*; Raph Mafma, Lindsey Wagner, and Sabrina Fonseca, *Understanding the Catalysts for Citizenship Application: User Research on Those Eligible to Naturalization* (Washington, DC: New America Foundation, 2019).

55. These suggestions have been empirically tested for effectiveness. See Mafma, Wagner, and Fonseca, *Understanding the Catalysts*; and Thai V. Le et al., *Paths to Citizenship: Using Data to Understand and Promote Naturalization* (Center for the Study of Immigrant Integration, University of Southern California, Dornsife, 2019).

56. For comprehensive analysis of application fees, see William Kandel, *U.S. Citizenship and Immigration Services (USCIS) Functions and Funding* (Washington, DC: Congressional Research Service, May 15, 2015), 16; William Kandel and Chad Haddal, *U.S. Citizenship and Immigration Services' Immigration Fees and Adjudication Costs: Proposed Adjustments and Historical Context* (Washington, DC: Congressional Research Service, July 16, 2010), 15; and US Commission on Immigration Reform, *Becoming an American: Immigration and Immigration Policy*, Executive Summary (Washington, DC: US Commission on Immigration Reform, 1997). A resurgence of concern about application fees arose in 2016 and 2018 amid increases.

57. Kandel and Haddal, *U.S. Citizenship*.

58. Manuel Pastor and Jared Sanchez, "Promoting Citizenship: Assessing the Impacts of the Partial Fee Waiver" (Los Angeles: Center for the Study of Immigrant Integration brief, University of Southern California, Dornsife, 2016). The USCIS in 2016 experimented with the principle of incentivizing naturalization by providing not only fee waivers for low-income applicants but also fee reductions for higher-income applications specifically for naturalization. In 2019, a proposal to raise fees for naturalization and other immigration benefits was introduced and then delayed as it is reviewed in court. "USCIS Fee Schedule and Changes to Certain Other Immigration Benefit Request Requirements," US Citizenship and Immigration Services, November 14, 2019, 84 Fed. Reg. 62280, https://www.govinfo.gov/content/pkg/FR-2019-11-14/pdf/2019-24366.pdf. See Additional Information on Filing a Reduced Fee Request, Form I-912 and I-942, U.S. Citizenship and Immigration Service, last updated August 13, 2018, https://www.uscis.gov/reduced.

59. A nonimmigrant is defined by the USCIS as "a foreign national who is admitted to the United States for a specific temporary period of time in a specified class of visa, and who does not intend to remain permanently." INA § 101(a)(15)(15)(B)–(V).

60. The problems of international students on F-visas extend to other temporary visas that do not permit dual intent. The E-2 treaty trader visa permits dual intent but

prohibits adjustment of status without waiving rights provided for in the treaty. In contrast, the H-1B, L, and O visa typically permit dual intent.

61. Since October 2017, USCIS has instructed its officers to apply the same level of scrutiny to both initial petitions and extension requests for nonimmigrant visa categories, reversing prior practice of affording deference to prior petitions. "Rescission of Guidance Regarding Deference to Prior Determinations of Eligibility in the Adjudication of Petitions for Extension of Nonimmigrant Status," Policy Memorandum, US Citizenship and Immigration Services, October 23, 2017, https://www.uscis.gov /sites/default/files/USCIS/Laws/Memoranda/2017/2017-10-23Rescission-of-Deference -PM6020151.pdf.

62. Some of these policies challenging legal migration are summarized in the 2019 Unified Regulatory Agenda. The White House proposals would shift immigrant admissions from family-based to employer-based high-skilled worker visas

63. Kit Johnson, "Universities as Vehicles for Immigrant Integration," *Fordham Urban Law Journal* 46 (2019): 580–601.

64. Technology companies like Google, Apple, and Facebook have always been protective of foreign workers, who are vital to their businesses, and they have therefore supported H-1B visas and resisted restrictive employment laws that dampen foreign competition, such as the Hire America, Buy America Executive Order. Donald J. Trump, "Presidential Executive Order on Buy American and Hire American," White House, April 18, 2017, https://www.whitehouse.gov/the-press-office/2017/04/18 /presidential-executive-order-buy-american-and-hire-american. High-tech companies have filed amicus briefs in opposition to the travel ban and lobbied Congress and the White House to raise caps on the H-1B and other visas benefiting their employees.

65. Calls for a pathway to citizenship for DREAMers have been made repeatedly. After years of unenacted legislative proposals, in June 2019, the US House of Representatives passed an American Dream and Promise Act that would permit a green card and then citizenship for DREAMers. The Senate did not get on it.

66. Jason Cade, for example, urges equitable enforcement that encourages legalization via adjustment of status, cancellation of removal, U visas, Special Immigrant Juvenile Status, or unlawful presence waivers. Jason Cade, "Enforcing Immigration Equity," *Fordham Law Review* 84 (2015): 661–724.

67. Amanda Frost, "Cooperative Enforcement in Immigration Law," *Iowa Law Review* 103, no. 1 (2017): 1–52.

68. Jeanne M. Atkinson and Thomas K. Wong, "The Case for National Legalization Program," *Journal on Migration on Human Security* 6 (2018): 161–66 (suggesting screening without executive or legislative action based on study of eligibility).

69. Shoba Wadhia, *Beyond Deportation: The Role of Prosecutorial Discretion in Immigration Cases* (New York: New York University Press, 2015).

70. Irene Bloemraad and Els de Graauw, "Immigrant Integration and Policy in the United States: A Loosely Stitched Patchwork," in *International Perspectives: Immigration and Inclusion*, ed. James Frideres and John Biles (Montreal: McGill–Queen's University Press, 2012), 205–34.

71. Judith Shklar, *American Citizenship: The Quest for Inclusion* (Cambridge, MA: Harvard University Press, 1991). Recall Pocock's description of the Greek polis as a model of political citizenship. J. G. A. Pocock, "The Ideal of Citizenship since Classical Times," in *Theorizing Citizenship*, ed. Ronald Beiner (Albany: State University of New York Press, 1995), 29–52.

72. Noncitizens are barred from voting, jury duty, and public employment. On noncitizen voting, see Jamin Raskin, "Legal Aliens, Local Citizens," *University of Pennsylvania Law Review* 141 (1993): 1391, 1401–16; Gerald M. Rosberg, "Aliens and Equal Protection: Why Not the Right to Vote?," *Michigan Law Review* 75 (1977): 1092–136; and Ron Hayduck, *Democracy for All: Restoring Immigrant Voting Rights in the U.S.* (New York: Routledge, 2006). On jury duty, California governor Edmund Brown in 2013 vetoed a rare attempt to permit noncitizens to serve jury duty in State Assembly Bill 1401. On public employment, case law originating with *Sugarman* bars noncitizens from many government jobs. Sugarman v. Dougall, 413 U.S. 634 (1973).

73. Elizabeth F. Cohen, "Dilemmas of Representation, Citizenship, and Semi-Citizenship," *Saint Louis University Law Journal* 58 (2014): 1047–70.

74. The turbulent history of Americanization movements and the tension of integration and civic nationalism are analyzed by Noah Pickus, *True Faith and Allegiance* (Princeton, NJ: Princeton University Press, 2009).

75. For a summary of the scholarship on the similarities and differences of pluralism and civic nationalism as modes of integration, see Per Mouritsen, "The Resilience of Citizenship Traditions: Civic Integration in Germany, Great Britain, and Denmark," *Ethnicities* 13 (2013): 86–109; and Christian Joppke, "Beyond National Models: Civic Integration Policies for Immigrants in Western Europe," *West European Politics* 30 (2007): 1–22.

76. Nabila Ramdani, "Laïcité and the French Veil Debate," *Guardian*, May 23, 2010.

77. Ellen Barry and Martin Selsoe Sorensen, "Denmark's Harsh Laws for Immigrant Ghettos," *New York Times*, July 1, 2018.

78. The historical and philosophical underpinnings of similar programs appear in Suzanne Mettler, *From Soldiers to Citizens: The G.I. Bill and the Making of the Greatest Generation* (Oxford: Oxford University Press, 2005). The Obama proposals are discussed in White House, "Task Force on New Americans: One-Year Progress Report," December 2015, https://obamawhitehouse.archives.gov/sites/default/files/image/tfna_progress_report_final_12_15_15.pdf.

79. Michael J. Sullivan, *Earned Citizenship* (Oxford: Oxford University Press, 2019).

80. New Deal for New Americans.

81. A key contributor to the scholarship about civic nationalism and multiculturalism in Europe is Christian Joppke. Joppke, "Beyond National Models"; Christian Joppke, "The Retreat of Multiculturalism in the Liberal State," *British Journal of Sociology* 55 (2004): 237–57. The tension between these civic ideals in the United States can be illustrated by the cultural threat observed by Samuel Huntington and theories of earned citizenship for military service of undocumented immigrants. Samuel P. Huntington, "The Hispanic Challenge," *Foreign Policy*, October 28, 2009, https://foreignpolicy.com/2009/10/28/the-hispanic-challenge/.

82. Shklar, *American Citizenship*. Recall the history of slavery and the women's movement as largely a movement about the right to work, plus numerous (failed) antipoverty movements.

83. Graham v. Richardson, 403 U.S. 365 (1971).

84. Matthews v. Diaz, 426 U.S. 67 (1976).

85. Plyler v. Doe, 457 U.S. 202 (1982).

86. The notion of persons residing under color of law, or PRUCOL; Alessia v. Novello, 712 N.Y.S.2d 96 (App. Div. 2000); Bruns v. Mayhew, 750 F.3d 61 (2014).

87. "Pre-Existing Condition Insurance Plan Program," US Department of Health and Human Services, 77 Fed. Reg. 52614, 52616 (Aug. 30, 2012); 45 C.F.R. §152.2, https://www.govinfo.gov/content/pkg/FR-2012-08-30/pdf/2012-21519.pdf.

88. "Inadmissibility on Public Charge Grounds," *Federal Register* 84, no. 157 (August 14, 2019), https://www.govinfo.gov/content/pkg/FR-2019-08-14/pdf/2019-17142.pdf. More generally, see Cybelle Fox, "Unauthorized Welfare: The Origins of Immigrant Status Restrictions in American Social Policy," *Journal of American History* 102 (2016): 1051–74.

89. Commonwealth of Australia, *Government Response to the Report of the Australian Citizenship Council: Australian Citizenship . . . a Common Bond* (Canberra: Commonwealth of Australia, 2001).

90. Fox, "Unauthorized Welfare."

91. Fox. Critical race theorists such as Evelyn Nakano Glenn have written extensively about the second-class citizenship of racial minorities and women on the basis of income inequality and class. Evelyn Nakano Glenn, *Unequal Freedom* (Cambridge, MA: Harvard University Press, 2002). Cultural incorporation tends to be confined to language rights and religious accommodation cases in the US context and tends to be weaker than group-based rights in the Canadian and European tradition. Cf. Marshall, "Citizenship and Social Class"; Rogers Brubaker, *Citizenship and Nationhood in France and Germany* (Cambridge, MA: Harvard University Press, 1992).

92. Yick Wo v. Hopkins, 118 U.S. 356 (1886); INA § 1152(a)(1)(A) (providing that "no person shall . . . be discriminated against in the issuance of an immigrant visa because of the person's race, sex, nationality, place of birth, or place of Residence").

93. Zadvydas v. Davis, 553 U.S. 678 (2001).

94. Johnson, "Universities as Vehicles," endorses a similar idea.

95. The campaign website is available here: https://www.youarewelcomehereusa.org/read-me/.

96. The Open Doors survey from the Institute of International Education shows a decline of 2.2 percent undergraduate and 5.5 percent graduate new enrollment from 2016 to 2017, preceding the Muslim travel ban. "Open Doors: Research and Insights," Institute of International Education, 2017, https://www.iie.org/en/Why-IIE/Announcements/2017/11/2017-11-13-Open-Doors-Data. The Institute of International Education annual reports show a majority of international students (57 percent) report that the social and political environment are key factors in their enrollment decisions and that they have felt the effects of the environment on changes in the visa

process as of 2018. "Open Doors Survey and Report on International Educational Exchange," Institute of International Education, 2017, https://www.iie.org/en/Why-IIE/Announcements/2017/11/2017-11-13-Open-Doors-Data.

97. Canada's constitution and federal laws contain a broad mission of integration that goes further than the United States' commitment. These laws reflect a consensus regarding the spirit and ideals of the Canadian Bill of Rights (1960), the Canadian Charter of Rights and Freedoms (1982), the Multiculturalism Act of Canada (1988), and the Immigration and Protection Act of 2001.

98. Among those engaged in the normative discussion, see Linda Bosniak, Elizabeth F. Cohen, and Hiroshi Motomura, whose work is described in chapter 2.

99. Pressures to assimilate in Denmark and other Scandinavian countries that favor civic nationalism over multiculturalism and concerns about cultural diversity in the United States raise these issues. For the flavor of the debate, see Joppke, "Retreat of Multiculturalism"; and Sullivan, *Earned Citizenship*.

100. Huntington, *Who Are We?*

101. Some of the theorists referenced in this book include Linda Bosniak, Joseph Carens, Elizabeth Cohen, Sarah Song, Rogers Smith (on citizenship), Ian Haney Lopez and Evelyn Nakano Glenn (on race and gender), and T. H. Marshall (on class).

102. These operational difficulties have been an ongoing matter of policy discussion. In 1980, an Office of Management and Budget budget examiner told a study team of the House Government Operations Committee that "some of the INS's problems in handling resources result from a long-standing conflict between enforcement and service responsibilities" and complained that "the agency put too much emphasis on enforcement and too little on service." Milton Morris, *Immigration: The Beleaguered Bureaucracy* (Washington, DC: Brookings Institution, 1985), 121. Congress created a commission to study the issue in Immigration Act of 1990, Pub. L. No. 101-649. The US Commission on Immigration Reform released a final report in 1997 recommending a major structural overhaul of immigration because INS could not be both a benefits agency and an enforcement agency and perform both functions effectively. In hearings for the Immigration Reform and Improvements Act of 1998, H.R. 3904, 105th Cong. (1998), a proposal for division of INS responsibilities into an enforcement arm housed within the Department of Justice and a benefits agency housed within the State Department went unheeded; a similar proposal to remove enforcement from the INS and place it within the Department of Justice arose in the Border Security and Enforcement Act of 1997, H.R. 2588, 105th Cong. (1997). The creation of the Department of Homeland Security in the Homeland Security Act of 2002, H.R. 5005, 107th Cong. (2002), retained the separation of immigration courts in the Department of Justice but kept both Immigration and Customs Enforcement and USCIS within the Department of Homeland Security.

103. One serious attempt was the US Commission on Immigration Reform under Barbara Jones, which studied the problem for five years and garnered support from President Clinton and Congress in 1995 and 1997. The government has

given little attention to integration, and the presidential election of 2020 is repeating the pattern.

104. Charles R. Epp, *Making Rights Real: Activists, Bureaucrats, and the Creation of the Legalistic State* (Chicago: University of Chicago Press, 2010); Els de Graauw, *Making Immigrant Rights Real: Nonprofits and the Politics of Integration in San Francisco* (Ithaca, NY: Cornell University Press, 2016).

105. Official declarations of the Trump administration are collected on WhiteHouse.gov and the Department of Homeland Security webpage. Campaign statements and Twitter posts are collected in news media.

106. Many of these policy changes are described in American Immigration Lawyers Association, *Deconstructing the Invisible Wall: How Policy Changes by the Trump Administration Are Slowing and Restricting Legal Immigration* (Washington, DC: American Immigration Lawyers Association, 2018); Chen and New, "Silence and the Second Wall."

107. *Deconstructing the Invisible Wall*; Chen and New, "Second Wall."

108. *Deconstructing the Invisible Wall*; Colorado State Advisory Committee to the US Commission on Civil Rights, *Citizenship Delayed: Civil Rights and Voting Rights Implications of the Backlog in Citizenship and Naturalization Applications*, September 2019 (reprinted in *University of Colorado Law Review* Forum 91 (2019), http://lawreview.colorado.edu/citizenship-delayed-civil-rights-and-voting-rights-implications-of-the-backlog-in-citizenship-and-naturalization-applications/).

109. "Inadmissibility on Public Charge Grounds," US Department of Homeland Security, August 14, 2019, 84 Fed. Reg. 41292, https://www.federalregister.gov/documents/2019/08/14/2019-17142/inadmissibility-on-public-charge-grounds. The public charge rule has been enjoined and implementation delayed as a result of multiple lawsuits as of 2020.

110. Cassandra Burke Robertson and Irina D. Manta, "(Un)Civil Denaturalization," *New York University Law Review* 94, no. 3 (2019): 402–71; Cassandra Burke Robertson and Irina D. Manta, "Litigating Citizenship," *Vanderbilt Law Review* 73 (forthcoming 2020); Amanda Frost, *Unmaking Americans: A History of Citizenship Stripping in the United States* (Boston: Beacon Press, 2021).

111. Tom R. Tyler, *Why People Cooperate: The Role of Social Motivations* (Princeton, NJ: Princeton University Press, 2010).

112. Robert D. Putnam, "E Pluribus Unum: Diversity and Community in the Twenty-First Century: The 2006 Johan Skytte Prize Lecture," *Scandinavian Political Studies* 30 (2007): 137–74.

113. Maria Abascal and Delia Baldassari, "Love Thy Neighbor? Ethnoracial Diversity and Trust Reexamined," *American Journal of Sociology* 121 (2015): 722–82.

114. Asad L. Asad and Matthew Clair, "Racialized Legal Status as a Determinant of Health," *Social Science and Medicine* 199 (2018): 19–28.

115. Emily Ryo, "Fostering Legal Cynicism through Immigration Detention," *Southern California Law Review* 90 (2017): 999–1053.

116. "Immigration System Is at 'Breaking Point,' Homeland Security Warns," NPR, March 28, 2019, https://www.npr.org/2019/03/28/707509464/immigration-system -is-at-breaking-point-homeland-security-warns; Michael D. Shear, Miriam Jordan, and Manny Fernandez, "The U.S. Immigration System May Have Reached a Breaking Point," *New York Times*, April 10, 2019. An American Bar Association report, said, "This is a critical moment in the administration of justice within our immigration system. Systems that were already strained by lack of legislative reform and inconsistent policies are now at the breaking point." American Bar Association, "ABA Commission Recommends Major Changes to U.S. Immigration System," March 20, 2019, https://www.americanbar.org/news/abanews/aba-news-archives/2019/03/aba -commission-recommends-major-changes-to-u-s--immigration-syst/. Full report is located at https://www.americanbar.org/content/dam/aba/publications/commission _on_immigration/2019_reforming_the_immigration_system_volume_2.pdf.

117. Paul Kane, "'Get So Close—and Nothing Happens': Congress's Record on Immigration Is Repeated Failures," *Washington Post*, June 23, 2018.

118. John Burnett, "See the 20+ Immigration Activists Arrested under Trump," NPR, March 16, 2018, https://www.npr.org/2018/03/16/591879718/see-the-20-immigration -activists-arrested-under-trump.

119. Jennifer Safstrom, "Inside the ACLU's War on Trump," *New York Times*, July 2, 2018.

120. Many immigration enforcement policies under the Trump administration have stoked fear in immigrants, ranging from highly publicized raids, to hard-fought battles to include a question about citizenship on the Census, to confusing rules about whether accepting public benefits will lead to ineligibility for a green card, to the travel ban. Many of these policies never go into effect, or have limited results when they do, leaving analysts to conclude that the fear is the point of many policies. Gavrielle Jacobivitz, "Trump's Immigration Proposals Don't Need to Happen to Cause Harm," HuffPost, August 2, 2019, https://www.huffpost.com/entry/trump-immigration -chilling-effects-public-charge-census_n_5d42ef7ce4b0acb57fc890bc; Jose A. Del Real, "When It Comes to the Census, the Damage Is Done," *New York Times*, June 27, 2019; Helena Bottemiller Evich, "Immigrants, Fearing Trump Crackdown, Drop Out of Nutrition Programs," Politico, September 3, 2018, https://www.politico.com/story/2018/09 /03/immigrants-nutrition-food-trump-crackdown-806292.

121. Tatiana, interview with the author, Boulder, Colorado, November 13, 2017.

122. Esen, interview with the author, Boulder, Colorado, February 27, 2018.

Appendix: Research Methods and Data

1. The interviews were conducted under University of Colorado research grants and an IRB protocol 16-0668.

2. "Immigrants in Colorado," American Immigration Council, October 4, 2017, https://www.americanimmigrationcouncil.org/research/immigrants-colorado.

3. Nathaniel Minor, "Colorado's Refugee Population Summarized in Four Charts," Colorado Public Radio News, February 1, 2017, https://www.cpr.org/2017/02

/01/colorados-refugee-population-explained-in-4-charts/; "Veteran Population," National Center for Veterans Analysis and Statistics, 2016, https://www.va.gov/vetdata/veteran_population.asp.

4. "Student Statistics," University of Colorado International Student and Scholar Services, 2019, https://www.colorado.edu/isss/about-us/student-statistics.

5. Audrey Singer, "The Rise of New Immigrant Gateways," Brookings Institution, Living Cities Census Series, February 1, 2004; Lisa Martinez, *We Have a Dream: Undocumented Youth and the Politics of Immigration* (New York: New York University Press, forthcoming).

6. Michael A. Rodriguez, Maria-Elena Young, and Steven Wallace, *Creating Conditions to Support Healthy People: State Policies That Affect the Health of Undocumented Immigrants and Their Families* (Los Angeles: UCLA Blum Center on Poverty and Health, 2015).

7. Colorado ASSET Bill, Senate Bill 13-033 (2013, extended in 2018).

8. Colorado Road and Community Safety Act, Senate Bill 139 (2014, extended in 2020).

9. Children's Health Insurance Program Reauthorization Act of 2009; Implement Medicaid Delivery and Payment Initiatives, Colorado House Bill 09-1353.

10. Statement of Governor John Hickenlooper on Syrian Refugees, November 16, 2015, https://www.colorado.gov/gov-hickenlooper-statement-syrian-refugees; John Aguilar, "Colorado Communities Welcome Refugee Resettlement," *Denver Post*, January 8, 2020, https://www.denverpost.com/2020/01/08/refugee-resettlement-colorado-trump-executive-order/.

11. Justin Wingerter, "Colorado's ICE Restrictions Could Earn It 'Sanctuary' Label and Jeopardize Federal Grants," *Denver Post*, June 21, 2019, https://www.denverpost.com/2019/06/21/colorado-sanctuary-city-trump-federal-grants/.

12. Colorado Employment Verification Law, 8-2-122 (amended House Bill 16-1114) (2016).

13. Lisa Martinez, "(Navigating) The Rocky Terrain of Immigration Politics in the American West," in *We Have a Dream: Undocumented Youth and the Politics of Immigration Reform* (New York: New York University Press, forthcoming).

14. Larger incentives for the DACA students were made possible by collaboration with other Colorado immigration scholars interested in issues of integration.

Bibliography

Abascal, Maria. "Tu Casa, Mi Casa: Naturalization and Belonging among Latino Immigrants." *International Migration Review* 51 (2015): 291–322.

Abascal, Maria, and Delia Baldassari. "Love Thy Neighbor? Ethnoracial Diversity and Trust Reexamined." *American Journal of Sociology* 121 (2015): 722–82.

Abrams, Kathryn. "Contentious Citizenship: Undocumented Activism in the Not-1More Deportation Campaign." *Berkeley La Raza Law Journal* 26 (2016): 46–69.

———. *Open Hand, Closed Fist: Undocumented Immigrants Mobilize in the Valley of the Sun.* Unpublished manuscript, December 2019.

———. "Performative Citizenship in the Civil Rights and Immigrants' Rights Movements." In *A Nation of Widening Opportunities: The Civil Rights Act at 50*, edited by Ellen D. Katz and Samuel R. Bagenstos, 1–28. Ann Arbor: Michigan Publishing Services, 2015.

Abrego, Leisy. "Legal Consciousness of Undocumented Latinos." *Law and Society Review* 45 (2011): 337–69.

———. "Legitimacy, Social Identity, and the Mobilization of Law: The Effects of Assembly Bill 540 on Undocumented Students in California." *Law and Social Inquiry* 33 (2008): 709–34.

Abrego, Leisy, and Sarah M. Lakhani. "Incomplete Inclusion: Legal Violence and Immigrants in Liminal Legal Statuses." *Law and Policy* 37 (2015): 265–93.

ACLU Southern California. "Muslims Need Not Apply: How USCIS Secretly Mandates the Discriminatory Delay and Denial of Citizenship and Immigration Benefits to Aspiring Americans." Webinar, August 20, 2013. https://www.youtube.com/watch?v=Nqfzc6DW9EM.

Ager, Alastair, and Alison Strang. *Indicators of Integration: Final Report.* Home Office Development and Practice Report 28. London: Home Office, 2010.

Agnieszka, Kubal. "Conceptualizing Semi-legality in Migration Research." *Law and Society Review* 47 (2013): 555–87.

Aguilar, John. "Colorado Communities Welcome Refugee Resettlement." *Denver Post*, January 8, 2020. https://www.denverpost.com/2020/01/08/refugee-resettlement-colorado-trump-executive-order/.

Aleinikoff, T. Alexander, David Martin, Hiroshi Motomura, Maryellen Fullerton, and Juliet Stumpf. *Immigration and Citizenship.* 8th ed. St. Paul, MN: West Academic, 2016.

American Bar Association, Commission on Immigration. *Reforming the Immigration System: Proposals to Promote Independence, Fairness, Efficiency, and Professionalism in the Adjudication of Removal Cases.* Washington, DC: American Bar Association, Commission on Immigration, 2019. https://www.americanbar.org/content/dam/aba/publications/commission_on_immigration/2019_reforming_the_immigration_system_volume_2.pdf.

American Immigration Lawyers Association. *AILA's Guide to U.S. Citizenship and Naturalization Law.* Washington, DC: American Immigration Lawyers Association, 2014.

——. *Deconstructing the Invisible Wall: How Policy Changes by the Trump Administration Are Slowing and Restricting Legal Immigration.* Washington, DC: American Immigration Lawyers Association, 2018.

Amuedo-Dorantes, Catalina, and Mary J. Lopez. "Impeding or Accelerating Assimilation? Immigration Enforcement and Its Impact on Naturalization Patterns." Center for Growth and Opportunity at Utah State University, 2019. https://www.growthopportunity.org/research/working-papers/impeding-or-accelerating-assimilation.

Antonio Vargas, Jose. *Dear America: The Story of an Undocumented Citizen.* New York: HarperCollins, 2019.

Aptekar, Sofya. "Citizenship and Naturalization among Immigrant Members of the U.S. Military: Meanings and Mechanisms." Paper presented at the Law and Society Association Annual Meeting, May 30, 2017.

——. "Citizenship in the Green Card Army." In *Immigration Policy in the Age of Punishment: Detention, Deportation and Border Control,* edited by David Brotherton and Philip Kretsedemas, 257–75. New York: Columbia University Press, 2018.

——. *The Road to Citizenship: What Naturalization Means for Immigrants and the United States.* New Brunswick, NJ: Rutgers University Press, 2015.

Arendt, Hannah. *The Origins of Totalitarianism.* New York: Schocken Books, 1951.

Asad, Asad L., and Matthew Clair. "Racialized Legal Status as a Social Determinant of Health." *Social Science and Medicine* 199 (2018): 19–28.

Atkinson, Jeanne M., and Thomas K. Wong. "The Case for National Legalization Program." *Journal on Migration on Human Security* 6 (2018): 161–66.

Banks, Angela. "The Curious Relationship between 'Self-Deportation' Policies and Naturalization Rates." *Lewis and Clark Law Review* 16 (2012): 1149–213.

Banting, Keith. "Is There Really a Retreat from Multiculturalism? New Evidence from the Multiculturalism Policy Index." *European Comparative Politics* 11 (2013): 577–98.

Barry, Catherine N. "Moving on Up? U.S. Military Service, Education, and Labor Market Mobility among Children of Immigrants." PhD diss., University of California, Berkeley, 2013.

Barry, Ellen, and Martin Selsoe Sorensen. "Denmark's Harsh Laws for Immigrant Ghettos." *New York Times*, July 1, 2018.

Bernard, William S. "Cultural Determinants of Naturalization." *American Sociological Review* 1 (1936): 943–53.

Bloemraad, Irene. *Becoming a Citizen*. Berkeley: University of California Press, 2006.

———. "Does Citizenship Matter?" In *The Oxford Handbook of Citizenship*, edited by Ayelet Shachar, Rainer Baubock, Irene Bloemraad, and Maarten Vink, 524–50. New York: Oxford University Press, 2017.

———. "North American Naturalization Gap." *International Migration Review* 36 (2002): 193–228.

———. "Theorising the Power of Citizenship as Claims-Making." *Journal of Ethnic and Migration Studies* 44 (2017): 4–26.

Bloemraad, Irene, and Els de Graauw. "Immigrant Integration and Policy in the United States: A Loosely Stitched Patchwork." In *International Perspectives: Immigration and Inclusion*, edited by James Frideres and John Biles, 205–34. Montreal: McGill–Queen's University Press, 2012.

Bloemraad, Irene, and Alicia Sheares. "Understanding Membership in a World of Global Migration: (How) Does Citizenship Matter?" *International Migration Review* 51 (2018): 823–67.

Blum, Cynthia. "Rethinking Tax Compliance of Unauthorized Workers after Immigration Reform." *Georgetown Immigration Law Journal* 21 (2007): 595–620.

Borjas, George. *Heaven's Door: Immigration Policy and the American Economy*. Princeton, NJ: Princeton University Press, 2011.

———. *Immigration Economics*. Cambridge, MA: Harvard University Press, 2014.

Bosniak, Linda. *The Citizen and the Alien*. Princeton, NJ: Princeton University Press, 2006.

———. "Citizenship Denationalized." *Indiana Journal of Global Legal Studies* 7 (2000): 447–509.

———. "Status Non-citizens." In *The Oxford Handbook of Citizenship*, edited by Ayelet Shachar, Rainer Baubock, Irene Bloemraad, and Maarten Vink, 314–36. New York: Oxford University Press, 2017, 314–36.

Bratsberg, Bernt, James F. Ragan Jr., and Zafar M. Nasir. "The Effect of Naturalization on Wage Growth: A Panel Study of Young Male Immigrants." *Journal of Labor Economics* 20 (July 2002): 568–97.

Brennan, Jason. *The Ethics of Voting*. Princeton, NJ: Princeton University Press, 2012.

Brubaker, Rogers. *Citizenship and Nationhood in France and Germany*. Cambridge, MA: Harvard University Press, 1992.

Burciaga, Edelina M., and Aaron Malone. "Rocky Mountain Dreaming: Undocumented Young Adults in Colorado." Panel presentation at the Migrant Illegality across Uneven Legal Geographies convening, Providence, RI, October 2018.

Burciaga, Edelina M., and Lisa Martinez. "Political Contexts and Undocumented Youth Movements." *Mobilization* 22 (2017): 451–71.

Burnett, John. "See the 20+ Immigration Activists Arrested under Trump." NPR, March 16, 2018. https://www.npr.org/2018/03/16/591879718/see-the-20-immigration-activists -arrested-under-trump.

Butler, Judith. *Precarious Life*. New York: Verso, 2004.

Cade, Jason. "Enforcing Immigration Equity." *Fordham Law Review* 84 (2015): 661–724.

Carens, Joseph. *The Ethics of Immigration*. Oxford: Oxford University Press, 2013.

Carrillo, Dani. "Politics and Group Belonging: Predictors of Naturalisation Behaviour in France." *Journal of Ethnic and Migration Studies* 41 (2015): 1932–57.

Casaperalta, Edyael. "The New Atravesados: Tech Workers in the Digital Borderlands." *Rio Bravo: A Journal of the Borderlands* 24 (2019): 105–20.

Center for Economic Progress. *The IRS Individual Taxpayer Identification Number: An Operational Guide to the ITIN Program*. Chicago: Center for Economic Progress, 2014.

Chacon, Jennifer. "Citizenship Matters: Conceptualizing Belonging in an Era of Fragile Inclusions." *UC Davis Law Review* 52 (2018): 1–80.

———. "Producing Liminal Legality." *Denver University Law Review* 92 (2015): 709–67.

Chang, Robert S. "Whitewashing Precedent: From the Chinese Exclusion Case to Korematsu to the Muslim Travel Ban Cases." *Case Western Law Review* 68 (2018): 1183–222.

Chen, Ming H. "Citizenship Denied: Implications of the Naturalization Backlog for Noncitizens in the Military." *Denver University Law Review*, 97. Forthcoming 2020.

———. "Regulatory Rights: Civil Rights Agencies, Courts, and the Entrenchment of Language Rights." In *The Rights Revolution Revisited: Institutional Perspectives on the Private Enforcement of Civil Rights in the U.S.*, edited by Lynda Dodd, 100–122. Cambridge: Cambridge University Press, 2018.

———. "Where You Stand Depends on Where You Sit: Immigrant Incorporation in Federal Workplace Agencies." *Berkeley Journal of Employment and Labor Law* 33 (2012–13): 359–430.

Chen, Ming H., and Zachary New. "Silence and the Second Wall." *Southern California Interdisciplinary Law Journal* 27 (2019): 549–87.

Chenoweth, Jeff, and Laura Burdick. *A More Perfect Union: A National Citizenship Plan*. Washington, DC: Catholic Legal Immigration Network, 2007.

Cheong, Pauline, Rosalind Edwards, Harry Goulbourne, and John Solomos. "Immigration, Social Cohesion, and Social Capital: A Critical Review." *Critical Social Policy* 27 (2007): 24–49.

Chin, Gabriel Jack. "The Plessy Myth: Justice Harlan and the Chinese Cases." *Iowa Law Review* 82 (1996): 151–82.

Cohen, Elizabeth F. "Dilemmas of Representation, Citizenship, and Semi-Citizenship." *Saint Louis University Law Journal* 58 (2014): 1047–70.

———. *The Political Value of Time*. Cambridge: Cambridge University Press, 2018.

———. *Semi-Citizenship in Democratic Politics*. New York: Cambridge University Press, 2009.

Colorado Department of Human Services, Refugee Services Program. *The Refugee Integration Survey and Evaluation (RISE) Year Five: Final Report: A Study of Refugee Integration in Colorado.* Colorado Department of Human Services, Refugee Services Program, 2016. https://drive.google.com/file/d/10S9Xp9Hw2PGOT -3C3is6pnPPrwtyxolf/view.

Colorado State Advisory Committee to the US Commission on Civil Rights. *Citizenship Delayed: Civil Rights and Voting Rights Implications of the Backlog in Citizenship and Naturalization Applications.* September 2019. Reprinted in *University of Colorado Law Review* Forum 91 (2019). http://lawreview.colorado.edu /citizenship-delayed-civil-rights-and-voting-rights-implications-of-the-backlog -in-citizenship-and-naturalization-applications/.

Cook-Martin, David. *The Scramble for Citizens: Dual Nationality and State Competition for Immigrants.* Palo Alto, CA: Stanford University Press, 2013.

———. "Temp Nations? A Research Agenda on Migration, Temporariness, and Membership," *American Behavioral Scientist* 63, no. 9 (2019): 1389–403.

Correa, Michael Jones. *Between Two Nations.* Ithaca, NY: Cornell University Press, 1998.

Cort, David. "Spurred to Action or Retreat? The Effects of Reception Contexts on Naturalization Decisions in Los Angeles." *International Migration Review* 46 (2012): 483–516.

Coutin, Susan Bibler. "Denationalization, Inclusion, and Exclusion: Negotiating the Boundaries of Belonging." *Indiana Journal of Global Legal Studies* 7 (2000): 585–91.

Coutin, Susan Bibler, Sameer M. Ashar, Jennifer M. Chacon, and Stephen Lee. "Deferred Action and the Discretionary State: Migration, Precarity, and Resistance." *Citizenship Studies* 21, no. 8 (2017): 951–68.

Cuison Villazor, Rose, and Pratheepan Gulasekaram. "Sanctuary Networks." *Minnesota Law Review* 103 (2019): 1209–83.

de Graauw, Els. "Cities and the Politics of Immigrant Integration." *Journal of Ethnic and Migration Studies* 42, no. 6 (2016): 989–1012.

———. *Making Immigrant Rights Real: Nonprofits and the Politics of Integration in San Francisco.* Ithaca, NY: Cornell University Press, 2016.

Del Real, Jose A. "When It Comes to the Census, the Damage Is Done." *New York Times*, June 27, 2019.

Dunst, Charles, and Krishnadev Calamur. "Trump Moves to Deport Vietnam War Refugees." *Atlantic*, December 12, 2018.

Eagley, Ingrid, Steven Shafer, and Jana Whalley. "Detaining Families: A Study of Asylum Adjudication in Family Detention." *California Law Review* 106 (2018): 785–868.

Elias, Stella Burch. "The New Immigration Federalism." *Ohio State Law Journal* 74 (2013): 703–52.

———. "Testing Citizenship." *Boston University Law Review* 96 (2016): 2093–169.

Engel, David, and Frank Munger. *Rights of Inclusion: Law and Identity in the Life Stories of Americans with Disabilities.* Chicago: University of Chicago Press, 2003.

Enriquez, Laura. "Participating and Belonging without Papers: Theorizing the Tension between Incorporation and Exclusion for Undocumented Immigrant Young Adults." PhD diss., University of California, Los Angeles, 2014.

Epp, Charles R. *Making Rights Real: Activists, Bureaucrats, and the Creation of the Legalistic State*. Chicago: University of Chicago Press, 2010.

Ettlinger, Nancy. "Precarity Unbound." *Alternatives* 32, no. 3 (2007): 319–40.

Evich, Helena Bottemiller. "Immigrants, Fearing Trump Crackdown, Drop Out of Nutrition Programs." Politico, September 3, 2018. https://www.politico.com/story/2018/09/03/immigrants-nutrition-food-trump-crackdown-806292.

Fitzgerald, David Scott, and David Cook-Martin. *Culling the Masses: The Democratic Origins of Racist Immigration Policy in the Americas*. Cambridge, MA: Harvard University Press, 2014.

Fix, Michael, Jeffrey S. Passel, and Kenneth Sucher. *Trends in Naturalization*. Urban Institute Immigration Studies Program Brief No. 3. Washington, DC: Urban Institute Immigration Studies Program, 2003.

Fox, Cybelle. "Unauthorized Welfare: The Origins of Immigrant Status Restrictions in American Social Policy." *Journal of American History* 102 (2016): 1051–74.

Freeman, Gary P., Luis Plascencia, Susan Gonzalez Baker, and Manuel Orozco. "Explaining the Surge in Citizenship Applications in the 1990s: Lawful Permanent Residents in Texas." *Social Science Quarterly* 83 (2002): 1013–25.

Frisch, Max. *Überfremdung I, in Schweiz als Heimat? Versuche über 50 Jahre [Switzerland as Home? Attempts over 50 Years]* (Frankfurt: Suhrkamp Verlag 1991).

Frost, Amanda. "Cooperative Enforcement in Immigration Law." *Iowa Law Review* 103, no. 1 (2017): 1–52.

———. *Unmaking Americans: A History of Citizenship Stripping in the United States*. Boston: Beacon Press, 2021.

García Hernández, César. *Crimmigration Law*. Chicago: American Bar Association, 2015.

Gelbaum, Emily. *Building a Second Wall: USCIS Backlogs Preventing Immigrants from Becoming Citizens*. Chicago: National Partnership for New Americans, October 27, 2017.

Gilbertson, Greta, and Audrey Singer. "The Emergence of Protective Citizenship in the USA: Naturalization among Dominican Immigrants in the Post-1996 Welfare Reform Era." *Ethnic and Racial Studies* 26 (2003): 25–51.

Gleeson, Shannon. "From Rights to Claims: The Role of Civil Society in Making Rights Real for Vulnerable Workers." *Law and Society Review* 43, no. 3 (2009): 669–700.

Gomez, Laura. *Inventing Latinos: A New Story of American Racism*. New York: New Press, 2020.

Gonzales, Richard. "America No Longer a 'Nation of Immigrants,' USCIS Says." NPR. February 22, 2018. https://www.npr.org/sections/thetwo-way/2018/02/22/588097749/america-no-longer-a-nation-of-immigrants-uscis-says.

Gonzales, Roberto G. *Lives in Limbo*. Berkeley: University of California Press, 2015.

Gonzales, Roberto G., and Angie Bautista-Chavez. *Two Years and Counting: Assessing the Growing Power of DACA*. Washington, DC: American Immigration Council, 2014.

Gonzales, Roberto G., Sayil Camacho, Kristina Brant, and Carlos Aguilar. "The Long-Term Impact of DACA: Forging Futures Despite DACA's Uncertainty, Findings from the National UnDACAmented Research Project." Immigration Initiative at Harvard, 2019. https://immigrationinitiative.harvard.edu/files/hii/files/final_daca_report.pdf.

Gonzales, Roberto G., Marco A. Murillo, Cristina Lacomba, Kristina Brant, Martha C. Franco, Jaein Lee, and Deepa S. Vasudevan. "Taking Giant Leaps Forward: Experiences of a Range of DACA Beneficiaries at the 5-Year Mark." Center for American Progress, June 2017. https://www.americanprogress.org/issues/immigration/reports/2017/06/22/434822/taking-giant-leaps-forward/.

Gonzales, Roberto G., Veronica Terriquez, and Stephen P. Ruszczyk. "Becoming DACAmented: Assessing the Short-Term Benefits of Deferred Action for Childhood Arrivals (DACA)." *American Behavioral Scientist* 58 (2014): 1852–72.

Gonzalez, Richard. "America No Longer a 'Nation of Immigrants,' USCIS Says." NPR. February 22, 2018. https://www.npr.org/sections/thetwo-way/2018/02/22/588097749/america-no-longer-a-nation-of-immigrants-uscis-says.

Gonzalez-Rose, Jasmine. "The Exclusion of Non-English Speaking Jurors." *Harvard Civil Rights-Civil Liberties Law Review* 46 (2011): 497–549.

———. "Litigating Citizenship." *Vanderbilt Law Review* 73 (2020): 101–53.

Gulasekaram, Pratheepan, and S. Karthick Ramakrishnan. *The New Immigration Federalism*. New York: Cambridge University Press, 2015.

Hajnal, Zoltan, and Taeku Lee. *Why Americans Don't Join the Party: Race, Immigration and the Failure (of Political Parties) to Engage the Electorate*. Princeton, NJ: Princeton University Press, 2011.

Haney Lopez, Ian. *White by Law*. New York: New York University Press, 1996.

Hayduck, Ron. *Democracy for All: Restoring Immigrant Voting Rights in the U.S.* New York: Routledge, 2006.

Holpuch, Amanda. "Trump's War on Refugees Is Tearing Down US' Life-Changing Resettlement Program." *Guardian*, June 26, 2019.

Hugo Lopez, Mark, Ana Gonzalez-Barrera, and Jens Manuel Krogstad. "Hispanics and Their Views of Immigration Reform." Pew Research Center, 2018. https://www.pewresearch.org/hispanic/2018/10/25/views-of-immigration-policy/.

Huntington, Samuel P. "The Hispanic Challenge." *Foreign Policy*, October 28, 2009. https://foreignpolicy.com/2009/10/28/the-hispanic-challenge/.

———. *Who Are We? The Challenges to America's National Identity*. New York: Simon and Schuster, 2004.

Iñiguez-López, Diego. *Democracy Strangled: Second Wall of Barriers to Citizenship Risks Preventing Hundreds of Thousands of Immigrants from Naturalizing and Becoming Voters in Presidential Election of 2020*. Chicago: National Partnership for New Americans, March 2019. https://drive.google.com/file/d/1t1oWo6zc97qBpeXq93f5ycjFJfdBAlo6/view.

———. *Tearing Down the Second Wall: Ending USCIS's Backlog of Citizenship Applications and Expanding Access to Naturalization for Immigrants*. Chicago: National Partnership for New Americans, July 2, 2018, https://www.immigrationresearch.org/system/files/Naturalization_Backlogs_Second_Wall.pdf.

Inskeep, Steve. "Immigration System Is at 'Breaking Point,' Homeland Security Warns." NPR, March 28, 2019. https://www.npr.org/2019/03/28/707509464/immigration-system-is-at-breaking-point-homeland-security-warns.

Institute of International Education. "Fall International Enrollments Snapshot Reports." 2018.

———. "Open Doors Survey and Report on International Educational Exchange." 2017. https://www.iie.org/en/Why-IIE/Announcements/2017/11/2017-11-13-Open-Doors-Data.

Jacobivitz, Gavrielle. "Trump's Immigration Proposals Don't Need to Happen to Cause Harm." HuffPost, August 2, 2019. https://www.huffpost.com/entry/trump-immigration-chilling-effects-public-charge-census_n_5d42ef7ce4b0acb57fc890bc.

Jasso, Guillermina, Douglas S. Massey, Mark R. Rosenzweig, and James P. Smith. The New Immigrant Survey. Princeton University. Accessed December 13, 2019. http://nis.princeton.edu/project.html.

Jiménez, Tomás. *Immigrants in the United States: How Well Are They Integrating into Society?* Washington, DC: Migration Policy Institute, Summer 2011.

Johnson, Kevin. "Race Matters: Immigration Law and Policy Scholarship, Law in the Ivory Tower, and the Legal Indifference of the Race Critique." *University of Illinois Law Review* 2000, no. 2 (2000): 525–58.

Johnson, Kevin, and Bill Ong Hing. "National Identity in a Multicultural Nation: The Challenge of Immigration Law and Immigrants." *Michigan Law Review* 103 (2005): 1347–90.

Johnson, Kit. "Opportunities and Anxieties: A Study of International Students in the Trump Era." *Lewis and Clark Law Review* 22 (2018): 413–90.

———. "Universities as Vehicles for Immigrant Integration." *Fordham Urban Law Journal* 46 (2019): 580–601.

Jones-Correa, Michael, and Els de Graauw. "The Illegality Trap: The Politics of Immigration and the Lens of Illegality." *Daedalus* 142 (2013): 185–98.

Joppke, Christian. "Beyond National Models: Civic Integration Policies for Immigrants in Western Europe." *West European Politics* 30 (2007): 1–22.

———. "The Retreat of Multiculturalism in the Liberal State." *British Journal of Sociology* 55 (2004): 237–57.

Jordan, Miriam. "New Scrutiny Coming for Refugees from 11 'High-Risk' Nations." *New York Times*, January 29, 2018.

Kahanec, Martin, and Mehmet Serkan Tosun. "Political Economy of Immigration in Germany: Attitudes and Citizenship Aspirations." *International Migration Review* 43 (2009): 263–91.

Kandel, William. *U.S. Citizenship and Immigration Services (USCIS) Functions and Funding.* Washington, DC: Congressional Research Service, May 15, 2015.

Kandel, William, and Chad Haddal. *U.S. Citizenship and Immigration Services' Immigration Fees and Adjudication Costs: Proposed Adjustments and Historical Context.* Washington, DC: Congressional Research Service, July 16, 2010.

Kane, Paul. "'Get So Close—and Nothing Happens': Congress's Record on Immigration Is Repeated Failures." *Washington Post*, June 23, 2018.

Kelly, John. "Memorandum on Enforcement of the Immigration Laws to Serve the National Interest." U.S. Department of Homeland Security, Washington, DC,

January 20, 2017. https://www.dhs.gov/sites/default/files/publications/17_0220_S1
_Enforcement-of-the-Immigration-Laws-to-Serve-the-National-Interest.pdf.

Kim, Claire Jean. "The Racial Triangulation of Asian Americans." *Politics and Society*
27 (1999): 105–38.

King, Desmond. *Making Americans: Immigration, Race, and the Origins of the Diverse
Democracy.* Cambridge, MA: Harvard University Press, 2000.

Kirk, David S., Andrew V. Papachristos, Jeffrey Fagan, and Tom R. Tylor. "The Paradox of Law Enforcement in Immigrant Communities." *Annals of the American
Academy of Political and Social Science* 641, no. 1 (2012): 79–98.

Kretsedemas, Phillip. *Migrants and Race in the U.S.: Territorial Racism and the Alien/
Outside.* New York: Routledge, 2014.

Kubal, Agniezka. "Conceptualizing Semi-legality in Migration Research." *Law and
Society Review* 47 (2013): 555–87.

Kymlicka, William. *Multicultural Citizenship: A Liberal Theory of Minority Rights.*
Oxford: Oxford University Press, 1995.

Lah, Kyung, and Alberto Moya. "Motivated by Fear, Some Immigrants Are Turning
to Citizenship." CNN, December 7, 2016. http://www.cnn.com/2016/12/07/politics
/citizenship-surge-after-donald-trump-election/index.html.

Le, Thai V., Manuel Pastor, Justin Scoggins, Dalia Gonzalez, and Blanca Ramirez. *Paths
to Citizenship: Using Data to Understand and Promote Naturalization.* University of
Southern California, Dornsife, Center for the Study of Immigrant Integration, 2019.

Lenhardt, Robin, and Jennifer Gordon. "Citizenship Talk: Bridging the Gap between
Immigration and Race Perspectives." *Fordham Law Review* 75 (2006): 2493–519.

Levitt, Peggy. *The Transnational Villagers.* Berkeley: University of California Press, 2001.

Logan, John, Sookhee Oh, and Jennifer Darrah. "The Political and Community Context of Immigrant Naturalization." *Journal of Ethnic and Migration Studies* 38
(2012): 535–54.

Lopez, Gustavo, and Jens Manuel Krogstad. "Key Facts about Unauthorized Immigrants Enrolled in DACA." Pew Research Center, September 25, 2017. https://
www.pewresearch.org/fact-tank/2017/09/25/key-facts-about-unauthorized
-immigrants-enrolled-in-daca/.

Lopez, Mary J., and Catalina Amuedo-Dorantes. "Impeding or Accelerating Assimilation? Immigration Enforcement and Its Impact on Naturalization Patterns."
Centre for Research and Analysis of Migration Discussion Paper Series, 2018.

Lowell, B. Lindsay. "H-1B Temporary Workers: Estimating the Population." University of California–San Diego Working Paper No. 12, May 1, 2000.

Macklin, Audrey. "Who Is the Citizen's Other? Considering the Heft of Citizenship."
Theoretical Inquiries in Law 8 (2007): 333–66.

Majma, Raph, Lindsey Wagner, and Sabrina Fonseca. *Understanding the Catalysts for
Citizenship Application: User Research on Those Eligible to Naturalize.* Washington, DC: New America Foundation, May 2019.

Malkin, Cheryl. "New Citizens Celebrate with Tears, Smiles and Song." *Lancaster
Eagle-Gazette*, April 3, 2017.

Marcelo, Philip. "Gang Database Made Up Mostly of Young Black, Latino Men." AP News, July 30, 2019.

Markowitz, Peter. "Undocumented No More: The Power of State Citizenship." *Stanford Law Review* 67 (2015): 869–915.

Marrow, Helen. "Immigrant Bureaucratic Incorporation: The Dual Roles of Professional Missions and Government Policies." *American Sociological Review* 74 (2009): 756–76.

———. *New Destination Dreaming: Immigration, Race, and Legal Status in the Rural American South*. Palo Alto, CA: Stanford University Press, 2011.

Marshall, T. H. "Citizenship and Social Class." In *Citizenship and Social Class: And Other Essays*. New York: Cambridge University Press, 1950, 30–39.

Martinez, Lisa. *We Have a Dream: Undocumented Youth and the Politics of Immigration Reform*. New York: New York University Press, forthcoming.

Massey, Douglas. *Categorically Unequal: The American Stratification System*. New York: Russell Sage Foundation, 2007.

Massey, Douglas, Jorge Durand, and Nolan J. Malone. *Beyond Smoke and Mirrors: Mexican Immigration in an Era of Economic Integration*. New York: Russell Sage Foundation, 2003.

Massey, Douglas, and Nolan Malone, "Pathways to Legal Immigration." *Population Research and Policy Review* 21, no. 6 (2002): 473–504.

Massey, Douglas, and Karen Pren. "Unintended Consequences of U.S. Immigration Policy: Explaining the Post-1965 Surge from Latin America." *Population and Development Review* 38, no. 1 (2012): 1–29.

McGlynn, Adam, and Jessica Lavariega Monforti. "The Poverty Draft? Exploring the Role of Socioeconomic Status in U.S. Military Recruitment of Hispanic Students." American Political Science Association Annual Meeting Paper, 2010.

McHugh, Margie, and Madeleine Morawksi. "Immigrants and WIOA Services: Comparisons of Sociodemographic Characteristics of Native- and Foreign-Born Adults in the United States." Migration Policy Institute, April 2016. http://www.migrationpolicy.org/research/immigrants-and-wioa-services-comparison-sociodemographic-characteristics-native-and-foreign.

McIntosh, Molly F., Seema Sayala, and David Gregory. *Non-citizens in the Enlisted U.S. Military*. Alexandria, VA: Center for Naval Analysis, 2011.

Menjívar, Cecilia. "Liminal Legality: Salvadoran and Guatemalan Immigrants' Lives in the United States." *American Journal of Sociology* 111, no. 4 (2006): 999–1037.

———. "The Power of the Law: Central Americans' Legality and Everyday Life in Phoenix, Arizona." *Latino Studies* 9 (2011): 377–95.

Menjívar, Cecilia, and Daniel Kanstroom, eds. *Constructing Immigrant "Illegality": Critiques, Experiences, and Responses*. New York: Cambridge University Press, 2013.

Mettler, Suzanne. *From Soldiers to Citizens: The G.I. Bill and the Making of the Greatest Generation*. Oxford: Oxford University Press, 2005.

Miller, David. "Irregular Migrants: An Alternative Perspective." *Ethics and International Affairs* 22, no. 2 (2008): 193–97.

Montero, David. "Becoming a U.S. Citizen in the Time of Trump." *Los Angeles Times*, February 5, 2017. http://www.latimes.com/nation/la-na-naturalization-colorado -20170205-story.html.

Moran, Rachel. "Undone by Law: The Uncertain Legacy of *Lau v. Nichols.*" *Berkeley La Raza Law Journal* 16 (2008): 1–10.

Morris, Milton. *Immigration: The Beleaguered Bureaucracy.* Washington, DC: Brookings Institution, 1985.

Mosaad, Nadwa, Jeremy Ferwerda, Duncan Lawrence, Jeremy M. Weinstein, and Jens Hainmueller. "Determinants of Refugee Naturalization in the United States." *Proceedings of the National Academy of Science* 115 (2018): 9175–80.

Motomura, Hiroshi. *Americans in Waiting.* New York: Oxford University Press, 2007.

———. *Immigration outside the Law.* New York: Oxford University Press, 2014.

Mouritsen, Per. "The Resilience of Citizenship Traditions: Civic Integration in Germany, Great Britain, and Denmark." *Ethnicities* 13 (2013): 86–109.

Nakano Glenn, Evelyn. "Constructing Citizenship: Exclusion, Subordination, and Resistance." *American Sociological Review* 76, no. 1 (2011): 1–24.

———. *Unequal Freedom.* Cambridge, MA: Harvard University Press, 2002.

Nam, Yunju, and Wooksoo Kim. "Welfare Reform and Elderly Immigrants' Naturalization: Access to Public Benefits as an Incentive for Naturalization in the United States." *International Migration Review* 46 (2012): 656–79.

New, Zachary. "Ending Citizenship for Service in the Forever Wars." *Yale Law Journal Forum* 129 (2020): 552–66.

Ngai, Mae. *Impossible Subjects: Illegal Aliens and the Making of Modern America.* Princeton, NJ: Princeton University Press, 2004.

Nicholson, Michael D. "The Facts on Immigration Today: 2017 Edition." Center for American Progress, April 20, 2017. https://www.americanprogress.org/issues /immigration/reports/2017/04/20/430736/facts-immigration-today-2017-edition/.

Núñez, D. Carolina. "Mapping Citizenship Status, Membership, and the Path in Between." *Utah Law Review* 2016, no. 3 (2016): 477–533.

Olivas, Michael. *No Undocumented Child Left Behind: "Plyler v. Doe" and the Education of Undocumented Children.* New York: New York University Press, 2012.

———. *Perchance to DREAM: A Legal and Political History of the DREAM Act and DACA.* New York: New York University Press, 2020.

Omi, Michael, and Howard Winant. *Racial Formation in the United States.* New York: Routledge, 1986.

Ong, Paul. "Defensive Naturalization and Anti-immigrant Sentiment." *Asian American Policy Review* 22 (2011): 39–55.

Organisation for Economic Co-operation and Development. *Naturalization: A Passport for the Better Integration of Immigrants?* Paris: Organisation for Economic Cooperation and Development, 2011.

Papameditriou, Demetrios, Alexander Aleinikoff, and Deborah Meyers. *Reorganizing the Immigration Function: Toward a New Framework for Accountability.* Washington, DC: Carnegie Endowment International Migration Policy Program, 1998.

Paret, Marcel, and Shannon Gleeson, eds. "Building Citizenship from Below: Precarity and Agency through a Migrant Lens." Special Issue. *Citizenship Studies* 20, no. 3–4 (2016).

Parker, Kunal. *Making Foreigners: Immigration and Citizenship Law in America, 1600–2000.* New York: Cambridge University Press, 2015.

Pastor, Manuel, and Jared Sanchez. "Promoting Citizenship: Assessing the Impacts of the Partial Fee Waiver." Center for the Study of Immigrant Integration, University of Southern California, Dornsife. 2016. https://dornsife.usc.edu/assets/sites/731/docs/CSII_Citizenship_Brief_May2016_Final_Web.pdf.

———. *Rock the (Naturalized) Vote: The Size and Location of the Recently Naturalized Voting Age Citizen Population.* University of Southern California, Dornsife, 2012. https://dornsife.usc.edu/csii/rock-the-naturalized-vote/.

Patler, Caitlin, and Whitney Pirtle. "From Undocumented to Lawfully Present: Do Changes to Legal Status Impact Psychological Well-Being among Latino Immigrant Young Adults?" *Social Science and Medicine* 199 (2018): 39–48.

Peters, Floris, Maarten Vink, and Hans Schmeets. "The Ecology of Immigrant Naturalisation: A Life Course Approach in the Context of Institutional Conditions." *Journal of Ethnic and Migration Studies* 42 (2016): 359–81.

Pham, Huyen, and Pham Hoang Van. "Subfederal Immigration Regulation and the Trump Effect." *New York University Law Review* 94 (2019): 125–70.

Pickus, Noah. *True Faith and Allegiance.* Princeton, NJ: Princeton University Press, 2009.

Pocock, J. G. A. "The Ideal of Citizenship since Classical Times." In *Theorizing Citizenship*, edited by Ronald Beiner, 29–52. Albany: State University of New York Press, 1995.

Portes, Alejandro, and Jozsef Borocz. "Contemporary Immigration: Theoretical Perspectives on Its Determinants and Modes of Incorporation." *International Migration Review* 23 (1989): 606–30.

Portes, Alejandro, and Min Zhou. "The New Second Generation: Segmented Assimilation and Its Variants." *Annals of the American Academy of Political and Social Science* 530 (1993): 74–96.

Putnam, Robert D. "E Pluribus Unum: Diversity and Community in the Twenty-First Century: The 2006 Johan Skytte Prize Lecture." *Scandinavian Political Studies* 30 (2007): 137–74.

Ramakrishnan, S. Karthick, and Irene Bloemraad, eds. *Civic Hopes and Political Realities: Immigrants, Community Organizations, and Political Engagement.* Santa Monica, CA: Russell Sage Foundation, 2008.

Ramdani, Nabila. "Laïcité and the French Veil Debate." *Guardian*, May 23, 2010.

Ramji-Nogales, Jaya, Andrew I. Schoenholtz, and Philip G. Schrag. *Refugee Roulette: Disparities in Asylum Adjudication.* New York: New York University Press, 2011.

Raskin, Jamin. "Legal Aliens, Local Citizens." *University of Pennsylvania Law Review* 141 (1993): 1391–470.

Ratcliffe, Matthew, Mark Ruddell, and Benedict Smith. "What Is a 'Sense of Fore-shortened Future?': A Phenomenological Study of Trauma, Trust, and Time." *Frontiers in Psychology*, September 2014.

Rawstory. "Top Trump Official Ken Cuccinelli Faces Immediate Backlash for His 'Absurd' Rewrite of the Statue of Liberty Greeting." August 13, 2019. https://www.rawstory.com/2019/08/top-trump-official-ken-cuccinelli-faces-immediate-backlash-for-his-absurd-rewrite-of-the-statue-of-liberty-greeting/.

Redden, Elizabeth. "International Student Numbers in U.S. Decline." Inside Higher Ed, April 23, 2019. https://www.insidehighered.com/quicktakes/2019/04/23/international-student-numbers-us-decline.

Robertson, Cassandra Burke, and Irina D. Manta. "(Un)civil Denaturalization." *New York University Law Review* 94, no. 3 (2019): 402–71.

Robles, Frances. "Vetting Delays Snarl Path to Citizenship for Thousands in Military." *New York Times*, April 29, 2017.

Rodríguez, Cristina M. "Guest Workers and Integration: Toward a Theory of What Immigrants and Americans Owe One Another." *University of Chicago Legal Forum* 2007 (2007): 219–88.

Rosberg, Gerald M. "Aliens and Equal Protection: Why Not the Right to Vote?" *Michigan Law Review* 75 (1977): 1092–136.

———. "Language Disenfranchisement in Juries." *Hastings Law Journal* 65 (2014): 811–64.

Ryo, Emily. "Fostering Legal Cynicism through Immigration Detention." *Southern California Law Review* 90 (2017): 999–1053.

———. "Legal Attitudes of Immigrant Detainees." *Law and Society Review* 51 (2017): 99–131.

Safstrom, Jennifer. "Inside the ACLU's War on Trump." *New York Times*, July 2, 2018.

Said, Carolyn. "SimpleCitizen Aims to Be the TurboTax for Getting a Green Card." *San Francisco Chronicle*, August 24, 2016. https://www.sfchronicle.com/business/article/SimpleCitizen-enables-DIY-green-card-applications-9182812.php.

Salyer, Lucy. "Wong Kim Ark: The Contest over Birthright Citizenship." In *Immigration Law Stories*, edited by David Martin and Peter Schuck, 51–86. New York: Foundation, 2005.

Sassen, Saskia. *The Global City*. Princeton, NJ: Princeton University Press, 2001.

Saxenian, Anna Lee. "Silicon Valley's New Immigrant High-Growth Entrepreneurs." *Economic Development Quarterly* 16, no. 1 (2002): 20–31.

Schwartz, Felicia. "In Vetting Refugees, U.S. Plans to Assess Ability to Assimilate." *Wall Street Journal*, September 29, 2017.

Shear, Michael D., Miriam Jordan, and Manny Fernandez. "The U.S. Immigration System May Have Reached a Breaking Point." *New York Times*, April 10, 2019.

Shklar, Judith. *American Citizenship: The Quest for Inclusion*. Cambridge, MA: Harvard University Press, 1991.

Schneider, Mike. "Department of Homeland Security to Share Citizenship Data with Census Bureau." *Time Magazine*, January 6, 2020. https://time.com/5760108 /homeland-security-citizenship-data-census-bureau/.

Sifton, Blake. "In Pursuit of Asylum on the US-Canadian Border." Al Jazeera. September 18, 2017. https://www.aljazeera.com/indepth/features/2017/09/pursuit-asylum -canada-border-170911073915212.html.

Smith, Rogers. "Citizenship and Membership Duties toward Quasi-citizens." In *The Oxford Handbook of Citizenship*, edited by Ayelet Shachar, Rainer Baubock, Irene Bloemraad, and Maarten Vink, 817–37. New York: Oxford University Press, 2017.

———. *Civic Ideals: Conflicting Visions of Citizenship in U.S. History*. New Haven, CT: Yale University Press, 1997.

Song, Sarah. "The Boundary Problem in Democratic Theory: Why the Demos Should Be Bounded by the State." *International Theory* 4, no. 1 (2012): 39–68.

Sotomayor, Marianna. "Naturalizations Backlog Could Keep Thousands of Immigrants from Voting." NBC News, October 16, 2016. https://www.nbcnews.com/politics /immigration/naturalizations-backlog-could-keep-thousands-immigrants-voting -n661951.

Soysal, Yasemin. *Limits of Citizenship: Migrants and Postnational Membership in Europe*. Chicago: University of Chicago Press, 1995.

Spiro, Peter. *At Home in Two Countries: The Past and Future of Dual Citizenship*. New York: New York University Press, 2016.

———. *Beyond Citizenship*. New York: Oxford University Press, 2008.

Stave, Jennifer, Peter Markowitz, Karen Berberich, Tammy Cho, Danny Dubbaneh, Laura Simich, Nina Siulc, and Noelle Smart. *Evaluation of the New York Immigrant Family Unity Project*. New York: Vera Institute of Justice, November 2017.

Stevens, Jacqueline. *States without Nations: Citizenship for Mortals*. New York: Columbia University Press, 2009.

Stumpf, Juliet. "The Crimmigration Crisis: Immigrants, Crime, and Sovereign Power." *American University Law Review* 56 (2006): 367–419.

Sullivan, Michael J. *Earned Citizenship*. Oxford: Oxford University Press, 2019.

Tang, Eric. *Unsettled: Cambodian Refugees in the New York City Hyperghetto*. Philadelphia: Temple University Press, 2015.

Taxin, Amy. "Immigrants Are Rushing to Apply for Citizenship amid Trump's Immigration Moves." Associated Press, February 21, 2017.

Taylor, Paul, Ana Gonzalez-Barrera, Jeffrey S. Passel, and Mark Hugo Lopez. "Recent Trends in Naturalization, 2000–2011." Hispanic Trends. Pew Research Center, November 14, 2012. https://www.pewresearch.org/hispanic/2012/11/14/ii-recent -trends-in-naturalization-2000-2011/.

Tichenor, Daniel. *Dividing Lines: The Politics of Immigration Control in America*. Princeton, NJ: Princeton University Press, 2002.

Tilley, Charles. "Citizenship, Identity, and Social History." *International Review of Social History* 40, no. 53 (1995): 1–17.

Tyler, Tom R. *Why People Cooperate: The Role of Social Motivations*. Princeton, NJ: Princeton University Press, 2010.

US Citizenship and Immigration Services. Profiles on Naturalized Citizens. https://www.dhs.gov/profiles-naturalized-citizens.

US Commission on Immigration Reform. *Becoming an American: Immigration and Immigration Policy*. Executive Summary. Washington, DC: US Commission on Immigration Reform, 1997.

US Department of Homeland Security Office of Immigration Statistics. *Yearbook. Table 20 Petitions for Naturalization Filed, Persons Naturalized, and Petitions for Naturalization Denied: FY 1907 to 2018*. https://www.dhs.gov/immigration-statistics/yearbook/2017/table20.

US Department of Justice. "Attorney General Announces Zero-Tolerance Policy for Criminal Illegal Entry." April 6, 2018. https://www.justice.gov/opa/pr/attorney-general-announces-zero-tolerance-policy-criminal-illegal-entry.

———. "DOJ Creates Section Dedicated to Denaturalization Cases." February 26, 2020. https://www.justice.gov/opa/pr/department-justice-creates-section-dedicated-denaturalization-cases.

US Government Accountability Office. *Immigration Enforcement: Actions Needed to Better Handle, Identify, and Track Cases Involving Veterans*. Washington, DC: US Government Accountability Office, June 2019. https://www.gao.gov/assets/700/699549.pdf.

———. *Language Access: Selected Agencies Can Improve Services to Limited English Proficient Persons*. Washington, DC: US Government Accountability Office, April 2010. http://www.gao.gov/assets/310/303599.pdf.

Varsanyi, Monica. "Interrogating Urban Citizenship vis-à-vis Undocumented Migration." *Citizenship Studies* 10 (2006): 229–49.

Volpp, Leti. "The Citizen and the Terrorist." *UCLA Law Review* 49 (2002): 1575–600.

———. "Excesses of Culture: On Asian American Citizenship and Identity." *Asian American Law Journal* 17 (2010): 63–81.

———. "Obnoxious to Their Very Nature: Asian Americans and Constitutional Citizenship." *Citizenship Studies* 5 (2001): 57–71.

Wadhia, Shoba. *Banned: Immigration Enforcement in the Time of Trump*. New York: New York University Press, 2019.

———. *Beyond Deportation: The Role of Prosecutorial Discretion in Immigration Cases*. New York: New York University Press, 2015.

Walzer, Michael. *Spheres of Justice: A Defense of Pluralism and Equality*. New York: Basic Books, 1984.

Wang, Hansi Lo. "Green Card Holders Worry about Trump's Efforts to Curtail Immigration." NPR, February 21, 2017. https://www.npr.org/2017/02/21/516375460/green-card-holders-worry-about-trump-s-efforts-to-curtain-immigration.

Warikoo, Natasha and Irene Bloemraad. "Economic Americanness and Defensive Inclusion." *Journal of Ethnic and Migration Studies* 44 (2018): 736–53.

Washington Post. "FBI, ICE Find State Driver's License Photos Are a Gold Mine for Facial Recognition Searches." July 8, 2019.

Waters, Mary, and Tomás Jiménez. "Assessing Immigrant Assimilation: New Empirical and Theoretical Challenges." *Annual Review of Sociology* 31 (2005): 105–25.

Waters, Mary, and Marisa Gerstein Pineau, eds. *The Integration of Immigrants into American Society.* Washington, DC: National Academies Press, 2015.

Weber-Shirk, Joanna. "Deviant Citizenship: DREAMer Activism in the United States and Transnational Belonging." *Social Sciences* 4 (2015): 583–97.

Weil, Patrick. *The Sovereign Citizen: Denaturalization and the Origins of the American Republic.* Philadelphia: University of Pennsylvania Press, 2013.

White House. "Task Force on New Americans: One-Year Progress Report." December 2015. https://obamawhitehouse.archives.gov/sites/default/files/image/tfna_progress_report_final_12_15_15.pdf.

Wolfinger, Raymond W., and Jonathan Hoffman. "Registering and Voting with Motor Voter." *PSOnline* 34, no. 1 (2001): 85–92.

Yamamoto, Eric K., Maria Amparo Vanaclocha Berti, and Jaime Tokioka. "Loaded Weapon Revisited: The Trump Era Import of Justice Jackson's Warning in Korematsu." *Asian American Law Journal* 24 (2017): 5–47.

Yang, Philip Q. "Explaining Immigrant Naturalization." *International Migration Review* 28, no. 3 (1994): 449–77.

Zhou, Min. "Segmented Assimilation: Issues, Controversies, and Recent Research." *International Migration Review* 31 (1997): 975–1008.

Index

Page numbers in *italic* indicate tables and figures.